Murder Spree

Murder Spree

Damon and Rowan Wilson

Magpie Books, London

Constable & Robinson Ltd
55-56 Russell Square
London WC1B 4HP
www.constablerobinson.com

First published as *Murder Most Foul*
by Robinson Publishing Ltd, 1994

This paperback edition published by Magpie Books,
an imprint of Constable & Robinson Ltd 2011

A copy of the British Library Cataloguing in
Publication Data is available from the British Library

ISBN 978-1-78033-292-5

Printed and bound in the EU

1 3 5 7 9 10 8 6 4 2

Contents

For Virginia and Carolyn

The Deptford Paintshop Murders

At 7.15 on the morning of 27 March 1905, a milkman and his delivery boy saw two young men hurriedly leaving Farrow's paintshop at 34, Deptford High Street, south east London. The boy noticed that they had left the door ajar and called after them, but the pair strode away without looking back. Ten minutes later, a workman was passing the shop when he saw an old man with a blood-drenched face peering from the doorway. In most areas, this would have been an arresting sight, but there were several slaughterhouses in Deptford, and the locals were used to seeing blood-soaked men going to and from work. The old man said nothing, but simply pulled the door closed.

Just after half-past eight, Willy Jones, the Farrows' shop-boy, arrived for work, and was disturbed to find the front door still locked. The Farrows were early risers, and the shop was always open by 8.30. After his shouts failed to raise a response he went to fetch Mr Chapman, the landlord. Fearing that the elderly couple had suffered an accident, Chapman told the boy to climb in the back window. There, in the back parlour, Jones found Thomas Farrow lying in a pool of blood. He had been savagely beaten to death, and the walls and ceiling were spattered with blood. Mrs Farrow was discovered on the bed upstairs, similarly beaten, but still faintly breathing.

It did not take the police long to reconstruct the crime. Neighbours reported that the Farrows would often open the shop early if someone called before half-past eight. Thomas Farrow was only partially dressed when found, so it seemed likely that he had been summoned from his bed by somebody at the door. Two stocking masks were found at the scene of the crime and the pattern of bloodstaining showed that the first blows had been struck in the front part of the shop. This suggested that two or more masked men had thrust their way in when Farrow unfastened the lock and attacked him on sight. The blood trail led to the back parlour where the most brutal blows seemed to have been struck. After, or perhaps during the struggle, Mrs Farrow was assaulted upstairs. When the assailants fled, the probably delirious Thomas Farrow staggered to the front door and closed it on the latch, then went back to the parlour to die.

The stamina of the Farrows, both in their seventies, astounded the examining doctors. Both had been struck repeated, violent blows with a heavy, blunt weapon like a crowbar. After completing his examination, the pathologist was astonished to hear that Thomas Farrow had managed to move at all after so severe a beating.

Mrs Farrow lived on for four more days, but never regained consciousness.

The motive for the assault seemed to be theft. The small, metal cash-box which the Farrows kept under their bed, had been forced open and looted. Willy Jones, the shop-boy, told detectives that he thought it had contained around eleven pounds – hardly, it seemed, adequate reason for such premeditated violence.

However, further investigation uncovered local rumours that the couple had kept all their life's savings on the premises. It was untrue – Mr Farrow banked the shop's takings regularly each week.

The killers had left behind only one clue – a single bloody thumbprint on the metal cashbox. This was rushed to the newly formed Central Fingerprint Branch at Scotland Yard to be photographed and enlarged. It was then checked against the prints of all those who might have touched the box since the attacks, including the victims. (This was the first recorded instance of fingerprints being taken from a corpse.) It matched none of them. The unit then checked the print against the 80,000 sets of fingerprints they had on file, but none of these matched either. It seemed plain that the police would have to catch someone before the bloody thumbprint might prove more useful.

Medical examination placed the time of the attacks at around 7 a.m. This made the two young men seen leaving the shop at 7.15 the prime suspects. The killers' knowledge of the Farrows' habits and, presumably, the false rumours about the hoard of money implied local men. Furthermore, the fact that they chose to kill, rather than simply overpowering the old couple suggested that they had feared identification, even though they were wearing masks. It seemed possible that the Farrows were acquainted with their attackers.

The movements of local criminals were checked, and investigators soon learned that two brothers, Alfred and Albert Stratton, had been keeping a low profile since the morning of the murders. The brothers fitted the description of the two men seen leaving the shop, and were of the right age group – Alfred was twenty-two and Albert was twenty. Both had a criminal record for burglary, and a reputation for rebellion. An interview with Hannah Cromarty, Alfred's girl-friend, revealed that he had been out on the streets at the time of the attack, and had returned home in an excited state. Finally Mrs Tedman, Albert's land-lady, told the police that she had found two black stocking masks under his mattress, shortly before the paintshop raid.

The brothers were located when they returned to the area a week later, and arrested. At the initial magistrate's hearing, in which the police applied for an extended period of custody for the suspects, Alfred and Albert were abusive and obnoxious. It may have been this behaviour that prompted the magistrate to grant the application, despite the doubt he expressed concerning the lack of tangible evidence.

The investigating officers now had a week to persuade the Strattons to give their fingerprints. The law did not require suspects to do so, and Alfred and Albert were less than cooperative. However, they were eventually persuaded to comply, perhaps believing that such a strange request could do them little harm. As it turned out, they had made the most fateful decision of their lives – the print on the cash box perfectly matched the right thumb of Alfred Stratton.

The import of fingerprint evidence, and what it might ultimately mean at the trial, seems to have eventually come home to Alfred, the eldest. At the preliminary hearing at Greenwich Police Court he confessed to the theft, but blamed the murders on Albert. His brother retaliated with a similar accusation, placing the blame on Alfred. The court was then adjourned to move to the larger Police Court at Tower Bridge. Here, represented by a solicitor for the first time, the brothers retracted their confessions, and a Crown Court trial was set for 5 May, at the Old Bailey.

The defence saw that they must destroy the validity of the thumbprint evidence to win the case. For this purpose they prepared to attack the accuracy of Scotland Yard's method of fingerprinting itself, and retained the services of two experts in the field to do so. For their part, the prosecution realized that they must defend the abilities of the Central Fingerprint Branch if they were to have any chance of securing a conviction.

The unique individuality of the skin ridges – now known as papillary lines – on a human's finger-tips had been known for centuries in China, where they were used as personalized seals on documents. However, it was not until 1823 – when the Czech physiologist, Johann Purkinje, published a description of the recurrent patterns he had noted on finger-tips – that the subject came under the scrutiny of western science. Even so, the tremendous import to criminology of such a realization remained unexplored for a further fifty-seven years.

In 1880, the October issue of the influential science magazine *Nature*, published a letter from a Scottish doctor, then teaching physiology in Tokyo. Dr Henry Faulds had noticed the striking individuality of fingerprints found on Japanese pottery. Two years later, he had been able to use this knowledge to help an investigation into a local burglary. He pointed out that the fingerprints of an arrested suspect did not match those made in soot by the thief at the scene of the crime. The man was released and the real culprit eventually apprehended. In his letter to *Nature*, Faulds suggested that a system of cataloguing and storing fingerprints would be invaluable to any modern police force.

An ex-Civil Servant named William Herschel read
Faulds' letter and sent a reply to *Nature*, fully agreeing
with the doctor's views, and mentioning that he had
used just such a method to identify illiterate natives in
India in 1860. Dr Faulds, a highly irascible man, misread
Herschel's letter as an attempt to steal the credit for the
discovery. He dashed off a series of infuriated letters
to all the influential men he could think of – including
Charles Darwin – and, in 1885, returned to Britain to
begin a life-long quest to assert his priority over any
other pretenders to the discovery.

Unfortunately for Dr Faulds, his indignant letters only
seem to have alienated the scientific establishment of the
time. When Sir Francis Galton, a cousin of Darwin's,
began to study fingerprints in 1888, he was referred by
the editor of *Nature*, not to Faulds, but Herschel. Sir
Francis' interest delighted the retired Civil Servant – his
superiors in India had all but accused him of insanity –
and he unhesitatingly handed Sir Francis all his research
material.

After three years of studious research, Galton published a paper in *Nature*, stating that not only were
fingerprints as individual and random as snowflakes,
but they also had recurring themes which would allow
cataloguing. The most commonly observed of these
features, he said, were patterns he referred to as arches,
loops and whorls.

Dr Faulds was, characteristically, outraged. He sent
a fuming letter to *Nature*, claiming that it was he,
not Galton, who had invented fingerprint identification. This was, of course, untrue. Faulds had merely
suggested that cataloguing was possible; it was Galton
who actually discovered how it might be achieved.

Galton published a full account of his findings in a

book called *Fingerprints*, in 1892. Another Englishman called Edward Henry, the Inspector General of Police in Bengal, read the work with fascination, but realized that Galton's system was still too primitive to be of much help to the police. Ideally, he thought, an officer should be able to telegraph a simple code, describing a fingerprint, to a central filing unit, which could then swiftly check to see if they had a duplicate already on record. If this were ever to be possible, they would need a more precise method of cataloguing.

As Henry puzzled over the problem, a police officer in Argentina named Juan Vucetich, was putting a basic system of fingerprinting to use. Under his instruction, the officer investigating the murder of two peasant children in the town of Necochea, searched the murder site for bloody fingerprints. He found one on the door which proved that the mother herself, and not the man she had accused, was guilty. It was the first time that fingerprinting had been used to solve a murder case.

Vucetich's system was based on four different types of fingerprint pattern, rather than Galton's three. Edward Henry eventually settled on five basic patterns; Galton's whorls, arches and loops, with the loops and arches subdivided into two groups each. However, this was still not enough to allow a swift and absolutely accurate identification of a fingerprint.

Henry eventually saw that the answer lay not in the central part of the fingerprint's pattern, but the 'leftover' spaces around it. The circular pattern in most fingerprints leaves small triangles, or 'deltas', around the edges. Henry devised an accurate way of measuring and cataloguing these deltas which allowed short, but totally precise descriptions of a fingerprint to be filed.

In 1896, Inspector General Henry ordered the Bengal Police Force to employ his new system. Its introduction was so successful that by May 1901, he was promoted to Assistant Commissioner at Scotland Yard. Two months later, he created the Central Fingerprint Branch. However, despite the successes of fingerprinting worldwide, the new unit was regarded as strictly experimental by his superiors.

The unit's first important success was at the 1902 Derby. Of the 54 suspects arrested for pickpocketing, 29 proved to have been offenders previously fingerprinted by the branch. Any of these that claimed to be first-time offenders were pointed out to the magistrates and treated with suitable severity.

The first Crown case to turn on the evidence of a fingerprint was that of Harry Jackson, also in 1902. While committing a burglary, he made the mistake of touching some wet paint. The fingerprint was matched with Jackson's and the jury was sufficiently convinced by the process to convict him. He was sentenced to seven years.

Prosecuting in the Jackson case was Richard Muir, QC; a highly reputed barrister who would never have touched a common burglary case if it were not for his certainty that fingerprinting was a major leap forward in law enforcement. This was why, three years later, he gladly took on the prosecution of the Stratton brothers with only a single thumbprint to link them with the murders.

Added to the difficulty of convincing the jury that this was enough evidence to convict two men, Muir soon realized that the judge, Sir Arthur Moseley Channel, was far from satisfied that the fingerprinting process was accurate. If the defence managed to convince Sir

Arthur that such identification was open to reasonable
doubt, he might throw the entire case out of court.

Muir opened the prosecution's case by calling Willy
Jones, followed by the detectives that had inspected the
crime scene. With the brutality of the attacks thus firmly
fixed in the jury's minds, he called Hannah Cromarty,
Alfred's girlfriend. She told the court that Alfred had
left, via her bedroom window, at six o'clock on the
morning of 27 March. He had returned two hours later,
she said, panting and in an obviously disturbed state. He
had changed his coat and rubbed black polish into his
brown boots, then, warning Hannah not to tell anyone
that he had been out that morning, left in a hurry.

Mrs Tedman, Albert's landlady, was then called to
give evidence as to the two black stocking masks she had
found under his mattress. The defence made some effort
to put her in a bad light by forcing her to admit that she
had been rifling the bed for money when she found them,
but, by and large, let the matter of the stockings pass.

The main witness for the defence was Henry Faulds,
the same irascible Scottish doctor who claimed to be
the sole discoverer of fingerprint identification. Muir
had earlier called Inspector Charles Collins, of the
Central Fingerprint Branch, who had testified that he
had found eleven distinct points of similarity between
Alfred Stratton's thumbprint and the one found on the
cashbox. Faulds now ridiculed this evaluation. There
were, he said, probably eleven or more *dissimilar* points
to be found between the two prints. As the man who had
worked longest in the field – twenty-five years, in fact –
it was his opinion that the bloody thumbprint, and the
Central Fingerprinting Branch's analysis of it, were not
sufficient evidence to link Alfred with the murders.

Copies of the two prints were passed among the

jury to emphasise Dr Faulds' testimony. He pointed out that some of the papillary ridges did not match; some were thinner, others fatter. The jury, to whom the whole subject of fingerprinting was new, could not have known that even with these differences the chance of two thumbprints being so similar were millions to one against. The Crown's case needed urgent reinforcement.

To refute Dr Faulds' claim, Muir called Inspector Collins back for cross-examination. He explained to the court that the width of the scrolling on a fingerprint was affected by the pressure exerted upon it at any one time. Alfred Stratton's thumbprint had been taken gently, while the bloody thumbprint had been left by somebody wrenching open the cashbox, and thus clutching it tightly. The Inspector went on to demonstrate by taking fingerprints from the members of the jury; first gently, then under mild pressure, then pressed forcefully to the card. The results left no room for argument; Faulds was wrong, Collins was right.

The defence now called their second expert witness, Dr J.G. Garson. Unlike Faulds, Garson was no establishment outsider. He was a vice-president of the Anthropological Institute, had given evidence to the Belper Committee on new forensic methods in 1900, and had invented his own independent method of fingerprint identification. Garson claimed that Edward Henry's – and thus Scotland Yard's – system of identification was inaccurate. He then went on to describe his own system in such detail that the judge was eventually forced to interrupt him to ask what his dissertation had to do with the case in hand.

As Richard Muir stood up to cross-examine Garson, he held up a sheet of paper. He asked if the doctor recognized it as the letter he had sent to the prosecution several weeks before the commencement of the trial, offering his services as an expert witness to *support* the Crown's evidence. Garson stammered that it was indeed his letter, but that he 'had meant to be an independent witness ...' Judge Channell cut him off brusquely saying: 'I would say a completely untrustworthy one. Kindly leave the witness box.' The case for the defence was in ruins.

It has since been suggested that the oddly inexpert evidence offered by Faulds and Garson might have been motivated by self-interest. In the case of Dr Faulds it is clear that he would have jumped at any opportunity to discredit his 'enemies' and get his name in the papers. Dr Garson, however, had rather more to gain from the trial.

In their book *Fingerprints*, Douglas Browne and Alan Brock revealed that in Garson's letter to the defence – sent on the same day that he had written to the prosecution – he offered 'to bring the existing fingerprint system into disrepute.' They suggest that, on being taken up by the defence, Garson must have realized that he and his system of fingerprinting had much to gain in reputation, by the acquittal of the Stratton brothers. Such a judgement would have undermined the Henry system and left Scotland Yard searching for an alternative which Garson would have been eager to supply.

The last hope left to the defence was that in his summing-up, Judge Channell would instruct the jury that the thumbprint evidence was insufficient to convict the brothers. He did not go so far, but did say that it was his belief that the jury 'would not act on such evidence alone.'

It is, of course, unknown how the jury came to their decision, but they found Alfred and Albert guilty of both murders. The brothers were hanged on 23 May 1905.

2

The Spinster's Sovereigns

Many murderers have left their mark on criminal history for their brutality, violence or cunning, and this is the main reason that their exploits still arouse a certain morbid fascination. But even in such dubious company, Frederick Seddon, whose trial was the sensation of 1912, lacks distinction. One account of his case is entitled simply: The Meanest Murderer. In spite of which, the Seddon poisoning case is one of the most dramatic ever staged at the Old Bailey.

On Wednesday 20 September 1911, a man called Frank Vonderahe went to call on his cousin, Miss Eliza Barrow, who lived in the top flat at 63, Tollington Park, Islington – a house owned by a highly successful insurance agent called Frederick Seddon. It was not that Vonderahe was particularly fond of his cousin. Forty-nine-year-old Miss Barrow was eccentric, sly, mean, stupid and inclined to alcoholism, as well as being physically unhygienic. But she was also rich. Her £4,000 or so in cash and property was worth, by modern standards, over £100,000, and in the event of her decease, the Vonderahes could expect to inherit some of her money. Until the previous year, Miss Barrow had lived with the Vonderahes, but had moved out after a quarrel – she was also suspicious and cantankerous.

The door was opened by a servant called Mary Chater. When Vonderahe asked for Miss Barrow, she looked surprised. 'Didn't you know? Miss Barrow is dead and buried.'

Vonderahe was staggered. 'No! When?'

'Last Saturday.'

Vonderahe asked if he could see Miss Barrow's landlord, Frederick Seddon, but was told he was out and would not be back for another hour. Vonderahe went home and told his wife the news – they lived only two streets away. An hour later, both went back to the Seddons' house, but were told that he was still out – at the theatre.

Vonderahe was angry and suspicious. What little he knew about Seddon aroused his distrust. Seddon was a business man through and through, an insurance agent from Lancashire who would go a long way to secure a bargain. If Miss Barrow had died on his premises, then there was almost certainly going to be a tug of war for her worldly possessions.

Vonderahe went to see his brother Albert, and they agreed that their two wives should call on Seddon and ask for details of Miss Barrow's final illness – and, if possible, collect her possessions.

The next morning, the two Mrs Vonderahes were admitted to the parlour by Maggie, Seddon's fifteen-year-old daughter, and kept waiting for some time. Finally the door opened, and Seddon and his wife came into the room. Seddon was a thin man with an almost bald head, a handlebar moustache, and cold and supercilious eyes.

He began by looking at his watch and telling the

women that he had little time to spare. (Mrs Frank
Vonderahe thought she recognized the watch as Miss
Barrow's.) He then asked who they were, and when
they told him, he handed them a carbon copy of a
letter addressed to Frank Vonderahe. It stated that Miss
Barrow had died on Thursday 14 September, and that
her funeral would take place on Saturday. It added that
three days before her death, Miss Barrow had made a
will leaving all her estate to a ten-year-old boy called
Ernie Grant – who lived with her – and his sister Hilda,
and appointing Seddon as her executor. The original
letter, Seddon claimed, had been sent to the Vonderahes
at their address in Evershot Road.

Mrs Vonderahe said she had never received it. That,
replied Seddon, was probably because he had sent it to
their previous address in Corbyn Street, and it had not
been forwarded. But in any case, they could have copies
of the letter, the will and a memorial card. The latter
contained the sugary lines:

> A dear one is missing and with us no more,
> That voice so much loved we hear not again,
> Yet we think of you now the same as of yore,
> And know you are free from trouble and pain.

Seddon put these items in an envelope, handed it to
one of the women, and made it clear by his manner that
he now expected them to leave.

The two women had noticed that Mrs Seddon – a
plain, tired-looking woman who had once been pretty –
seemed to be upset. But she was obviously totally under
her husband's thumb. When she tried to speak, Seddon
interrupted: 'Sit still, my dear. Don't upset yourself. I
can say all there is to say.'

Mrs Frank Vonderahe asked if her husband could come and talk to Seddon that evening, but he answered impatiently: 'That's impossible, I'm going away tomorrow. Anyway, I've wasted enough time on you. I'm a businessman, and can't be troubled by people asking questions.' With that he showed them the door.

The women were upset and offended. Seddon had not even tried to be pleasant. He had treated them as if they were his social inferiors – and, moreover, as if he thought that all they were interested in was the dead woman's money. The fact that there was some truth in this made it none the less unpalatable.

Frank and Albert Vonderahe were angry and even more suspicious. The excuse about sending the letter to the previous address was patently untrue – Frank Vonderahe was always receiving letters that had been forwarded. So why should Seddon lie about informing them of their cousin's death? There could be only one reason: that he intended to get his hands on her money.

When Frank Vonderahe called again at the Seddons' house, he learned that they had gone away to Southend for a holiday. Possibly Seddon realized that he was exciting suspicion, for a week later, Ernie Grant – Miss Barrow's ward – came to call on Frank Vonderahe. But he was accompanied by Seddon's two sons, and it was impossible to talk to him privately. This made Vonderahe more suspicious – and irritable – than ever. When the boys left, he told them to tell Seddon that he would call on him in about a week's time.

He made good his promise on 9 October 1911, and took with him a friend to act as witness. Seddon kept them waiting twenty minutes, then strode into the room – again accompanied by his wife – with an air of

supreme confidence. 'Mr Frank Vonderahe?' he asked.
Vonderahe admitted his identity. 'And your brother
Albert Vonderahe?' Frank explained that the other man
was a friend called Thomas Walker, and Seddon looked
surprised and irritated. He took his place at the fireside,
and lit a cigar.

'Now, what do you want?'

Vonderahe could see that Seddon was determined to
browbeat him – he suspected that during the twenty
minutes they had been kept waiting, Seddon had been
fortifying himself with a few drinks. In fact, Seddon gave
him very little chance to speak. He was an extremely
fluent talker, and exuded self-assurance as he waved
his cigar. He told Vonderahe that he heard he had
been making enquiries about Miss Barrow's financial
affairs, and when Vonderahe admitted it, Seddon's
reply was that he didn't see why he should give any
information. He himself would be perfectly happy to
talk to a solicitor about it. He added airily: 'I'm prepared
to spend a thousand pounds to prove that all I have done
is legal.' Seddon obviously hoped that the mention of this
huge sum would make Vonderahe feel he didn't stand a
chance.

Vonderahe wanted to know who now owned the
'Buck's Head' public house – which had brought Miss
Barrow £150 a year. 'I do,' said Seddon, 'I bought it on
the open market. I also own the barber's shop next door.
I'm always open to buy property. This house I live in is
my own, and I own seventeen other properties.'

According to Seddon, Miss Barrow's cashbox had
contained only a little over £4 on her death. Yet
Vonderahe had seen it stuffed with sovereigns and
£5 notes when Miss Barrow had lived with them in
Corbyn Street.

Vonderahe also wanted to know why Miss Barrow had been buried in a pauper's common grave at Finchley, when she could have been buried in the family vault at Highgate.

'I thought the vault was full up,' replied Seddon promptly. He seemed to have a ready answer to everything.

'How much did you pay for the "Buck's Head"?' asked Vonderahe.

'That is for the proper authorities to find out,' replied Seddon smartly. He was obviously pleased with the way he was handling this conversation. His manner seemed to imply: 'And there's not a damn thing you can do about it.'

So Vonderahe took his leave, angrier than ever, and determined to find a way to bring this arrogant bully crashing from his high horse.

He and his brother talked it over. They were quite certain that the 'Buck's Head' had never been on the open market. So here was another lie in which they had detected the glib insurance agent. As to the will signed by Miss Barrow, it merely left Ernie Grant and his sister her 'personal possessions', and these, according to Seddon, were worth only £16. So what had become of Miss Barrow's fortune of £4,000 or so? The answer, they suspected, was that it had gone into Seddon's pocket. The Vonderahes decided that it was time to inform the police of their suspicions. Frank Vonderahe lost no time in writing a letter to Sir Charles Mathews, the Director of Public Prosecutions..

It is not easy to convince the authorities that an exhumation is necessary, but when their enquiries revealed that Miss Barrow had died after several days of diarrhoea and vomiting, they agreed that it sounded extremely suspicious. The death certificate, signed by Seddon's doctor – a man named Sworn – stated that she had died of heart failure/epidemic diarrhoea. But apparently Sworn had not even called at the house to inspect the body. And any doctor with experience in police work knew that arsenic poisoning produces symptoms of diarrhoea and vomiting.

The doctor who was asked to conduct the exhumation was the relatively young Bernard Spilsbury, who had acquired a certain celebrity in the previous year, when he had given evidence in the trial of Crippen. Oddly enough, the graveyard in which Miss Barrow had been buried – the Islington Borough Cemetery – had also been the scene of the interment of what remained of Cora Crippen after her body had been dug up from Crippen's cellar. Spilsbury was accompanied by his friend and colleague, Dr (later Sir) William Willcox.

Seddon's first intimation that all was not well was when a messenger – who proved to be a coroner's officer – handed him a slip of paper that informed him that he was required to attend the inquest of the body of Miss Eliza Barrow on 15 November. He spent the night awake, making notes about his side of the story. Frank Vonderahe later recorded with understandable satisfaction that after his sleepless night, Seddon looked twenty years older. Yet if he knew that all his plans were unravelling, he did not show it at the inquest. In any case, this was adjourned awaiting the results of the post mortem conducted by Spilsbury and Willcox. A few days later, Spilsbury noted that he had been unable to detect any sign of disease in Miss Barrow's body, but that it was exceptionally well preserved. This phrase was more ominous than it sounds, for there is one poison that has the effect of preserving a body: arsenic. And arsenic is what Dr Willcox went on to detect in Miss Barrow's internal organs. Death, he concluded, was due to acute arsenical poisoning.

On 4 December, Seddon was arrested on a charge of murdering his lodger with arsenic. He cried indignantly: 'Absurd! What a terrible charge! Wilful murder! It is the first of our family that has ever been charged with such a crime. Are you going to arrest my wife as well?'

That exclamation was the first of Seddon's major mistakes. Would a totally innocent man, who knew nothing about his lodger's death, ask if his wife was being charged as well? Would he not, rather, protest strenuously that it must all be an absurd mistake?

Seddon was remanded in custody. By the time he appeared at the re-opened inquest, he was his usual confident self, laughing as he ate sandwiches and drank tea. He was inclined to be as loquacious as ever, and the coroner had to warn him that he had better save his comments for later. The reason became clear when a verdict of wilful murder by some person or persons unknown was returned.

Chief Inspector Alfred Ward was placed in charge of the case. He was aware that he had a difficult task in front of him. Seddon was a respectable member of the middle classes, and had never been in trouble with the law. The case against him was purely circumstantial. What Ward had to find was where Seddon had obtained the arsenic.

Ward's enquiries showed that Frederick Henry Seddon had been born in Lancashire in 1872, and he became an 'insurance man' at the age of 19. His company, the London and Manchester Industrial Insurance Company, found him intelligent, hard working and determined to rise in the world. By the age of 24 he was a district superintendent in Islington. His memory for figures was prodigious, and his book-keeping immaculate. He had engaged in various property deals, and by 1911 his income was £750 a year. He had bought the fourteen room house at 63, Tollington Park in 1909, and lived there with his wife Margaret, five children, and his 73-year-old father. But even here Seddon showed his meanness; he put up a partition in one of the rooms and crowded six members of the household into it.

He was a lay preacher, a Freemason, and a highly active chapelgoer. But Ward's enquiries suggested that his life was not quite blameless. There was gossip about affairs with women at whose homes he had to call in the absence of their husbands. Until the year of Miss Barrow's death he had been a teetotaller, but he had since taken up drinking – although there was no suggestion that he did so to excess. Although well-off by any standards, he apparently stinted his wife on housekeeping money, to such an extent that she had once been on the point of leaving him.

In 1910, Seddon advertised the top floor of his house for rent at 12s 6d a week, and on 25 July, Miss Barrow agreed to take it. She was a woman of 49, overweight and hard of hearing, and she was accompanied by a nine-year-old boy named Ernie Grant – the son of a dead relative – and by a middle-aged couple named Hook. Hook, it seemed, was Ernie's uncle; Miss Barrow had lived with Ernie's family for six years before the death of Ernie's mother, and now seemed deeply and genuinely attached to Ernie. Hook, it seemed, had been her sweetheart at one time, and now she had agreed to let the Hooks live rent free, in exchange for being taught cooking and housekeeping by Mrs Hook.

This arrangement did not last. The Hooks, like Miss

Barrow, were prone to a tipple, and after only a week
there was a quarrel, and Miss Barrow asked Seddon to
evict the Hooks. Seddon later claimed that he intended
to evict them all, but decided to allow Miss Barrow and
Ernie to stay. As Hook took his leave, he shouted that
Seddon was after her money, and added: 'And I defy you
and a regiment like you to get it.' This seems to have been
the first time that Seddon realized that his slovenly lodger
was wealthy. In fact, she was rather less wealthy than he
was; but Seddon was a miser, and anyone with money
enjoyed his respect.

Miss Barrow was also a miser; Frank Vonderahe
would remark later 'She had a great regard for money,
and in the ordinary course of things would not give four
farthings for a penny.' Yet during the course of the next
six months she developed such trust in Seddon that she
virtually allowed him to take charge of every penny she
possessed. How did he do it? Unfortunately, we shall
never know. But it *is* possible to make a few educated
guesses.

Vonderahe's account (which was published in 1916 in
a book called *Survivors' Tales of Famous Crimes*) makes
it clear that Seddon overflowed with the self-confidence
of a hard-headed businessman, one who believes himself
to be a winner in the game of life. His ascent, after all,
had been fairly rapid. Within five years of starting on
the lowest rung of the insurance ladder, he had become a
district superintendent. An insurance salesman needs to
be a smooth and convincing talker, and to be capable of
exerting a certain charm; Seddon's local acquaintances
seem to agree that he could do both. He was known
among his fellow masons as excellent company. His rise
had given him enormous confidence in his own abilities.
So he presented himself to Miss Barrow as the kindly,

successful man of the world, a man accustomed to think in thousands, and willing to give her the benefit of his free advice. No doubt he also made her feel that he and she differed from common people like the Hooks and the Vonderahes because they belonged to a kind of natural gentry. And since he was also wealthy, she had no reason to fear that he was interested in getting his hands on her money.

It is also recorded that Eliza Barrow and Frederick Seddon shared one rather peculiar taste: they loved to actually *handle* gold coins; like the miser of tradition, they loved to let them run through their fingers. It is recorded that when Miss Barrow had pound notes, she lost no time in changing them into gold sovereigns. The sight of Seddon sitting at a table, counting out sovereigns into bags, must have filled her with an emotion akin to love. No one (as far as I know) has suggested that Miss Barrow experienced a romantic attachment to Seddon – yet it is not inconsistent with the facts. She was a lonely old maid, locked, like Scrooge, into a world of negative emotions. Seddon was not unattractive; he was just the sort of man she probably wished she had married. Of course, Seddon was already married – to a woman eight years his junior, while Miss Barrow was nine years his senior. This is the kind of situation that makes a man seem more attractive than ever.

The facts suggest another interesting possibility. Seddon was a teetotaller until soon after Miss Barrow came to live in his house. Is it not conceivable that he began to drink in order to keep Miss Barrow company, and that it was while sharing a bottle of sweet sherry that he persuaded her to allow him to take charge of her money?

All this is speculation. What we know is that in the

autumn of 1911, Miss Barrow agreed to part with £1,600 in India stock in exchange for an annuity of £103 4s per annum, or about £2 a week – roughly 6½ per cent. He took over the leasehold of the 'Buck's Head' for a further £1 a week, or £52 per annum. Since Vonderahe remarks that the pub brought her an income of £105 per annum, and the adjoining barber's shop a further £52, it seems incredible that she should have allowed Seddon to take over both properties in exchange for the same amount of money that the barber's shop brought her. We have to assume that she was completely under Seddon's spell.

In July 1911, Miss Barrow – alarmed by a bank failure – closed her bank account and drew out £216, which she insisted on having in gold sovereigns. To a man like Seddon, the presence of so much gold in his house must have aroused a kind of lust. In August, the Seddons went on a three-day holiday to Southend-on-Sea, taking Eliza Barrow with them.

On 1 September 1911, Miss Barrow complained that she was feeling unwell. Seddon's own medical attendant, Dr Sworn, called that day and found her suffering from diarrhoea and vomiting. Three days later she had ceased to suffer from diarrhoea, but the bilious attacks continued. Dr Sworn suggested that she should be moved into hospital – and for a moment Seddon's heart must have been in his mouth; but she parsimoniously revolted at the idea, and she remained and grew worse. On 11 September, Seddon's sister, Mrs Longley, came to stay at 63, Tollington Park. She was shocked by the filth and smell in Miss Barrow's room, but when she mentioned this to her brother, he simply remarked that he had a delicate stomach and could not stand the smell either. During all this time, Miss Barrow insisted that ten-year-old Ernie Grant should continue to share her bed, although he had his own bedroom.

On the evening of 11 September, Miss Barrow decided to make a will, and asked Seddon to draft it for her – according to Seddon, he urged her to call in a solicitor but she refused. (He was almost certainly lying.)

On the evening of 13 September, Miss Barrow's condition had worsened. Seddon went out to the theatre, and came back in a state of indignation because he claimed that he had been given change for two shillings instead of half-a-crown. At 11.30, Miss Barrow sent Ernie Grant with a message to Mrs Seddon: 'I am dying.' Margaret Seddon found her groaning on the floor, and sat by her bed for the rest of the night, while Seddon himself sat outside the bedroom door reading a newspaper and smoking his pipe. The following morning, at 6.20, she died. Seddon called at Dr Sworn's surgery, and the doctor handed him a death certificate, stating that she had died of epidemic diarrhoea. Seddon then went to an undertaker and told him that Miss Barrow had only left £4. The only way that a funeral could be arranged for so little was by consigning her to a common grave. This is what happened two days later, on Saturday 16 September 1911. Incredibly, Seddon asked the undertaker for 'commission', and accepted 12s 6d.

This, then, is the story that Chief Inspector Ward learned as he conducted enquiries into the death of Eliza Barrow. In his account in *Survivors' Tales of Famous Crimes*, Vonderahe claims that he had been in the habit of seeing his cousin about three times a week, but this is almost certainly untrue. Several writers on the case have stated that she was on bad terms with the Vonderahes, and had left their house after a quarrel which ended with her spitting in Mrs Vonderahe's face.

There can be little doubt that one of the considerations that led Seddon to poison Miss Barrow was the fact that she seemed to be friendless. This explains the lack of consideration – not to say contempt – with which he treated the Vonderahes after her death: he saw them as vultures swooping on a battlefield. And this, as we can now see clearly, was his major miscalculation. If he had invited them to the funeral and showed them the will leaving her possessions to Ernie Grant, everyone would have been satisfied.

The first problem facing Chief Inspector Ward when he took over the case was to prove that Seddon had access to arsenic. Routine enquiries at every chemist's shop in the area revealed that on 26 August, four days before the onset of Miss Barrow's illness, Maggie Seddon – the eldest daughter – had bought Mather's flypapers at the shop of a chemist called Walter Thorley, in Crouch Hill. Such flypapers were sheets of ordinary absorbent paper impregnated with arsenic, and they were hung from the ceiling or placed on the mantelpiece soaked in sugared water. To extract the arsenic merely required steeping them in hot water. In 1889, a Liverpool housewife, Florence Maybrick, had been convicted of poisoning her husband because the maid had given evidence concerning flypapers that were steeped in the washbowl in her bedroom.

The trial of the Seddons – for Margaret Seddon had also been arrested in mid-January – opened at the Old Bailey on 4 March 1912. The evidence was, of course, purely circumstantial: no one had seen Seddon introducing poison into Miss Barrow's food or drink, and there was no real evidence that he had purchased poison. (Willcox never believed that Seddon had used flypapers; he suspected rat poison.)

Sir Rufus Isaacs, the Attorney General, led for the prosecution, supported by Travers Humphreys. Edward Marshall Hall led for the defence. When Marshall Hall had read the account of the death of Miss Barrow, he had remarked: 'This is the blackest case I have ever been in.' It was unusual for him to agree to take a case unless he was fairly convinced of the innocence of his client; this seems to have been the exception. He also felt strongly that Seddon should not appear in the witness box, remarking: 'If the evidence does not convict this man, his conceit will.' And indeed, Seddon's conceit was instrumental in seriously undermining his case, for when he heard that the Attorney General himself was prosecuting him, he was delighted at the idea of crossing swords with him, and determined to appear as a witness in his own defence.

Humphreys outlined the case for the Crown. He told the story of how Miss Barrow had come to live at the Seddons', how she had drawn out £216 in July 1911, how she had made over her remaining assets to Seddon, and how she had died in agony. He described how Seddon had arranged for the body to be buried in a pauper's grave, although there was a family vault in Islington, and had taken Miss Barrow's watch to a jeweller to have her name removed from the case. He also described how, after that, Seddon suddenly had plenty of cash in hand. His two assistants saw about £200 in sovereigns in his basement office, and were certain this was not money they had collected. He had put £80 into his bank account, and discussed paying off the mortgage on his house. Soon after, the Seddons both began using £5 notes that were known to have belonged to Miss Barrow, and Seddon had given a false name and address when changing some of these. (In those days, a £5 note – now worth more than £100 – was not easy to change, and particulars had to be furnished.) Clearly, Seddon had suddenly acquired a large sum of ready cash.

The Vonderahes then gave their evidence, followed by the Hooks, who described how they had been handed a note from Miss Barrow by Seddon's daughter Maggie, which declared they had treated her badly and would have to leave. The Hooks had no doubt that Seddon had talked her into writing the note.

But the most important evidence so far was that of Dr Willcox. He had taken over the examination of Miss Barrow after Spilsbury had concluded that there was no evidence of any physical illness, and had soon discovered arsenic in her organs. Willcox had used the famous test devised by James Marsh in the 1830s. The suspected arsenic is heated with zinc and sulphuric acid, and the gas given off passed through a small nozzle and set alight. The zinc and sulphuric acid produce hydrogen, which is inflammable; but if arsenic is present, it combines with the hydrogen to create arsine gas, and if this is ignited and a cold plate held against the flame, the result is a deposit on the plate, known as an 'arsenic mirror'.

With incredible thoroughness, Willcox had weighed the 'arsenic mirror', then – assuming that the arsenic was evenly distributed throughout the stomach – estimated how much arsenic must have been originally present. Willcox's estimate was that, in the vital organs alone (and not counting the rest of the body), there were more than two grains, which is about the fatal dose for arsenic. (Textbooks of toxicology estimate this at between two and three grains.) The total could have been as much as five grains.

But Marshall Hall was equally famous for his thoroughness, and he raised an objection that almost destroyed the prosecution. Miss Barrow had originally weighed ten stone (140 lbs), but her two months in the ground had reduced her weight to a mere 60 lbs, less than half. (The human body is more than 50 per cent water, which evaporates after death.) So the poison Willcox had found must have been concentrated by more than half. And in that case, the dose would have been a little over a grain – not enough to cause death. Willcox might have replied – but did not – that he had concentrated on the stomach, and that if he had extended his examination to other parts of the body, the total would have been much greater. Marshall Hall had scored a telling point.

He went on to make another. When someone is poisoned by arsenic, the chemical gets into the hair. Willcox had found arsenic at the end of the hair close to the scalp, and about half as much in the far end. But, said Marshall Hall, it would take about a year for arsenic to reach the far end of the hair, and the prosecution was alleging that Seddon had started to poison Miss Barrow only sixteen days before her death.

Willcox was shaken. Marshall Hall was implying that Miss Barrow had absorbed arsenic from some other source – such as the flypapers in her room – long before September 1911. If that possibility could be established in the minds of the jury, Seddon was virtually a free man.

Marshall Hall's biographer has remarked that if he had sat down then, he might well have won his case. But as the cross-examination continued, Willcox suddenly saw the answer. Miss Barrow's body, he now realized, had lain in a coffin in which there was a certain amount of bloodstained fluid, and the arsenic was probably absorbed from this fluid. Marshall Hall shook his head and looked sceptical. But Willcox determined to prove his point. He went home, took a lock of hair from the head of a female patient, and soaked it in the same fluid. Another medical man then took over the experiment and washed the hair – as had been done with Miss Barrow's – then tested it for arsenic. It proved to contain precisely the same amount as Miss Barrow's. For a while, the case had hung upon a hair, but the experiment left no doubt that Willcox's theory was correct.

Yet even so, Seddon might still have escaped on the grounds that all the evidence was circumstantial – British juries hate to convict on circumstantial evidence. But in spite of all Marshall Hall's efforts to persuade him not to give evidence, the vain insurance agent wanted to demonstrate his brilliance, and insisted on entering the witness box. To begin with – as Marshall Hall examined him – it looked as if he was justified; he spoke with clarity and common-sense. But at this point Sir Rufus Isaacs took over, and almost immediately scored a telling point. 'Did you like Miss Barrow?' he asked. Seddon was taken aback. 'Did I like her?' He thought hard. 'She was not a woman you could be in love with, but I deeply sympathised with her.' Analysed in retrospect, it can be seen as a straightforward and honest answer: he didn't like her, but her miserly nature aroused fellow feeling. In court, it sounded as if he was merely being evasive, and trying to obscure the fact that he regarded her simply as a nasty and smelly old woman.

Another exchange did Seddon even more harm. Accused of counting Miss Barrow's sovereigns immediately after her death, he exploded: 'I am not a degenerate. That would make it out that I am a greedy, inhuman monster . . . I would have had all day to count it.' The bathos of the last statement completely destroyed the effect of his only spontaneous outburst of the trial.

In his own opinion, Seddon probably felt that he had been devastating. What he failed to grasp was that this long cross-examination left the jury in no doubt about his character. He was certainly intelligent – Marshall Hall called him 'the ablest man I ever defended' – but he was also cold, calculating and pathologically mean. The extent of his meanness was further revealed when his wife went into the witness box. She looked nervous, pale and downtrodden, and when the jury learned that Seddon continually bullied her to reduce the housekeeping bills, and that on one occasion she had even been about to leave him because of his meanness, it seemed plain that they had decided that she was a victim of the calculating miser now in the dock.

In his final speech, Marshall Hall did his best. He emphasized that his client was a relatively wealthy man, who had no need to commit murder. Seddon had benefited by her death to the extent of a mere £1 8s a week, and 'people do not commit murders for one pound ten shillings a week.' His problem was that by now the jury felt that Seddon would commit murder for sixpence. At the end of four hours, Marshall Hall ended with the kind of emotional plea for which he was famous. Great scientists, he said, had been giving evidence against the Seddons. But science could not create the spark of life. And if the jury condemned the Seddons, 'that vital spark will be extinguished, and no science known to the world can ever replace it.'

Sir Rufus Isaacs, summing-up for the prosecution, was devastating. He left the jury in no doubt that, whether the evidence was circumstantial or not, it was conclusive. For example, the boy Ernie Grant went to the same school as the children of the Vonderahes. If he had gone to school on the morning of Miss Barrow's death, he would certainly have told the Vonderahe children. But the child did not go to school; instead, Seddon sent him down to Southend . . . So many facts revealed Seddon's careful calculation and his dishonesty, there could only be one answer to the question of how the arsenic had found its way into Miss Barrow's stomach.

The summing-up by Mr Justice Bucknill was equally devastating for Seddon (although he hinted fairly clearly that he thought Mrs Seddon should be acquitted). After that, it took the jury only one hour to find Seddon guilty and to acquit Mrs Seddon. In the total silence that followed, Seddon kissed his wife on the lips. She was then taken away, weeping hysterically, to be released. Asked if he had anything to say before sentence was passed, Seddon cleared his throat and – to everyone's surprise – said: 'I have, sir', then embarked on a precise and lucid account of his financial dealings with Miss Barrow. At the end, he raised his hand in a masonic salute – he knew the judge was a fellow Mason – and declared: 'I swear by the Great Architect of the Universe that I am innocent.'

The judge was obviously shaken by this. In his reply, he reminded Seddon that although they were members of the same brotherhood, it did not encourage crime. He ended by imploring Seddon to make his peace with God. Seddon's reply was: 'I am at peace.' After the death sentence he drank a glass of water, still looking unmoved, then was taken away.

Seddon's appeal was dismissed. And a petition for a reprieve – surprisingly signed by 300,000 people – was rejected by the Home Secretary. In prison, Seddon was calm, and continued to maintain his innocence. But he showed some emotion when told of the poor price that his property had fetched. 'Well, that finishes it!' He was hanged on 18 April 1912, at Pentonville.

In his introduction to the *Notable British Trials* volume on Seddon, Filson Young seems to take the view that Seddon was unfairly treated. In his summing up, the judge emphasized every single point that could be made against him, but neglected those in his favour. One example of the latter concerns Maggie Seddon and the purchase of the poison. It was alleged that Maggie had bought the poison at the shop of Walter Thorley in Crouch Hill. Maggie denied this, and may well have been telling the truth – Thorley knew Maggie by sight (she was a friend of his daughters), yet at first told the police he could not identify the fair-haired girl who bought the flypapers.

Soon after his arrest, Seddon decided that someone ought to purchase some similar flypapers and test it to see how much arsenic could be obtained from it. Maggie was accordingly sent to another chemist, Robert Price, to buy them. He asked her name, and when told it was Seddon, decided not to supply her, since he preferred not to get involved in the case.

When Maggie was questioned by the police, the question was framed in such a way that her statement seemed to deny that she had ever been in Price's shop. And in due course, this statement was used by the prosecution to discredit Maggie's denial of buying the other flypapers in Walter Thorley's shop.

Filson Young is certainly correct to point out that all this was extremely dubious – after all, if Maggie's denial of buying the flypapers had been accepted by the jury, her father might well have been acquitted. In fact, Marshall Hall raised this question in his final speech, but by then the time to sway the jury was past.

Filson Young's point seems to be that if the presentation of the evidence had been more balanced, Seddon would probably have been acquitted. He might also have added that the jury probably convicted Seddon as much for his meanness and arrogance as for the murder of Miss Barrow. The fact remains that when the evidence is examined in retrospect, and all Seddon's actions taken into account, it is virtually impossible to believe that he was innocent.

After Seddon's execution, his wife married again, and she and the family moved to California. On 17 November 1912, while she was still in Liverpool waiting to sail, the *Weekly Dispatch* published two articles signed by Mrs Seddon describing her miserable life with him, and declaring that she had seen her husband administer the final dose of poison to Miss Barrow, and that he then terrorized her into silence with a revolver. *John Bull* pursued the story, and two weeks later, published an affidavit to the effect that Mrs Seddon had done it for money, and to put an end to gossip about her being her husband's accomplice in murder.

In his *Life of Marshall Hall*, Edward Marjoribanks seems unconvinced. He points out that Seddon *did* own a revolver. And he tells how, when his solicitor went to his house, Seddon pointed at a picture on the dining-room wall, showing a husband shooting his wife's lover, and commented: 'I'd have shot them both – that's the kind of man I am.'

Looking back on the case, it seems highly likely that Mrs Seddon knew about the poisoning while it was going on. One writer objects that Seddon was far too mean to take his wife into his confidence, since she would have demanded a share of the proceeds – the answer to which is that Mrs Seddon was too browbeaten to demand anything. The truth is probably that if the jury had known all the facts, Mrs Seddon would also have gone to the gallows. Yet it is impossible not to feel that, if that had happened, it would have been as great a miscarriage of justice as Frederick Seddon's acquittal.

3

The Brides in the Bath

At about 7.35 on the evening of 18 December 1914, a landlady named Louisa Blatch was ironing in her kitchen when she heard a splashing sound from the bathroom overhead. The sound was not unexpected, since her new lodger, Mrs Margaret Lloyd, had gone into the bathroom a few minutes ago – Mrs Blatch had run the bath for her. But as Mrs Blatch continued her ironing, there was a squeaking sound, as if someone was grabbing the side of the bath with wet hands, and then a sigh. A few minutes later, the sound of an organ pealed from the sitting-room next door; it was playing 'Nearer My God to Thee.' This seemed odd, for Mrs Blatch had heard Mrs Lloyd's husband – who was now playing the organ – going up the stairs in the direction of the bathroom. Evidently he had come down very quietly – or perhaps it was one of the other lodgers going upstairs.

The music continued for perhaps ten minutes. Then Mrs Blatch heard the front door slam. A few minutes later, the doorbell rang. It was Mrs Lloyd's husband, a tall gentleman with a moustache – although perhaps gentleman was not the right word, since Mr Lloyd had a cockney accent and dropped his aitches; he was definitely not of the same social class as his wife, who spoke like a lady.

'I'm sorry,' said Mr Lloyd, 'I forgot I had a key.' He explained that he had been out to buy his wife some tomatoes for supper, and asked if she had finished her bath. Mrs Blatch said she had not seen her, and Mr Lloyd went upstairs.

A moment later he called: 'My God, there's no answer.'

'Perhaps she's in the bedroom.'

There was a pause, followed by a cry of alarm 'Come and help me. She's in the bath.'

Mrs Blatch was unwilling to enter a bathroom with a strange gentleman, but was eventually persuaded to forget her principles. In the darkened bathroom, Mr Lloyd was struggling to lift his wife out of the bath. Mrs Blatch felt her arm, and it was cold.

Mrs Blatch lost no time in running for a policeman. He arrived to find Mr Lloyd trying to give his wife artificial respiration on the bathroom floor. But when a doctor arrived soon afterwards, he quickly pronounced Mrs Lloyd dead.

It was the second time in twenty-four hours that Dr Stephen Bates had seen Mrs Lloyd. The evening before, Mr Lloyd had brought her along to see him, explaining that his wife had a headache, and was suffering from dizzy spells. Mrs Lloyd had certainly seemed oddly lethargic and passive. Dr Bates had concluded that she might be sickening for flu. Her death in the bath seemed to confirm that verdict; it was Dr Bates' opinion that the hot water had caused an attack of syncope – or, in plain English, a fainting fit.

On Sunday 3 January, the *News of the World* carried a story headlined: BRIDE'S TRAGIC FATE ON

DAY AFTER WEDDING! which began: 'Particularly
sad circumstances under which a bride of a day met
her death were investigated at an Islington inquest
on Margaret Elizabeth Lloyd, thirty-eight, wife of a
land agent of Holloway.' The verdict had been one of
accidental death.

In the village of Aston Clinton in Buckinghamshire,
a retired coal merchant named Charles Burnham read
the item in the *News of the World*, and was suddenly
gripped by suspicion. His own daughter, a nurse called
Alice, had drowned in almost identical circumstances
only a year before; her husband, to whom Mr Burnham
had taken an instant and violent dislike, had been called
George Joseph Smith. Could this Lloyd person be the
same man? Mr Burnham cut out the newspaper story,
and sent it, together with a letter, to the police at nearby
Aylesbury.

At about the same time as Mr Burnham was reading
his *News of the World*, Mr Bill Haynes of Blackpool
was engaged in the same activity. It so happened that
Mr Haynes had helped to carry the body of Charles
Burnham's daughter out of the bathroom after she had
been found dead. Like Mr Burnham, he concluded that
this seemed like more than coincidence. When he told
his wife that he was taking the *News of the World* over
to Alice Burnham's ex-landlord, Sarah Haynes raised
objections; she wanted to read it first. So Bill Haynes
went out and – with some difficulty – managed to buy
another copy. With this he called upon Joe Crossley
of 16, Regent Road. There happened to be a family
gathering at the Crossleys that Sunday morning, and
they all read the inquest report and agreed that it
was highly suspicious. Joe Crossley decided to write
to Scotland Yard.

Within a few days, both these letters, together with the inquest report and a clipping from a Blackpool newspaper about Alice Burnham's death, landed on the desk of Detective Inspector Arthur Neil of the Kentish Town Police Station – the lodging at 14, Bismarck Road, Highgate, where Mrs Lloyd had died, fell within his precinct. The inspector agreed that the two cases sounded suspiciously similar.

His first step was to visit Bismarck Road. There he was shown the large tin bath in which Mrs Lloyd had drowned, and was told that Mr Lloyd had ordered the cheapest possible funeral for his wife. Dr Bates was able to tell him that there were no signs of violence on the body, except for a bruise on the elbow. He verified that Lloyd had shown no sign of grief.

A detective sergeant named Dennison also had a story for Neil. Before Lloyd and his wife had taken rooms with Mrs Blatch, they had first called at the boarding of a Mrs Lokker, where one of the tenants had allowed Lloyd to pay a deposit of six shillings. Mr Lloyd had asked to see the bath, and had complained that it was a 'bit small', but probably large enough for someone to lie down in. The Lloyds had then left, saying they would return later. When the landlady returned, she had objected to tenants who could not provide references, and had asked Detective Sergeant Dennison – who was a friend – to return Mr Lloyd's deposit and ask him to leave. Lloyd and his bride had duly been turned away, and had then located Mrs Blatch's house half a mile away.

This interest in the bath intensified Neil's suspicions. Further enquiries revealed that Mrs Lloyd had made a will a few hours before her death, making her husband sole heir – Lloyd had already been in touch with a lawyer named Davies about the will. She had also gone to the local savings bank and had drawn out all her money. A few days later, Dr Bates was able to tell Inspector Neil that the Yorkshire Insurance Company had contacted him, telling him that John Lloyd had taken out a life insurance policy for £700 on his wife.

The next step was to find out more about the death of Alice Burnham. The Blackpool police supplied the information, and it left Neil in no doubt that John Lloyd and George Smith were the same person. Smith and his newly married wife Alice had arrived in Blackpool on 10 December 1913, and had found rooms at the Crossleys. Interestingly enough, this was the second lodging they had called at; Mr Smith had rejected the first because it had no bath. He had also insisted on inspecting the bathroom before taking rooms at the Crossleys.

The day after settling in, Mr Smith had asked Mrs Crossley to recommend a doctor – his wife was suffering from a headache. Dr George Billing could find nothing much wrong with Mrs Smith, although he observed that she had a slight heart murmur. He prescribed heroin and caffeine.

The next day, Mrs Smith asked if she might have a bath later. She climbed into it around eight in the evening. As the Crossleys sat eating high tea in the kitchen, someone noticed a patch of water on the ceiling, and Mrs Crossley asked her daughter-in-law Alice to go and ask Mrs Smith not to overfill the bath. Alice objected that the new tenants might think they were grumbling. A few minutes later, Mr Smith came into the kitchen, and placed a bag on the table. 'I've brought some eggs for Mrs Smith's breakfast.' He stayed around for a while talking about Blackpool's new fire engine, then said goodnight. Moments later, he was calling: 'Fetch the doctor.' He had found his wife in the bath with her head below the water.

The coroner's verdict was 'Heart failure in the bath. Accidental drowning.'

Smith, like Lloyd, had told the undertaker that he wanted the cheapest burial possible; he even agreed to have her buried in a public grave, then changed his mind. This was, apparently, not due to conscience, but to the fact that his late wife's mother and brother had arrived in Blackpool for the funeral. But when the undertaker told him that, in that case, the funeral would have to be delayed for two days, Smith replied: 'I can't wait. Put her in that public grave, but don't tell her mother.' He carefully removed the rings from the body before the funeral. He had even objected to moving into another boarding house on the night of his wife's death – because of the cost – saying that he didn't mind sleeping alongside the body. The Crossleys were shocked at his callousness. And Mrs Crossley apparently had her suspicions that the death was not natural, for after the funeral she had been unable to restrain her feelings, and shouted 'Crippen!' after their departing lodger.

Smith and Lloyd certainly sounded remarkably alike.

From Alice Burnham's parents, Neil learned the story of how their daughter came to become Mrs Smith, and end in a pauper's grave.

Smith had met Alice in Southsea in a Methodist chapel in September 1913. Alice was 25 years old, 5 feet 6 inches tall, and distinctly plump. One of Smith's chroniclers, Arthur La Bern, remarks that 'she was by no means innocent in the ways of the wicked world.' When Smith met her she was a private nurse caring for an elderly patient. Smith told her that he had a private income, and showed her bank books to prove it. Alice

had some money saved – £100, which her father was
taking care of. On 25 October 1913, Smith and Alice
arrived at Aston Clinton for a visit. Mr Burnham took
an instant dislike to Smith that was so strong that he lost
no time in urging Alice – who was his favourite daughter
– to break off her engagement; when she refused he
ordered her out of the house. Smith married her at
the Portsmouth Registry Office on 4 November, and
promptly insured her life for £500. Then he urged his
wife – who had only £27 in cash – to write to her father
for her savings. Mr Burnham declined to send them,
declaring that they were safer in his hands, whereupon
Alice threatened to sue him. Typically, Smith demanded
– and got – interest on the money: £4 1s. When the
cheque arrived, Smith put it into his own account, then
got Alice to make out a will in his favour. Then he took
her on that fatal trip to Blackpool.

For the next three weeks, Neil continued his investigations, taking statements from 150 witnesses, including
one of Smith's ex-wives from Canada. On 23 January,
Neil contacted the Director of Public Prosecutions, Sir
Charles Mathews, who had never heard of a case of
murder by drowning, but was quite willing to believe
that this might be the first.

The history of George Joseph Smith, as unearthed by
Detective Inspector Neil, was as follows.

He was born at 92, Roman Road, Bethnal Green,
on 11 January 1872, the son of an insurance agent.
Nothing is known of the offence that caused a judge,
when George was only nine, to sentence him to eight
years in a reformatory, but it was almost certainly theft
– or a series of thefts. Only one thing is certain: that the
judge who dealt out this savage sentence bears much of
the responsibility for Smith's life of crime. One writer on

the case – L.C. Douthewaite – quotes a retired governor of Pentonville as saying: 'Sending a lad ... to prison for the purpose of curing him of crime is just about as sensible as it would be to send a patient suffering from nettlerash to a smallpox hospital.' Two years after returning home at the age of sixteen, Smith received seven days for a minor theft, and in the following year, six months' hard labour for stealing a bicycle. After this he seems to have spent three years in the army – the Northamptonshire Regiment; he was a gym instructor, and seems to have been proud of his muscular build and broad shoulders. In July 1896 he was in trouble again for larceny and receiving stolen goods, and was sentenced to a year's hard labour. He was calling himself George Baker, and had persuaded a woman to steal for him.

On his release from prison in 1897, he found another girl who was willing to risk her liberty to support him. He forged a reference for her, and she helped herself to £175 from a cashbox. Smith took the money, deserted the lady, and decided to move to Leicester, where he opened a baker's shop at 28, Russell Square with the £175. He was now calling himself George Oliver Love. One day, a buxom, pretty bootmaker's daughter named Caroline Thornhill came into the shop, and 'Love' offered her a job. Caroline was eighteen, Smith twenty-five. She refused, but changed her mind when she saw him dressed in a frock coat and top hat.

This attire justifies a digression. Smith was a big man, and this, together with the small grey eyes and the cockney accent, combined to create the impression of a thug with the intellectual qualifications of Bill Sykes. This appearance was unfavourable to inspiring trust in potential victims. Besides, like so many ambitious criminals, Smith liked to regard himself as a man of

sensitivity and intelligence. He quickly realized that a
frock coat and top hat did wonders for his appearance;
he ceased to look like a bruiser, and could create the
impression of a self-made businessman. He seems to
have been a natural musician who had learned to play
the organ 'by ear', and could pick up most tunes
within minutes. Smith also liked to explain that he
loved Shakespeare and Tennyson, and that he was the
son of 'George Smith, the figure artist.' Altogether, he
was a typical confidence man, his only drawback from
the professional point of view being that people's first
impressions of him were usually bad. Given a chance
to rectify this, he could usually convince the doubters –
particularly ladies – that he was a rough diamond who
deserved the benefit of the doubt.

So Caroline Thornhill, impressed by his frock coat,
became his shop assistant, and Smith was able to put
into operation the second part of his plan, which was
to seduce her. Here he found himself up against the
sexual prudishness of the working classes. Caroline's
father and brothers kept a close eye on her, and she
herself made it clear that she intended to remain a virgin
until she married. Smith had no alternative. Since all his
violent physical passions were now aroused, he married
her at St Matthew's Church on 28 January 1898. Her
father had taken an intense dislike to him, and refused
to come to the wedding. When the bride tried to cut the
wedding cake – baked by the bridegroom – it provided
an ominous portent by falling to pieces.

Caroline Love soon learned that her husband was
dictatorial and subject to fits of rage, when he was
perfectly capable of using his immense physical strength
to beat her black and blue. Six months later, when
the business collapsed, she left him, but he followed

her to Nottingham, and persuaded her to change her mind.

The bakery seems to have been Smith's last attempt to make an honest living. He and Caroline went to London, and Smith decided that it was time for her to support him. He looked in the advertisement columns for respectable citizens who needed a maid, and forged Caroline's references, sometimes even presenting himself, in his frock coat, as her previous employer. Few jobs lasted long, for Caroline was ordered to help herself to any valuables her employers left lying around; after which they hurriedly left the neighbourhood. They moved from London to Brighton, then to Hove and Hastings. In August 1899, a pawnbroker in Eastbourne became suspicious of an obviously working-class young woman trying to sell him some family silver, and whispered to his assistant to cycle to the police station while he kept her talking. Smith, who was waiting outside, saw the assistant pedal off in a hurry, and decided that it was time to abandon his wife to her fate (although it would have been easy enough to walk into the shop and drag her away before the police arrived.) He returned to their lodging, packed their belongings, then hurried to London, where he sold her possessions. Caroline pleaded guilty to stealing silver spoons and forks from her employer, Mr Burrows of Hastings, and was sentenced to a year in prison – although her solicitor stated that she was completely under the spell of her husband. Meanwhile, Smith married his London landlady – bigamously – at St George's, Hanover Square, and so found himself free lodgings. This landlady was later to testify that he had an 'extraordinary power' over her, and that this power lay in his eyes. 'When he looked at you for a minute or two you had the feeling you were being magnetised. They were little eyes that seemed to rob you of your will.' Marshall Hall, who was later to defend Smith on a charge of murder, was convinced that Smith's secret was that he possessed hypnotic powers.

Smith was as violent towards his new wife as he had been towards Caroline, and one night, after beating her 'until she was nearly dead', he helped himself to what he could lay his hands on and left her. Hearing that Caroline was out of prison, he wrote to her – presumably at her parents' home – and asked her to take him back. Caroline ignored the letter. He went to Leicester to try and persuade her, but her brothers soon made it clear that he was unwelcome.

On 11 November 1900, Smith was strolling down Oxford Street, hoping to make the acquaintance of a lady with savings in the bank, when Caroline saw him. She hurried to the nearest policeman and told him that the man looking in the shop window was George Love, who was wanted for receiving stolen goods. When the policeman asked him if this was true, Smith flew into a fury and tried to attack his wife with his stick; the constable bundled him into a passing cab, and had to restrain him by force until they arrived at Vine Street. There, oddly enough, Smith broke down in tears and confessed his guilt, blaming it all on his wife. The result was two years' hard labour. Meanwhile, Caroline left England for Canada, recognizing that her husband's vengeful nature would lead him to seek her out when he came out of prison.

Smith's activities between 1902 and 1908 have gone unrecorded, except that he was dismissed from employment in a West End club, presumably as a bouncer. In 1908 he met a widow named Florence Wilson on a public seat in Brighton, and when he learned that she had £33 13s in the bank, proposed marriage. He told her that he was an antique dealer and a 'man of means.' After their marriage, on 3 July 1908, he persuaded her to draw out £30 from her account, to 'go shares' with him in buying antiques. They then went on a trip to White City, where there was a Franco–British Exhibition. He left her on a seat while he went off 'to buy a newspaper', hurried back to Victoria Station, where they had left their luggage, and disappeared. After half an hour of mounting misgivings, Florence spoke to a policeman, who advised her to go and check on her luggage; she also hurried to Victoria Station cloakroom, and found that her husband had preceded her and taken everything. She used some of the £3 13s left in her post office account to buy herself a ticket back to her home in Worthing, and resumed her employment in a needlework shop, £30 (and some clothes) the poorer.

Smith now moved to Bristol, and set up in Gloucester Road as an antique dealer – no doubt with Florence's £30. He then advertised for a housekeeper at £16 a year. The only applicant was a round-faced woman of 28 named Edith Pegler, who lived in the same road. Smith solved the problem of paying her wages by marrying her. Oddly enough, he remained more or less faithful to Edith Pegler to the end of his life – although it seems probable that this was less because he loved her than because she had no money to steal, and provided him with a home to which he could return. On the one occasion when she enquired about his business, he shook his fist in her face and ordered her never again to commit the same indiscretion. For the next six-and-a-half years, Smith returned to Edith Pegler between long 'business' trips, and stayed until the money ran out. Then he would go off – seldom leaving her enough money to live on – in search of another victim.

One of these was a servant girl named Alice Reavil, whom he picked up in the sea-front gardens in Bournemouth. Smith was wearing white flannels and a boater. During an hour's conversation he told her that he received a regular £2 a week from some land he owned in Canada, and arranged to see her that evening. He told her then that his name was Charles Oliver James. Two weeks later they were married in the Woolwich Registry Office. As with Florence Wilson, Smith suggested pooling their cash and opening an antique shop. Alice sold her piano and some other belongings, which realized £14, and withdrew her entire savings – £76 6s – from the post office. Two days later, they went for a tram ride – during which he invited her to Halifax, Nova Scotia – and he left her on a seat in a public garden while he returned to their lodging in Battersea, and vanished with her trunk and possessions, worth about £50. These he presented to Edith Pegler, explaining that he had done a deal in second hand clothing.

In June 1909 he was in Southampton with Edith when his eye was taken by a woman named Sarah Freeman, who was a clerk. Smith seems to have had an instinct about women who could be persuaded to succumb, and Sarah Freeman aroused this instinct so strongly that he ordered Edith to return immediately to Bristol – claiming that he had to go abroad on a business deal. The conquest of Sarah Freeman took longer than that of other brides, and it was not until four months later – 29 October 1909 – that he married her in the Southampton Registry Office. Sarah had £50 in cash, but she had not initially told George Rose – as he called himself – that she also had £260 in the post office, and government stock worth £30. After pocketing the £50, he told her to sell the stock and withdraw the £260. They collected the money from the Lavender Hill post office, and despite his wife's protests, 'Rose' grabbed the lot. A few days later, she was notified that the £30 for her government stock had been transferred to the post office; this was also collected. After that Smith suggested a visit to the National Gallery. There he left her, as usual, on a bench, explaining that he wanted to go to the gents. It was half an hour or so before she became suspicious. She then discovered that her husband had succeeded in taking all her spare cash from her handbag, leaving only enough for her bus-fare back to their lodgings. There she found that everything had vanished, and had to borrow money to pay the rent.

This was his largest windfall so far, and Smith immediately bought a house at Southend for £270 and sent for Edith. But since he had no source of income, he had to borrow money to live on, using the house as security, and was soon as heavily in debt as ever. Finally, he and Edith moved back to Bristol.

In August 1910 he met a tall, shy girl with a sad, downturned mouth called Beatrice Constance Annie Mundy, generally addressed as Bessie, the daughter of a deceased bank manager. When Smith learned that she had £2,500 in gilt edged securities, he immediately proposed and was accepted. He was 38 and his bride seven years younger. Smith now called himself Henry Williams, and claimed to be a picture restorer. He seems to have persuaded Bessie to yield her virginity before the marriage – at least, they moved into 14, Rodwell Avenue, Weymouth, two days before the marriage, which was on 26 August. By this time, Smith had discovered, to his disgust, that Bessie's £2,500 was held in trust, and that Bessie received only £8 a month. Her only ready cash was £138 'for emergencies'; the rest was beyond his reach. Smith ordered her to send for the ready cash. It had arrived by 13 September, when he took Bessie for the statutory walk, and left her on a seat. Then he returned to the lodgings, where there was a telegram waiting for him – sent, of course, by himself – and told the landlady, Mrs Crabbe, that he had to leave immediately on business, and that his wife would pay the rent. When Bessie returned, she found a letter from her husband that claimed he had contracted venereal disease from her – although he explained that he was not accusing her of immorality with another man: he thought that it was probably the result of 'not keeping herself clean.' (Smith himself had an aversion to baths; Edith was to say that he had taken only one in the seven years she had known her, and had warned her that baths were injurious to the health.) He told her he would return to her when he was cured – which might take ten years. Smith always believed in leaving his options open.

In this case, it paid off. Bessie collapsed for three weeks and was nursed back to health in her brother's home in Poole, Dorset, then returned sadly to her spinsterish existence. Eighteen months later, in February 1912, Bessie went to stay at a boarding house in Weston-super-Mare, and on 14 March, went out to buy some flowers for her landlady, Mrs Sarah Tuckett. Returning home with a bunch of daffodils, she recognized the tall man staring out over the sea as her husband. She became pale, and Smith, who now noticed her, looked thunderstruck.

Unlike Caroline Thornhill, who had run for the nearest policeman, Bessie lacked fire; in fact, as soon as

Smith's hypnotic gaze fell on her, her heart yearned for the man she still loved. Smith, recognizing the yielding expression, told her that their parting had been a terrible misunderstanding, and that he had been looking for her for two years. Bessie instantly forgave him. She returned to Mrs Tuckett an hour-and-a-half late, explaining that she had met her husband and been reconciled to him. Two hours later, Smith himself arrived, and Mrs Tuckett took an immediate and instinctive dislike to him. Smith had now been struck by an inspiration, and explained that he had come to Weston-super-Mare on purpose, looking for his wife – although he failed to answer Mrs Tuckett's question about why he had not simply contacted her through her relatives. When Mrs Tuckett said she felt it her duty to wire Bessie's aunt about the return of the missing husband, Smith announced that he had to leave; Bessie said she would go with him. ('I suppose I may go with my husband?') She left her belongings behind, saying she would be back; but she never returned, and Mrs Tuckett never recovered the £2 10s rent she owed.

Smith had recovered his heiress – he must have felt that fate was taking a hand – but without ready cash. There was only one way to obtain the £2,500 in trust, and that was to persuade her to make a will in his favour, and kill her. But first he had to regain her trust. His first step was to take her to see a solicitor, whose job was to reconcile Smith to Bessie Mundy's family. Smith spun an absurd tale about why he had left her so suddenly – while his wife sat listening and gazing at him fondly – and agreed that he owed her £150 – he even gave her a note for that amount. (He took it back the moment they were outside.)

For the next two months, Smith and his bride moved

from place to place, staying in boarding houses. On 20 May 1912, Smith rented a house in Herne Bay and set up a sign that said: H. WILLIAMS, ART DEALER. In June, he was obliged to sell his house in Southend. On 8 July, he and his wife drew up wills in which either left the other their property in the event of decease. On 9 July, Smith bought a tin bath for £1 17s 6d – the price of which he persuaded the shopman to reduce from £2. The following day he took his wife to a local doctor, Frank Austin French, explaining that she had suffered an epileptic fit – Bessie sat by him passively, apparently agreeing with everything he said. The doctor prescribed bromide. On 12 July, Smith asked the doctor to call to see his wife, who was in bed. She looked hot and flushed – it was very hot weather – but otherwise seemed well. That evening, before going to bed, Bessie wrote a letter to her Uncle Herbert, explaining that she had recently had two 'bad fits', and that her husband wanted him to tell other relatives of her 'breakdown'.

The next morning, at 8 o'clock, the doctor received a note that said: 'Can you come at once? I am afraid my wife is dead.' When the doctor called, he found Bessie Mundy lying naked in a bath of water – the bath that Smith had bought four days earlier. It was only five feet long, and the dead woman was seven inches taller than that, so it was hard to see how she had drowned. But drowned she undoubtedly had – her head was still partly submerged in the water. They lifted her out on to the floor, and the doctor applied artificial respiration. As soon as it was clear that Bessie was dead, Dr French went off to call the police. When a policeman visited an hour later, the corpse was still lying uncovered on the floor. The body was laid out later in the day by a neighbour. By that time Smith had sent a telegram to her family announcing that 'Bessie died in a fit.'

The inquest two days later – on Monday 15 July – concluded with the verdict that Mrs Williams had died of an epileptic seizure while in the bath.

After selling the furniture of the house to the undertaker for £20 4s, Smith went to the solicitor who had drawn up the wills, and instructed him to obtain probate. An attempt by the Mundy family to block the settlement was unsuccessful, and within a few weeks of his 'wife's' death, Smith had laid his hands on £2,403 15s, by far the largest sum he had managed to obtain from any of his victims.

He sent for Edith to come and join him at Margate. Then he began to calculate how best to hang on to his fortune. Property still seemed by far the best investment – he liked the idea of being a landlord. So he spent £2,187 10s of his inheritance on various houses, into one of which – in Bristol – he moved with Edith Pegler. He told her that he had been to Canada and bought a Chinese statue, which he had sold for £1,000, then to Spain, where he had bought some jewellery that he expected to re-sell at a profit.

Smith lacked the temperament to be a good landlord; he harassed his tenants and quarrelled with them. But his success in disposing of Bessie Mundy seems to have inspired him with the idea of pursuing murder for profit. He and Edith moved into a house that he bought in Weston-super-Mare, and there he made the acquaintance of a governess called Burdett, who was in her late twenties, and in charge of two children. Smith told Edith that he had decided to insure the life of this young lady for £500 'as an investment.' He took Miss Burdett to see an insurance agent, then told Edith to accompany her to a doctor for the physical examination required by the insurance company. What precisely he had in mind is doubtful, although it is possible to hazard a guess: Miss Burdett would be invited to live in one of his houses, one with a bath ... But for some reason Smith changed his mind, and the scheme was dropped.

Smith also decided that landlordism was not for him, and resold the houses, losing £600. He decided that he would recoup the loss by finding himself another gullible lady; so, leaving Edith with only £5 (and taking the rest with him), he set off once more in search of a victim.

As he followed Smith's tortuous trail, Detective Inspector Neil was aware that this is where he had come in. For in October 1915, while staying in Southsea, Smith met the plump and not-inexperienced nurse Alice Burnham. Alice must have seemed something of a disappointment after Bessie Mundy, since she only had £100 in savings. But a visit to an insurance broker should remedy that ... Within a few weeks, Alice Burnham was insured for £500 (at a premium of £25), and had been instructed to write to her father, who had taken an instant dislike to her fiancé, for the £100 he was keeping for her. This was paid on 1 December 1913, and was immediately paid into Smith's bank account. Now everything was ready for the 'accident'.

This, as we have seen, happened in Blackpool, in the home of Mrs Crossley at 16, Regent Road, where they arrived on 10 December 1913. Two days later, Alice was dead.

Smith spent that Christmas with Edith Pegler's family, and Edith later recalled that he was in an excellent mood, wearing a paper hat, telling funny stories, and kissing girls under the mistletoe. She records that he even got the long end of the wishbone.

By 17 January 1914, Smith had obtained the £500 insurance money on Alice Burnham. By then he was living in furnished rooms in Cheltenham with Edith. He bought himself a pony and trap, but treated the pony with typical brutality if it disobeyed him. He decided to use his leisure in continuing a novel he had been writing for years – it was called *The Man Who Saw his Own Funeral* – and a poem called *When London Sleeps*. But he still kept Edith so short of housekeeping money that she once threatened to leave him – and was restrained by an outburst of violent rage, and a threat to hunt her down and kill her.

Bored with life as a gentleman, he set out again on his travels in mid-August. It was at this point in Bournemouth, on 7 September, he saw the maidservant Alice Reavil, to whom he represented himself as a Canadian with an income of £2 a week from his 'agent'. By 22 September, he had got his hands on Alice's savings of £76 and deserted her in London.

Back in Bristol with Edith, Smith now made the acquaintance of a clergyman's daughter named Margaret Lofty, who had been disappointed in love – the man who had asked her to marry him proved to be married already. She was also bored with being a companion of elderly ladies, and longed to have a husband. Margaret Lofty was walking near the Clifton suspension bridge when she was accosted by 'John Lloyd', whose instinct somehow informed him that she was another potential victim. Unfortunately, Margaret proved to have little ready cash – a mere £19 – but, like Alice Burnham, she would clearly be worth a great deal more when insured. This was done on 4 December, for £700. On 17 December, she married John Lloyd in Bath – it has never been discovered whether Smith chose it because of the name – and they set off for London and for the rooms in Bismarck Road, Highgate, where Margaret Lofty would die the following day in her bath . . .

This, then, was the substance of the dossier that Detective Inspector Arthur Fowler Neil compiled on George Joseph Smith (although at this stage he had not yet learned of Bessie Mundy's death in Herne Bay). To begin with, of course, he had no idea where to find Smith. But when Dr Bates told Neil that the Yorkshire Insurance Company had contacted him about a £700 policy taken out on Margaret Lofty, he knew it was merely a matter of time. He told Bates to notify the insurance company that there were no suspicious circumstances in Mrs Lloyd's death, and that insurance should be paid.

The undertaker had been able to tell Neil that 'Lloyd' had offered him a cheque, and had volunteered the information that his bank was 'next door'. Neil went to see the bank manager, who told him that Mr Lloyd had transferred his account to the branch in Shepherd's Bush. The manager of the Shepherd's Bush branch was unwilling to reveal his customer's present address, but was willing to tell Neil that Smith's solicitor was called W.P. Davies, whose address was in Shepherd's Bush Road. Mr Davies in turn was willing to divulge that his client Mr Lloyd had asked him to obtain probate of his wife's will.

Neil ordered constant surveillance of the office from the upper storey of a pub across the road. The police soon spotted their quarry, and followed him back to his lodging in Richmond Road, Shepherd's Bush. But before he could be arrested, Neil still had a great deal of work to do. This would take him another three weeks.

On 1 February 1915, Neil was again watching as

'Lloyd' entered the solicitor's office. When he came out again, Neil approached him. 'I am Detective Inspector Neil of the London Metropolitan Police. Are you John Lloyd?'

'Yes I am.'

'The John Lloyd whose wife was drowned in a bath on the night of 18 December, last, at Bismarck Road, Highgate?'

'Yes.'

'From my investigations I have reason to believe you are identical with George Smith whose wife was found drowned in a bath three weeks after her marriage in 1913 in Blackpool. You married Miss Lofty, your last bride, at Bath, Bristol, in the name of Lloyd.'

'Yes, that is so, but that doesn't prove that my name is Smith. I don't know the name of Smith . . .'

'Very well. I am going to detain you for making a false attestation on oath to the Registrar.' (Smith had made some mis-statements at the Registry Office in Bath.)

'Oh, if that's what you're making all the fuss over, I may as well tell you I am Smith.' He was evidently relieved to think that the police only wanted him for suspected bigamy.

So Lloyd/Smith was duly arrested and taken to Shepherd's Bush Police Station. He proved to have £150 in notes in his pocket. Alice Burnham's father came from Aston Clinton with his remaining daughter, and identified Smith as the man who had taken Alice away. Witnesses from Bath identified Smith as John Lloyd, and he was charged with making a false entry in the marriage register. When Neil asked him about the earlier death of Alice Burnham, Smith replied that that was just bad luck. 'Bad luck is all you can charge me with', he said defiantly.

Two weeks later, Smith had reason to worry that this calculation had been undermined; a police inspector in Herne Bay had read the newspaper publicity about the 'Brides in the Bath', and recollected the case of Bessie Williams — or Mundy. As a result of this information, Neil told Smith that he now had reason to believe that he was also Henry Williams, whose wife Bessie Mundy had died in her bath in Herne Bay. Obviously, coincidence could only be stretched so far. Smith's chief consolation was that he could only be charged with one murder at a time, and that a good defence lawyer might persuade the judge not to allow the jury to know about the other 'accidents'. In the army, Smith had been known as a 'barrack room lawyer', and he had undoubtedly taken the trouble to find out what happened in cases of men charged with multiple murder.

He must also have known that a good lawyer would emphasize the difficulty of drowning someone in the bath. The victim would be sure to struggle and scratch, and even if her attacker was strong enough to force her head under water, she would sustain bruises. But only one of Smith's victims — the last — had a small bruise, and that was on her elbow.

While he was still waiting to arrest Smith, Neil had declined the suggestion that the bodies should be exhumed. An exhumation is bound to attract the attention of the press, and their quarry might vanish. But three days after the arrest, on 4 February 1915, the pathologist Bernard Spilsbury was asked to take over the case. Spilsbury had achieved celebrity four years earlier during the Crippen case. Crippen had poisoned his wife Cora with hyoscine, in order to be able to marry his mistress Ethel le Neve, and had dismembered her body and buried it in the cellar. The identification of this body turned upon a piece of flesh with an operation scar; one doctor had declared that the scar was merely a fold in the flesh. Spilsbury's evidence convinced the jury otherwise. In another major case, the Seddon poisoning, Spilsbury had been in charge of the exhumation of Miss Barrow, although it was his colleague Willcox who calculated the fatal dose of arsenic in her organs.

Now Spilsbury's first step was the exhumation of the body of Smith's last 'wife', Margaret Lofty, from Islington cemetery. He examined it very carefully for evidence of violence, but could find none except the bruise on the elbow already noted by Dr Bates. The brain showed signs of congestion, which suggested death by suffocation. It was as if she had died of a sudden stroke.

The other two victims, when exhumed, also showed no sign of violence – but also no sign of any illness that might account for losing consciousness in the bath. Alice Burnham's faint 'heart murmur' was due to a slight thickening of the mitral valve, which should not have affected her health, and certainly not caused a heart attack.

Drowning is due to ingestion of water in the lungs. As self-evident as this sounds, it had not been recognized until the seventeenth century; the Romans thought drowning was due to swallowing water, which distended the stomach. This view had been disproved in the late seventeenth century by the pathologist G.B. Morgagni, who drowned cats and dogs and showed that their lungs were filled with foam. Now the post mortems left no doubt that Smith's three wives had died – very suddenly – of drowning. But how had he done it?

The bathtub in which Margaret Lofty had drowned was transferred to the Kentish Town Police Station.

As Spilsbury stared at it, he realized that it would be impossible for someone to drown in such a tub during a fainting fit. He was equally doubtful when he saw the tub in which Bessie Mundy had died. The second phase of an epileptic attack involves convulsions of the limbs, and these alone would have prevented the head from slipping under water.

Yet Dr French had said that Bessie Mundy had died with her head under water and her feet *above* the far end of the bath. Even allowing for the fact that her feet were at the sloping end of the bath, that sounded impossible – after all, she must have been sitting upright in the 'straight' end.

Unless, of course, someone had grabbed her by the knees or the ankles and simply raised her legs. But how long would it take for the victim to drown? Would she not struggle and kick, and splash water all over the bathroom?

Neil immediately decided that he had to experiment on a living woman. He hired an experienced swimmer who was roughly the same height and weight as Bessie Mundy; in her bathing costume, she climbed into the bath. First Neil tried to push her under by grabbing her shoulders; she made it almost impossible by holding on to the sides of the bath. Next – after warning her what he meant to do – Neil grabbed her by the ankle and gave a sudden heave. The girl's head vanished instantly under the water, and to Neil's horror, she immediately lost consciousness. They had to lift her out of the water and place her face downwards on the floor; even then, it was half an hour before she recovered. She explained that the last thing she felt was water rushing up her nose.

This, then, was the answer. If the head went under

the water as the feet were lifted in the air, water rushed up the nose and caused instant oblivion.

It was now easy to imagine how Smith had killed Bessie Mundy. He had gone into the bathroom, bent over her and kissed her, probably fondling her at the same time. Then, as she sighed and relaxed, his hands transferred to her ankles and jerked them upwards; within seconds she was unconscious. As a method of murder, it was almost humane.

Smith's solicitor Mr Davies approached the famous advocate Edward Marshall Hall to ask if he would be interested in taking the case; Marshall Hall's clerk replied that the fee required would be very high indeed. But several national newspapers were anxious to buy Smith's life story, and the sums they were willing to pay would satisfy even the most voracious advocate. But the Home Secretary, Sir John Simon, stepped in and declared that such a deal would be immoral. Marshall Hall failed to see his point, and the two men – who were old friends – quarrelled over the 'Brides in the Bath' case. Out of sheer stubbornness, Marshall Hall decided to accept the case.

Ever since his arrest, Smith had been behaving in a way that would damage his own case. He was obviously a man without any kind of self-discipline. In the cab with two policemen immediately after his arrest, he babbled all the way to the police station, insisting that he had no idea that Margaret Lofty had been insured, and therefore laying himself open to being revealed as a liar at an early stage of the investigation. In Bow Street Police Court, where a judge had to decide whether to send him for trial, Smith shouted and blustered, and constantly interrupted witnesses. It became obvious that Smith's technique was to play the injured innocent who was being framed by the police, and to dwell on minor details to try to obscure the major issues. When Mrs Blatch, the landlady from Bismarck Road, was asked whether she had declared that the organ had begun to play immediately after Mrs Lloyd had gone upstairs for her bath, she replied that she had not said 'immediately'. Smith interrupted to say that this was not true. The jailer by Smith's side warned him to be quiet but Smith shouted: 'It's no good telling me to be quiet. That is the word she said.' Again and again he made interruptions like: 'This is a lot of lies. I can't stand any more lies.' It made no difference. Smith was charged with the murder of Bessie Mundy and committed for trial at the Old Bailey.

The trial, which lasted nine days, opened on Tuesday 22 June 1915. For some reason, it excited extraordinary interest among women – as the trial of another lady killer, Henri Landru, was to do six years later – and some of them pressed so close to the dock that they were able to touch the accused man. They must have found his appearance disappointing. He had a sallow face, boney features, a narrow forehead, and a wide, sensual mouth. Only the penetrating stare of his grey eyes offered any explanation of his success as a seducer.

Marshall Hall was convinced that Smith possessed some hypnotic power, and had terminated his only interview with his client because he felt Smith was trying to hypnotize him. He knew well enough that his only chance of obtaining an acquittal was to concentrate on the charge in hand – the murder of Bessie Mundy – and try to prove that there was no case to answer. 'If you tried to drown a kitten it would scratch you, and do you think a woman would not scratch?' But Spilsbury's evidence, based on Neil's experiments in the bath, soon disposed of that objection. After that, Hall's only hope was to try to show that the case against Smith was weak in law. He was being tried only for one murder, yet the jury was being allowed to listen to evidence of a long criminal career, which was bound to create prejudice. (Marshall Hall's later appeal was based heavily on the same argument.)

The man who presented that evidence to the jury was Archibald Bodkin. Travers Humphries, who was appearing with Bodkin, described it later as 'one of the most deadly pieces of advocacy I have ever heard.' In effect, the defence was arguing that the death of three wives in the bath was an unfortunate coincidence; Bodkin made nonsense of that argument by listing a dozen other 'coincidences', beginning with bigamy and the taking out of life insurance, and including the fact that in each case Smith had tried to provide himself with an alibi by going out and buying food while his wife lay dead. (Arthur La Bern has also pointed out that Smith preferred to commit murder on Friday night or Saturday morning, so the victim's relatives would find it difficult to attend the inquest.) And when the judge, Mr Justice Scrutton, overruled Marshall Hall's attempt to exclude all evidence except that relating to Bessie Mundy (telling the jury that they must nevertheless not assume that Smith was a man of bad character), Marshall Hall must have known that his client's case was hopeless. No sensible jury could possibly believe in so many coincidences.

Marshall Hall's final speech was as brilliant as everyone had expected it to be. He emphasized that Spilsbury had admitted that he 'dare not say that' the death of Bessie Mundy 'could not have been an accident.' After praising British justice, he attacked the prosecution for

'Americanizing' it – that is, using the unlimited resources of the Crown to make the defence of a pauper almost impossible. (He was, of course, 'getting at' Sir John Simon.) He tried every device to appeal to the jury's sentiment, even throwing in a gratuitous reference to the young men who were now dying in the trenches. He asked with passion if they could really believe that a man could be such a depraved monster as the prosecution represented Smith to be. The answer, of course, was that they could and did.

The judge preceded his three-hour summing-up with a piece of amateur dramatics in which he asked the jury to imagine a husband stripping his wife in the bathroom, then tenderly picking her up in his arms, lowering her into the bath, and then raising her knees so that her head goes under water. Marshall Hall protested at this play-acting but was ignored. Then the judge went on to summarize all Smith's misdemeanours, with constant interruptions from the prisoner, who was manifestly losing his nerve and taking refuge in extravagant self-pity. When Mr Justice Scrutton asked why Smith had chosen not to go into the witness box, Smith shouted: 'What's the point? You'd believe me just as much there as here,' and the judge conceded with a solemn nod: 'That conceivably is true.'

It took the jury only 20 minutes to return with a guilty verdict. Smith became suddenly very pale. Before passing sentence, the judge remarked that 'I think exhortation to repentance would be wasted on you.'

Two days later, while awaiting his appeal, Smith wrote Edith Pegler a letter in which he declared that 'perjury, spite, malice and vindictiveness has done its best and caused me to be placed thus.' But he assured her of his undying love, and told her that he constantly prayed to 'the powers which govern my life and rule my fate to deliver me from bondage and set me free again to join you.' Two weeks later, just before his appeal, he begged her to forgive him and to be prepared to remain with him for the rest of his life when he was freed from prison, as he was sure that he would be. Both letters are oddly moving. After his appeal was turned down – as it inevitably was – on 29 July 1915, he told her: 'I have not asked for a reprieve nor made a petition and I do not intend to do so . . . My time is occupied in solemn and deep meditation.'

Anyone who had not studied the evidence would be convinced by these letters that Smith was innocent. In fact, the prison chaplain and the Bishop of Croydon were both convinced. The Bishop wrote: 'He told me – not under seal of confession – that for twenty years he has been a most wicked and abandoned man; that he has been steeped in every villainy, but never of murder.'

On Friday 13 August, before his execution, he partook of the Holy Sacrament and stated: 'I shall soon be in the presence of God, and I declare before Him that I am innocent.' After these last words, the executioner released the trap.

Two days after his execution, Smith's first bride, Caroline, remarried.

4

The Henpecked Poisoner

The setting was pure Agatha Christie – a pleasant country house with a large garden, complete with housekeeper, two maids and a gardener – overlooking the valley of the River Wye. The accused man was a highly respectable local solicitor, churchwarden, Freemason, Clerk of the Court and officer in the Territorial Army. To the townsfolk of Hay-on-Wye, a pleasant little market town with a mere 1,300 inhabitants, it seemed unbelievable that the dapper and diminutive Major Armstrong could be capable of trying to poison a fellow solicitor, and even more unlikely that he had poisoned his wife, to whom he had shown nothing but tender devotion – they wagered five-to-one in favour of an acquittal. Those who passed this vote of confidence on Major Armstrong were to lose their money.

Herbert Rowse Armstrong was born in Plymouth in May 1869, the son of a hard-working but unsuccessful colonial merchant; his childhood, while not exactly deprived, was far from well-to-do, and it may have been memories of his father's struggles to support the family that led Armstrong, in later years, to take such drastic steps to ensure his own financial survival.

The charity of two aunts enabled young Herbert

Armstrong to go up to Cambridge, where he studied at St Catherine's College. In spite of physical disadvantages – he was only five feet tall, and weighed about seven stone – he was understudy to the Cambridge cox in the boat race. He graduated in 1891, at the age of 22, and four years later was enrolled as a solicitor and public notary. His first job was as an articled clerk in Liverpool, where his family had moved many years before. He was hard-working, conscientious, loquacious and well-liked. His negative characteristics were egotism, a hunger for acclaim, personal vanity – there were those who said he walked like a strutting bantam cock – and an obsession with trivia. He was quite determined to be a highly-regarded member of the community, and to this end became a second lieutenant in the Territorial Army and an organizer of the local Sunday school.

In 1901 Armstrong became a junior in a solicitor's office in Newton Abbott, Devon, where he joined the Devon volunteers, and made the acquaintance of a high-minded young lady named Katherine Mary Friend, a passionate advocate of good works and opponent of alcohol and tobacco, whom he marked down as a possible spouse against the day when he would be able to afford that luxury. He was resigned to the notion that that day would be a long way off, for although he was an obsessive saver, the wages of a solicitor's clerk were poor.

In 1906, when he was 36, an opportunity to use his savings for promotion arose when he became managing clerk to a solicitor named Edmund Cheese, in Hay-on-Wye; Armstrong put his capital into the business.

Mr Cheese's office in Broad Street was unimpressive, part of a small converted shop, the other half of which was rented by an estate agent. But then, Mr Cheese's only rival in the legal department, Robert Griffiths, had equally unimpressive offices on the other side of the street. Armstrong moved in as a lodger with Mr Cheese and his wife, and continued to work hard – most of the business was conveyancing for local farmers. In June 1907, he finally married Katherine Friend, and they moved into a modest little house at nearby Cusop. By 1910, Armstrong was a partner, and they were able to move into an altogether more suitable house called Mayfield. In due course the Armstrongs were blessed with two girls and a boy.

Subsequent events make it clear that at some point, Armstrong became aware that his marriage had been a mistake. The initial attraction was probably based on the fact that Armstrong was outgoing and loquacious, while Katherine was withdrawn and shy. He liked to dominate. Marriage soon revealed that it was Armstrong who was to be dominated: Mrs Armstrong was strong-willed and domineering, with a tendency to obsessiveness and hypochondria. She was a thin, masculine-looking woman who was blind in one eye as a result of a cycle accident. Armstrong was soon pitied by his neighbours as a henpecked husband. He was allowed to smoke his pipe in only one room in the house, and never outdoors. The garden was Armstrong's domain; he had a passion for gardening; but if he was stealing a quiet smoke behind the rose bushes, and Mrs Armstrong's voice was heard, he hastily snuffed out the pipe and dropped it in his pocket.

No alcohol was permitted. If guests came to dinner, they were allowed a glass of wine, but if the servant came too close to the master of the house, his wife rapped out: 'No wine for the Major.' She criticized him in front of other people, and even berated him before the servants;

when he was late for dinner, she would ask how he could expect the servants to keep good time if he set a bad example. She had been known to drag him away from a tennis match because it was his bath night. There could be no doubt that Mrs Armstrong's desire to dominate her household – the children suffered equally – bordered on mental illness. It seems conceivable that Dylan Thomas may have had the Armstrongs in mind when he created Mr and Mrs Pugh in *Under Milk Wood*, where Mrs Pugh nags at the breakfast table while Mr Pugh reads *Lives of the Great Poisoners*. Armstrong certainly seems to have behaved like the unprotesting Mr Pugh, never betraying the slightest sign of mutiny.

If it had not been for the outbreak of the First World War, Armstrong might have spent his life merely dreaming of rebellion. But as an officer in the Territorials, he was one of the first to be called up. He was posted to the First Wessex Field Company of the Royal Engineers and became a captain. Posted as an adjutant to Bournemouth, he was able to keep in touch with the business in Hay-on-Wye. His partner Mr Cheese had died earlier in 1914, but Mr Cheese's nephew had agreed to fill Armstrong's shoes while he was in the army. On the whole, Armstrong did not regret the life he had left behind. The Territorials had been a kind of play-acting; this was the real thing. He was a highly efficient officer – his men may have found him too efficient – and loved the camaraderie of the Officers' Mess. He could smoke and drink without being rebuked, and enjoy the delights of authority. And – although we lack details on this point – he could also exercise his undoubted charm on the ladies of the town, a habit he carried back with him into civilian life, if the syphilis he contracted in 1920 is any indication.

He also fell in love – or at least, entered into a
flirtation with a certain enthusiasm. The woman's name
was Marion Gale, and she was a widow who lived with
her mother and niece near Bournemouth. He met her
through a woman in whose house he was billeted, and he
was soon visiting her at the cottage she shared with her
mother. She knew he was married, but it seems probable
that he told her something of his strained relations with
his wife. It is unlikely that she became his mistress – to
begin with, opportunities were lacking – but she seems
to have accepted that his feelings for her were warmer
than was proper for a married man. When Armstrong
was posted to France, they kept in touch. Armstrong
served for three months in a base depot behind the lines
near Rouen, and was there when the war ended in 1918.
By now he was Major Armstrong.

Return to Hay-on-Wye must have been rather like
going back to prison. During the war-years his business
had languished. His rival Robert Griffiths had lived on
in the town, and had taken a partner, Oswald Norman
Martin, who had just been demobilized with a head
injury that caused some facial paralysis. Martin was a
'local', and was liked and trusted by the farmers who
were his main customers; he even wrote a tax manual
which had a brisk sale. By comparison, Armstrong was
an outsider, a stuffy Englishman who liked to dress in
his old army uniform and call himself 'the Major'.
Armstrong was pleasant enough, but it must have been
obvious that his central characteristic was his need for
self-esteem. He wanted to rise in the world, to be liked,
respected, looked-up-to. So, of course, do most men; but
in Armstrong it amounted to an obsession.

It must also have been galling to find that his wife
was as intolerable as ever. She had become sour and

bad-tempered. She was also developing obsessive characteristics, but of a different kind. As her hypochondria increased, her desire for social contact diminished; as she passed people on the pavement, she drew her coat close around her. 'No wine for the Major' is a quotation from that post-war period, although the spirit of the edict had been in force since the beginning of their marriage.

As his domestic life deteriorated and his business languished, Armstrong began to spend more and more time in his garden. This was also, no doubt, why he began to purchase quantities of arsenic weedkiller.

On 10 November 1920, Armstrong took the train to Cheltenham, and found himself in the same compartment as another Hay resident, Miss May Lilwall. Miss Lilwall was later to recall that throughout that journey, the little Major had only one subject of conversation: the acquittal, on the previous day, of a fellow solicitor, Harold Greenwood, on a charge of poisoning his wife. Greenwood lived about fifty miles away in Kidwelly. Mabel Greenwood had died, after a bilious-type illness, on 16 June 1919, and her death was diagnosed as due to heart failure. Four months later, Harold Greenwood had married a much younger woman. Local gossip finally led to the exhumation of the body and the discovery that the death had not been due to heart failure but to arsenic poisoning. Greenwood was another enthusiastic gardener who had bought an arsenic-based weedkiller shortly before his wife's death. The prosecution case was that Greenwood had laced the Burgundy on the dining table with weedkiller, knowing that only his wife liked wine. But his daughter insisted that she had also drunk Burgundy from the carafe on the fatal day. The local doctor, who had given Mrs Greenwood a bismuth medicine, admitted that he kept the arsenic solution next to the bismuth in his surgery. These doubts were enough to lead the jury to acquit Greenwood (although it ruined his practice, and he died eight years later).

For some reason, Greenwood's acquittal elated Armstrong, and on that journey to Cheltenham, he talked of nothing else. It was later suggested that Armstrong had good personal reasons to feel elated, since he had been administering small doses of weedkiller to his wife since the previous year.

It had been in May 1919 that Katherine Armstrong first went to her doctor, Thomas Hincks, complaining of pains in her right arm. He diagnosed neuritis. In August Hincks saw her again, after Armstrong had asked for a sedative – he said she was having trouble sleeping – and noted that her speech was affected, and that her mental health seemed to be deteriorating. She told him she was unkind to her children and that she had defrauded tradespeople. Hincks detected a heart murmur which had not been present on his earlier examination.

Armstrong sent for his wife's sister Bessie to come and help look after her. He also consulted another doctor, Frederick Jayne, who found Mrs Armstrong 'pale, thin and listless', and noted that when she could be persuaded to speak, her conversation suggested that she was of unsound mind. Jayne and Hincks agreed that Mrs Armstrong ought to be sent to a mental home for treatment. She was admitted to Barnwood, a private asylum near Gloucester, in August 1920, and Armstrong paid £81 18s 0d in advance – a sum he could ill afford, since business was so poor.

There her health – both physical and mental – slowly improved. As she began to feel better, she begged her husband to allow her to come home. On 11 January 1921, Dr Hincks wrote to Dr Townsend, who was in charge of the asylum, asking for her to be discharged. Against Townsend's advice, Mrs Armstrong was allowed home in mid-January.

Her health was obviously much improved – she was again able to walk without assistance – but she was clearly depressed: she asked a visiting nurse, Muriel Kinsey, if it would kill someone if they threw themselves out of an attic window. The nurse reported this question to Major Armstrong. In late January 1921, a resident nurse moved into Mayfield, and slept in Mrs Armstrong's bedroom – the Major moved out to another room. But from then on, Mrs Armstrong became steadily weaker. She vomited frequently and complained that her feet felt as if they were made of lead; her skin became discoloured. On 22 February, soon after nine in the morning, she died. Dr Hincks made out the death certificate, giving the cause of death as gastritis, complicated by a heart condition and nephritis. She was buried in Cusop churchyard three days later.

Oddly enough, the Major had made a number of trips to London during his wife's illness, attending dances and meeting Marion Gale for dinner. It was on 23 November 1920, soon after his return from Cheltenham, that Armstrong observed a genital sore, and Dr Hincks diagnosed syphilis. The incubation period for syphilis is from four weeks to three months, so presumably it was on some trip to London while his wife was in the asylum that he contracted the infection. The chief significance of the incident is that it seems to confirm that Armstrong had acquired a taste for ladies of the town during his military service, and that it persisted after his return to civilian life – providing another motive for dissatisfaction with his marriage.

After the memorial service for Mrs Armstrong on Sunday 27 February, Armstrong announced to the assembled friends and relatives at Mayfield: 'I thought I ought to tell you that my wife has made a fresh will in which she has left everything to me . . .'

Katherine Armstrong had originally made her will in January 1917. In this she left bequests to her sister and the three children, and £50 a year to her husband. Her personal fortune amounted to about £2,300, and the interest on this had so far brought Armstrong about £100 a year. But it seemed that a new will had been drawn up in July 1920 in which she left the full amount (£2,278) to her husband. Armstrong later insisted that the will had been drawn up at his wife's request, and that it was signed by his wife in the presence of two witnesses, who also signed. But a letter written from the Barnwood asylum – months after the second will was signed – was to make it clear that Mrs Armstrong still thought that her only will was the one made in 1917. One of the two witnesses flatly denied ever signing the second will, while the other was vague about exactly what she had signed. Later study of the signature was to show that the second will was a forgery.

The first thing Armstrong did with his newly acquired fortune (£2,000 was a large sum of money in 1921) was to take a holiday in Italy, where, according to his diary, he seems to have escorted a number of young ladies – 'Susan', Miss Buchanan and Miss McRae – on various excursions. On his return he went to see Marion Gale at Bournemouth and tentatively raised the question of marriage. She explained – equally tentatively – that she was concerned about leaving her mother and niece. In August he made a definite proposal, and again Marion said she needed time to think; Armstrong suggested that they leave it for another year. In October, Marion came to Mayfield and stayed overnight. They were to meet several times more in London and Bournemouth, but after this, Armstrong's interest seemed to decline.

In fact, Armstrong had new problems on his mind – financial ones. He had been acting for two clients who wanted to buy part of an estate that was being sold near Brecon; they had each given Armstrong £250 towards the purchase price. The deal was supposed to be completed in February 1920, but Armstrong explained that there were 'problems'. It dragged on for more than another year, with Armstrong making various excuses – and failing to give the true one, that he no longer had the money. In July 1921, the solicitor who had been acting for the owner of the property died, and Armstrong's rival from across the street, Oswald Martin, was asked to take over negotiations for the purchasers. Acting on behalf of his clients, Martin told Armstrong either to complete the contracts by 20 October, or return the two deposits. On 20 October, Armstrong begged for another week's grace, which was granted. Then, oddly enough, Armstrong asked Mr Martin if he could come to tea that afternoon. Martin said he was busy. How about the next day? Or the day after that? Finally, Martin agreed to come to Mayfield on Monday 26 October.

He arrived soon after 5 p.m., and was shown around the garden. Then the housekeeper, Emily Pearce, made the tea. Armstrong handed Martin a buttered scone with the remark 'Excuse fingers.' Martin ate the scone, and also several slices of currant bread. To his surprise, Armstrong failed to bring up the matter of the deposits; instead they talked about office organization, and Armstrong turned to more personal matters and admitted he was lonely.

Mr Martin arrived home at 6.30. By 7.30, when supper was ready, he was feeling sick. At 9.15 he began to vomit, and continued to do so throughout the night. His wife, who had been a nurse, noticed that his heart was beating very fast. Dr Hincks was called the next morning and recommended a mustard plaster applied to the stomach. When Armstrong heard that his colleague was sick he hastened to call on him, and told Mrs Martin that it was most inconvenient that her husband was sick, since they had some business matters that had to be completed.

It was Martin's father-in-law, Fred Davies – the local pharmacist – who first began to suspect poison. He mentioned his suspicion to Dr Hincks, and remarked that he had sold Armstrong several lots of arsenic to be used as weedkiller. The doctor dismissed the idea. But after Fred Davies had visited his son-in-law, and seen him disgorging an extremely unpleasant vomit, he told them of his suspicions. The two men then went over the meals that Martin had eaten over the past few days. The only one he had not shared with his wife had been the tea with Major Armstrong.

Fred Davies shook his head and told the Martins that they ought to be on their guard against a second attempt at poisoning. The Martins looked at one another. It had struck them both simultaneously that a second attempt had already been made. Or rather, to be more precise, that the tea with Major Armstrong *had* been the second attempt.

On the morning of 20 September, only three days after Martin had written to Armstrong giving him notice that the property deal had to be completed, the postman had delivered a box of chocolates at the Martins' home. No letter or card was enclosed. That evening, the Martins ate one or two, but they were not fond of chocolates, and the next time the box was opened was when Martin's two brothers and their wives came to supper. This had been on 8 October. One of the wives, Dorothy Martin, ate one, and was violently ill in the night. She had recovered the next day, and they had all assumed that she had caught a stomach chill.

Now Fred Davies' warning raised another possibility. They handed him the remaining chocolates, and he noticed that some had been 'tampered with'. It looked as if a white powder had been inserted in them, then covered over with chocolate.

Davies took the chocolates – and his suspicions – to Dr Hincks, and Hincks agreed that they should be analysed. He also asked Martin to provide a specimen of urine for analysis. These were sent away to the Clinical Research Association in London.

Meanwhile, Armstrong continued to press Martin to come to tea again. Martin would always refuse. The invitations began to arrive several times a week. Armstrong would even ring Martin from across the road and say: 'I'm just about to pour tea – why don't you come over?' Martin was anxious not to allow Armstrong to suspect that he was under suspicion, but he felt he was running out of excuses.

The analysis took two weeks. When the report came, it verified that Martin's urine contained arsenic, and that two of the chocolates in the box had had cylindrical holes drilled into them, and been filled with white arsenic. Each chocolate contained a potentially fatal dose.

On the last day of 1921, a Saturday, three detectives called at Armstrong's office – in those days everyone worked on Saturday mornings – and Chief Inspector Alfred Crutchett read Armstrong a statement that

informed him that arsenic had been found in the chocolates and in Martin's urine, and that he was being
arrested on a charge of attempted murder. Armstrong
went pale, and for a moment his hands trembled. Then
he seemed to regain control, and said: 'Certainly, this
is a serious matter. I will help you all I can.' From that
moment on he displayed total self-control. That night,
Armstrong was confined in the Hay police cells.

In Armstrong's pockets at the time of his arrest were
three love letters from Marion – in which she addressed
him as 'my dearest' and signed herself 'Your ever loving
Marion' – and a small packet of white powder, which
proved to be arsenic. Armstrong was obviously prepared
in case Martin suddenly accepted an invitation to tea.

On Monday 2 January 1922, Armstrong appeared
in the court room in which he served as Clerk of the
Court. He was remanded in custody for a week. From
9 January until the evening of 12 January, the same
court heard evidence of how Armstrong had invited
Martin to tea, and about the poisoned chocolates.
Once again, Armstrong was remanded in custody – at
Worcester Jail – until 19 January. What undoubtedly
worried him most was a comment made by one of the
arresting officers, Superintendent Albert Weaver, about
'other matters pending.'

For by this time, the body of Katherine Armstrong
had been exhumed, and the famous pathologist Bernard
Spilsbury had found in it almost twice the fatal dose
of arsenic. Since it was ten months since she had been
buried, this indicated that the original amount had
been far larger. Even the wood of the coffin contained
arsenic.

On 19 January, before Armstrong's appearance in
court, Superintendent Weaver told him that he was being

charged with the murder of his wife. Armstrong replied: 'I repeat what I said before – I am absolutely innocent.' An hour later, when Mr St John Micklethwait, acting for the Director of Public Prosecutions, told the court that Armstrong was being charged with his wife's murder, there was uproar as reporters rushed out to phone their newspapers. Meanwhile, Mr Micklethwait went on to outline the case against Armstrong – how more than three grains of arsenic had been found in the body, how Armstrong had insisted on his wife returning home from the asylum – against the advice of its supervisor – and how Mrs Armstrong's recovery had been reversed from that moment. In the days that followed, Marion Gale appeared in court – wearing a veil and disguised under the pseudonym 'Madame X' – and described her relationship with Armstrong. The formidable Bernard Spilsbury gave evidence, describing the exhumation of Katherine Armstrong, and how he had found more than three-and-a-half grains of arsenic in the body. The fatal dose, Spilsbury believed, was administered within twenty-four hours of her death. On that same day – Friday 17 February 1922, Armstrong was committed for trial at Hereford Assizes.

Armstrong's children were looked after by a neighbour, Mary Tunnard, and one day Armstrong's eldest daughter, Eleanor, remarked: 'When mummy was ill, she told me to be very careful of the bottles of medicine, because if she took the wrong one, daddy would be blamed.' This comment was quickly passed on to Armstrong's lawyers – it could obviously be used by the defence to imply that Katherine Armstrong *had* taken the wrong medicine. But the defence team decided against it. When told of their decision Armstrong concurred: 'Yes, I agree. A little too like the Greenwood case ...'

Greenwood had been acquitted largely on his daughter's evidence.

The trial, in front of Mr Justice Darling, lasted from 3 to 13 April. Armstrong engaged the famous defence lawyer Sir Henry Curtis Bennett, but he seems to have been a thoroughly unhelpful client, at first declining to enlarge on his plea that he was not guilty. Bennett nevertheless believed that his chances of gaining an acquittal were high – after all, the evidence against Armstrong was purely circumstantial; no one had seen Armstrong administer poison. Armstrong's demeanour certainly suggested that he believed he would be acquitted – apart from that momentary loss of control at the time of his arrest, he seemed calm and confident.

One of the major questions raised on that first day of the trial was whether Armstrong's alleged attempts to poison Oswald Martin could be admitted as evidence. The jury was sent out while Mr Justice Darling listened to arguments on both sides. His final decision was that the Martin evidence was admissible, and that if he was making a mistake, the Court of Appeal could set it right. With that decision, one of the main hopes for Armstrong's acquittal disappeared.

Bennett's defence was based on the assertion that Katherine Armstrong had committed suicide, for which he had one convincing piece of evidence. After his arrest, Armstrong had told the police that he kept some arsenic in the drawer of his bureau – the implication being that his wife could have risen from her sick-bed and taken the fatal dose. The police had searched the bureau but found no packet of arsenic. Armstrong's solicitor, Thomas Matthews, also looked for it without success, and assumed it had been removed by the police. But when a police inventory of the articles they had removed contained no mention of arsenic, Matthews went back for a second search; this time he removed the drawer, and found a packet of arsenic behind it. Bennett felt this was his trump card, since – just as in the Greenwood case – it raised a serious doubt about who had administered the arsenic.

The obvious objection to this, of course, was that Mrs Armstrong had been showing signs of arsenic poisoning for a long time before her final illness. Moreover, everyone who had seen her during that last twenty-four hours agreed that she was far too weak to get out of bed and go in search of poison. Bennett's response to this was to ask Spilsbury whether it was not possible that she had taken the poison a week before her death, but that it had become 'encysted' – that is, encapsulated by mucus in the stomach – so that it only worked when it became free. Spilsbury would only agree that he could not entirely exclude this possibility. Two more medical experts, John Webster and Sir William Willcox, agreed that Mrs Armstrong must have ingested a great deal of arsenic over a long period for more than three grains to be found in the body ten months after death.

Even more convincing was the evidence of Eva Allen, the nurse who had been present in those last hours. She reported that Mrs Armstrong had said: 'Nurse, I'm not going to die, am I? Because I have everything to live for, my children and my husband.' These were clearly not the words of a woman who had just taken a massive dose of poison.

And what was Armstrong doing with a packet of arsenic in his pocket when he was arrested? His story was that he had divided the arsenic into twenty parts and made twenty individual packets, which he used for killing dandelions – his method, he explained, was to make a small hole beside the dandelion and pour arsenic into it. By mistake, he had used only nineteen packets, and left the twentieth in his pocket. But he failed to explain why he had gone to all the trouble of dividing the arsenic into twenty packets, instead of simply pouring it straight from the packet into the hole.

Bennett's bombshell about the finding of the arsenic behind the bureau drawer had less effect on the jury than he had hoped; the bureau was brought into the court building, and they had a chance to examine it. There was no cavity behind the drawer, and no obvious way in which a packet of arsenic could have jumped into the back of the drawer in such a way as to cause it to jam. The implication was that someone had placed the arsenic there after Armstrong's arrest, someone who had a strong desire to see Armstrong acquitted. The mystery of the arsenic in the bureau drawer has never been solved.

In his final speech for the prosecution, Sir Ernest Pollock, the Attorney General, emphasized that Mrs Armstrong had showed signs of arsenic poisoning long before her final illness, that these signs had vanished during her period in the asylum, and started again as soon as she returned home. The matter of the scone offered to Oswald Martin was also mentioned. The evidence of the maid and housekeeper showed that Armstrong himself had buttered the scone. Armstrong's action in offering it to Martin ('Excuse fingers') obviously spoke for itself — a more polite method would have been to offer the plate to his guest.

The judge's summing up was balanced, but he made it clear that he thought the suicide theory completely untenable. During that last day, Katherine Armstrong was too weak even to hold a cup of tea to her lips.

There could be no doubt that she had died of arsenic poisoning; what the jury had to decide was whether her husband had administered it.

Curtis Bennett was so confident of a 'not guilty' verdict that he went for a walk, believing that when he returned, he would hear an acquittal, or perhaps even meet Armstrong himself on his way home . . . But the jury took less time than expected to make up their minds; after a mere 48 minutes they signalled that they had arrived at a verdict. Curtis Bennett had stopped in a small post office when he heard what they had decided. The postmistress told him that her husband had just telephoned from Hereford to say that Armstrong had been found guilty. Bennett was shattered. 'It was unjust', he later told his family, 'a poor show'. This, of course, did not necessarily mean that he believed Armstrong innocent: only that, in view of the fact that all the evidence was circumstantial, he should never have been found guilty.

Darling need not have been concerned about his decision to admit the evidence about Oswald Martin; the Court of Appeal upheld it. Armstrong's appeal was dismissed; so was his request that the case should go to the House of Lords.

Armstrong made no final confession. On the day of his execution – 31 May 1922 – he walked firmly to the scaffold and stood quietly as a white cap was draped over his head and his legs were strapped together. Asked if he had anything to say, he declared: 'I am innocent of the crime for which I am condemned.' Because he was so light, the hangman made the drop exceptionally long – eight feet eight inches instead of the usual six feet. The hangman later claimed that Armstrong showed signs of collapse at the last minute, and that he had to release the trap quickly to prevent the condemned man from falling down. If true, this seems to have been the only sign of weakness that Armstrong showed after his arrest.

Armstrong, the only British solicitor to be hanged for murder, was buried in the yard of Gloucester Prison.

In Hay-on-Wye, Armstrong has remained something of a legend; there even seems to have been a certain amount of grudging admiration for him. Those who knew his wife certainly seem to feel that he deserved some sympathy; Mrs Chevallier, the wife of Armstrong's closest friend, remarked of Katherine Armstrong: 'I could have murdered her myself – she was an over-bearing, difficult woman.' Even so, those who have studied the case agree that there are certain pieces of the jigsaw that are missing. How could a solicitor – who knew better than most the possible consequences of his actions – have murdered his wife, and then, after getting away with it, commit the absurd folly of trying to poison a fellow solicitor? The suggestion that syphilis had affected his brain has to be dismissed in view of the fact that he contracted it long after he had started to poison his wife.

The best study of the case, Robin Odell's *Exhumation of a Murder* (1975), also has the best summary of the possible motives that drove Armstrong to murder. A little man, obsessed by the idea of being respected and esteemed, he must have found it intolerable to be married to a woman who made him smaller still. But having made the mistake of marrying this strange and eccentric lady – possibly with her money in mind – he had no alternative than to lie in the bed he had made for himself. The war changed all that. Armstrong tasted the pleasure of authority and of life in the Officers' Mess; he also met a woman who would have made him an altogether more suitable wife. Back in Hay-on-Wye, he found the old life unbearable and – like Dylan Thomas' Mr Pugh – decided it was time to rebel.

Anyone who has studied the history of poison knows that it is perhaps the cruellest way to kill – the violent illness, the vomiting, the painful enfeeblement. In order to kill the mother of his children over the course of two years, Armstrong must have hated her with morbid intensity. Robin Odell has suggested that Katherine Armstrong probably denied her husband sexual intercourse from a fairly early stage, but there are reasons to question this view. Armstrong and his wife always slept in the same bedroom. Even at the time when Mrs Armstrong was scolding her husband in front of the servants and criticizing him before guests, he remained thoughtful and considerate, which suggests that the couple had their more tender moments in the bedroom. By the time he returned to Hay-on-Wye, Marion Gale had made him aware of how much his marriage left to be desired. The henpecked husband never seems to have raised his voice to his wife; but once he decided he wanted to be rid of her, he became completely ruthless.

Armstrong must have believed that life without Katherine would be blissful. In fact, things began to go wrong almost immediately. The basic problem was Armstrong's lack of business sense. As a solicitor, he borrowed and lent money. One of his clients was John Williams Vaughan, who owned the Velnnewydd estate near Brecon – the estate that Armstrong was supposed to be selling. Armstrong had lent him £4,500, but the estate should have brought about £5,000 when it was sold, so Armstrong's money – or rather, the money of his clients – was theoretically safe. It has

never been fully explained why Armstrong continued
to delay this deal, but the police declared at one point
that 'Armstrong's financial affairs are in great dis-
order ... he is insolvent and has been improperly
using his clients' money.' When Oswald Martin was
asked to call him to account, Armstrong must have
felt desperate. He had been hoping to remarry and
settle down to a life of respectability – and increased
financial security – and now he was faced with public
disgrace and bankruptcy. The decision to poison Martin,
which strikes us as an insane miscalculation, must have
seemed to Armstrong the only solution. It would at
least buy him time enough to try and put things right.
It was a gamble, but he had already gambled once and
won ...

In conclusion, it is worth mentioning that the police
themselves considered another explanation – that
Armstrong was a mass poisoner, and that his wife was
not his first victim. Even Armstrong's lawyer Ronald
Bosanquet wrote: 'It is quite certain that Martin was
not the only person whom he had tried to murder.'
The death of Armstrong's partner Edmund Cheese,
which made Armstrong the owner of the practice,
was followed only twenty-four hours later by that of
Mrs Cheese. In 1921, a solicitor called Willi Davies
visited Armstrong at Mayfield to try to persuade him
to release money due to one of his clients. On the day
after the visit, Davies fell ill and had to be removed
to a nursing home, where he died three weeks later
– the cause of death was given as an abscess of the
appendix. This death was also highly convenient for
Armstrong.

When reporters heard about these suspicions – during
Armstrong's trial – they spent nights in Hay churchyard,

where the Cheeses were buried, hoping for another exhumation. It never came. The police had checked when Armstrong had first purchased arsenic, and when they learned that it was a week *after* the death of Mr Cheese, they decided to abandon that line of enquiry.

5

Who Killed PC Gutteridge?

On the morning of 26 September 1927, Dr Edward Richardson Lovell, a general practitioner in the town of Billericay, Essex, went out to begin his day's work around 9 a.m. and was upset to find that his car had been stolen. It was a blue Morris Cowley, registration number TW6120, with two doors and a canvas hood. Dr Lovell had locked and bolted the car in its wooden garage the previous evening, after making a note of the exact mileage on the clock. His next-door neighbour was able to tell him that he had heard the car – whose engine he recognized – being driven away at about 2.30 a.m. but had naturally assumed that the doctor had been called out. Dr Lovell lost no time in reporting the theft to the local police.

In fact, the car had already been found. A clerk named Albert McDougall, who lived at 21, Foxley Road, Brixton, was annoyed to find a car parked in the passageway at the back of his house when he set out for work that morning; he had to squeeze past it, and noticed that the radiator was still warm. When he returned that evening and found the car still there, he went and found a policeman, and brought him back to the house. Detective Sergeant Charles Hearn was summoned from the local station, and noted that the nearside mudguard was damaged, and that fragments of tree bark were sticking to the front springs. Hearn then committed an error that would horrify most modern policemen – he drove the car to the Brixton Police Station, thus destroying any fingerprints on the steering wheel. He probably became conscious of the extent of his mistake when someone noticed spots that looked like blood on the offside running board. Under the front passenger seat, Hearn found an empty cartridge case marked 'R.L.IV'; at the bottom of the case there was a tiny blister, due to some defect in the breech shield of the gun that fired it. The car's owner was soon traced, and Dr Lovell was informed that it had been found.

Another discovery made at 6 a.m. that day was not at first connected with the missing car. A dozen miles or so due east of Billericay, not far from Romford, the local postman saw a man's body against the bank near Howe Green. He stopped his mail van, and saw that the man, who was sitting with his legs sticking out, was their local constable, PC George William Gutteridge. His face was bloody, and there was a trail of blood leading into the middle of the narrow road. It took a local doctor only a few moments to recognize that the policeman had been shot to death; most of the back of the skull was blown away by an exit wound.

Gutteridge's whistle was hanging on its chain, and he was still holding a pencil stub; his notebook lay a few feet away. It was obvious that Gutteridge had encountered someone of whom he had reason to be suspicious, and had been murdered as he was preparing to take notes. Later examination showed that at least four shots had been fired. Two had struck him in the side of the head; then, when he had collapsed on the ground, two more were fired into each eye. The sheer brutality of the crime horrified the police, as it horrified the whole country when it was reported in the newspapers.

By the time Chief Inspector James Berrett, of Scotland Yard, arrived at mid-afternoon, he was aware of the theft of Dr Lovell's car, and the fact that the body had been found midway between Billericay and London. Moreover, a witness named Lady Decies had been awakened by shots sometime between 3 and 4 that morning, and had then heard a motorcar drive past in the direction of Romford. Admittedly, this was not on the most direct route from Billericay to London, but then, a car thief would obviously prefer to avoid main roads.

Within hours of the finding of the car, it looked as if the crime had been solved when a sailor in Basingstoke confessed to the murder. Berrett immediately drove there to see him. A little questioning revealed that the 24-year-old merchant seaman was an epileptic who was wasting police time.

The distance between Billericay and the site where the body was found was about 15 miles. Dr Lovell's note of the mileage on the clock revealed that the car had been driven 43 miles. That meant that the thief had taken a roundabout route which would have taken roughly an hour. It followed that PC Gutteridge had been shot at about 3.30. The bullets taken out of his head proved to be .455 calibre, the same as the cartridge case found under the passenger seat of the car. They were of an 'old fashioned' type, in which the bullet was propelled by 'black powder'; they were issued from the Woolwich Arsenal to the British Expeditionary Force in 1914, and later withdrawn because the Germans regarded them as belonging to the 'expanding' type forbidden by the Hague Convention.

Berrett requested a list of criminals known to use violence; it came a few days later, and was headed with the name 'Frederick Guy Browne'. But this was not because Browne was the prime suspect; merely because his name happened to be first in an alphabetical list. A check of his record revealed that he was a bicycle and car mechanic who had first been in trouble in 1911 – when he was thirty – for stealing and selling bicycles. A year later he was sentenced to hard labour for burglary, and ever since then had been in and out of prison. Browne was one of those highly dominant criminals whose reaction to prison is murderous resentment, and during a four-year term (for forgery) in 1923 he assaulted warders and smashed up his cell so often that he was transferred from Parkhurst to Dartmoor, where he served out his full term without remission. He was a man of immensely powerful physique, who had once sworn that he would never be taken alive again.

Berrett had a hunch that Browne might be the man they were looking for – or one of them. Dr Lovell had explained that his car was exceptionally difficult to start when it was cold (it seemed that all Morris Cowleys had this fault). The simplest way was to press the starting button while someone else swung the starter-handle. Alternatively, the driver could swing the starter handle then rush to the seat and push the starter. This argued either that Lovell's car had been stolen by two men, or by one man who was familiar with cars – like Browne.

But finding him proved difficult. He was believed to run a garage repair shop somewhere, but its address was unknown. In any case, Browne was only one of a long list of suspects – during the next two months the police interviewed more than a thousand.

Browne's address came to light by chance. In late November 1927, a van driver in Sheffield was forced to the wall by a car that passed him at speed. He succeeded in taking its number (numbers were shorter in those days) and reported the incident to the police. A local policeman spotted the car and interviewed the driver, who showed his driver's licence. In due course a summons for dangerous driving was sent to the London address shown on the licence, but this proved to be false, as was the name; the licence had been stolen. But at least the police had some idea of where to look for the car in Sheffield. The man they went to question was an ex-criminal named John Currie, a father of seven children, who had actually been in the car during the reckless driving incident. Inspired by a desire to minimize his own part in illegal activities – and perhaps by a reward offered by the *News of the World* – Currie told the police that the driver's real name was Frederick Guy Browne, and that he had been involved in a number of robberies. Browne could be found at the Globe Garage in Clapham Junction. For good measure he told them that the car Browne had been driving was an Angus Sanderson which had belonged to a Sheffield butcher named Benjamin Stow, who had given it in part exchange for another car – which Brown had stolen in Tooting.

Benjamin Stow, of 66, Bayland Street, told the police that he had exchanged his Angus Sanderson – plus £100 – for a Vauxhall. Although the numberplates had been changed, the police came to the conclusion that the Vauxhall was one that had been stolen from a Mrs Bridget Hulton in Tooting on 12 November, two weeks earlier.

Browne was now wanted on two charges – stealing

a car and dangerous driving. Now the only problem was to find him. He was a married man with a daughter, and his wife Caroline worked as a cook/housekeeper. The Globe Garage was situated at 7a, Northcote Road, Clapham, and another convict-acquaintance from Dartmoor, William Henry Kennedy, worked there as a book-keeper. But Browne never seemed to be home, and the police had no desire to alert him by asking his wife where he was to be found.

In January 1928, local police set up a surveillance operation on the garage. But Browne was away, picking up another criminal-acquaintance named Fred Counter, who had just been released from Dartmoor. On their way back to London on the afternoon of 20 January, Browne – who was wearing a chauffeur's uniform – was flagged down by a policeman who asked him to give his sergeant a lift into Andover. Browne obliged, and on the way there, they talked about the murder of PC Gutteridge. After dropping off the sergeant, Browne drove on to New Scotland Yard, where Fred Counter had to report to the Convict Registration Officer. Then, exhausted and badly in need of refreshment, he drove back to his garage in Clapham, arriving around 8 o'clock in the evening.

The police surveillance team noted his arrival and rang the local station. Half an hour later, Inspector Charles Leach, Inspector William Barker, and several armed policemen walked into the Globe Garage, and found Browne relaxing in his office. 'I am arresting you for stealing a Vauxhall car in Tooting last 12 November,' said Barker. 'What do I know about stealing a car?' Browne replied. He then asked to go to the lavatory, and Barker ordered two armed policemen to go with him. Their route took them past the Angus Sanderson car, parked in the cobbled courtyard behind the garage. A Detective Sergeant named Bevis decided to search the car, and a few minutes later rushed into the office and told Barker and Leach that he had found a loaded revolver. Barker had clearly been wise to send two armed policeman with Browne.

In Browne's pockets they found a driving licence under a false name, some burgling tools, and twelve .455 cartridges. They were all stamped 'R.L.IV' on the base. When the police found these, Browne said: 'That's done it. Now you've found them it's all up with me.' A second .455 Webley revolver was later found in the car.

Back in Browne's lodging, accompanied by Caroline Browne, the police found a loaded .22 nickel-plated revolver and a Smith and Wesson, also loaded. When Browne was shown the nickel-plated revolver at the Tooting Police Station, he commented: 'That would only tickle you unless it hit you in a vital part. If you'd stopped me in the car I should have shot five of you and saved the other for myself.' He added: 'I shall have to have a machine gun for you bastards next time.'

At half past midnight, Chief Inspector Berrett arrived, and told Browne he was investigating the murder of PC Gutteridge. Browne denied knowing anything about it. He also denied stealing cars. Berrett took a statement from him, which he signed.

The next day, the police discovered various stolen items in the Globe Garage, including the numberplates of Mrs Hulton's car, and some medical instruments that may have belonged to Dr Lovell. A full list of Browne's recent criminal activities included a burglary on 7 October at the Tooting home of Mrs Martha Betts, and a break-in at Tooting Junction railway station, in which he had stolen cigarettes and money. On 12 November he had stolen Mrs Hulton's Vauxhall. On 25 November he had stolen a Singer car. On 4 December, Browne and an accomplice had broken into Eynsham station and stolen parcels and a typewriter; a porter who had interrupted them was tied up, after which the thieves escaped by driving a stolen car along the tracks. On 7 December he stole a Buick car in Harringey, and on 11 December he broke into Bordon railway station and stole parcels and money. Only a day before his arrest he had broken into a shop in Herne Hill. Browne was virtually a one-man crime wave.

Berrett now drove to Sheffield to interview John Currie, who had given the police Browne's address. Although little is known about him – even his name was kept secret for many years – it seems clear that he had been involved in some of Browne's criminal activities, including the burglary at the home of Martha Betts. Currie now told the police that Browne's main accomplice was a man called 'Pat', whose surname was Kennedy. This was the Kennedy who worked at the garage as Browne's book-keeper, and who had not been seen since Browne's arrest.

Kennedy's landlady was traced, and explained that Kennedy and his wife had been staying with her for only one week when he had been called away by a telegram declaring that his sister was ill. This telegram had arrived on 21 January – the day after Browne's arrest. (It was later discovered that Kennedy had sent it to himself, hoping to persuade his landlady to return some of his rent-in-advance.)

It was not difficult to follow Kennedy's trail. He and his wife had been driven away from their lodgings in a hire car, whose driver was able to say that he had taken them to Euston Station. There a luggage porter described putting their luggage on the Liverpool night-train. A delivery man who had helped Kennedy to pack a tea-chest with his belongings described how Kennedy had taken him for a drink, and had told him he was working for the Irish government; he had produced a large pistol, which he said he had bought to protect his wife.

Kennedy was known to the Liverpool police. Ten years Browne's junior, with an Irish accent, he had twice been arrested for 'flashing', had often been charged with being drunk and disorderly, and had spent much of his adult life in prison for burglary. Like Browne, he had been in the army and been dishonourably discharged.

The Liverpool police enquired after Kennedy in his old haunts, and learned that he had been trying to buy cartridges for his revolver, a Savage automatic known as a 'Tin Lizzie'. One of his acquaintances was able to tell the police that Kennedy and his wife were living in a room at 119, Copperas Hill. Towards midnight on 25 January, four days after his flight, Kennedy was seen hastily walking down the street near his lodgings by police who were waiting for him. A police sergeant named Mattinson, who knew Kennedy from earlier days, hurried up behind him and placed his hand on his shoulder. Kennedy turned around, raised the automatic pistol, and pulled the trigger; there was just a click, and Mattinson grabbed the pistol and punched Kennedy in the face. The policemen who rushed up to support Mattinson stopped a passing taxi, and Kennedy was taken to the Warren Street station. When the gun was examined, it was found to be loaded; fortunately, Kennedy had left the safety catch on.

The next day, after a night in the cells, Kennedy was

taken back to London by train. At Scotland Yard, Berrett told him that he was being charged with aiding Browne in the theft of the Vauxhall car. He added that he was looking into the murder of PC Gutteridge, and asked Kennedy if he knew anything about it. Kennedy then asked if he could see his wife Patricia, and when she was brought in, told her that the police were questioning him about the murder of the policeman in Essex. 'You didn't murder him, did you?' she asked, and Kennedy answered: 'No, but I was there, and know who did.'

Kennedy then went on to dictate a statement in which he admitted being with Browne on the night of the murder, and in which he laid all the blame for the crime on Browne.

According to Kennedy, he had gone to work for Browne in November 1926; he was to be manager of the garage, and would sleep on the premises. He went on to describe how, on the evening of 26 September 1927, Browne had asked him to accompany him to steal a Raleigh car in Billericay. They entered the garage with a skeleton key, then prepared to wait until the car's owner went to bed. But when Browne went back to the garage, a dog began to bark at them, and Browne decided to abandon the attempt and find another car to steal. They walked to the other end of the village and found the garage owned by Dr Lovell. They waited until the doctor's lights went out, then broke into the garage with a tyre lever, pushed the car down to the road and drove off down the country lanes.

An hour later, when someone flashed a light at them, they stopped, and saw that it was a policeman. He asked who they were and where they had come from. Browne, according to Kennedy, was nervous, and stumbled in his answer. As the policeman took out his notebook,

Kennedy heard a report, and saw the policeman stagger backwards. Browne, Kennedy claimed, then got out of the car and told him to get out too. According to Kennedy, he had begged Browne: 'For God's sake don't shoot any more – the man's dying', but Browne had said: 'What are you looking at me like that for?', and shot the policeman through both eyes.

As they drove on, Kennedy re-loaded the revolver, and dropped the empty cartridge case. He threw the other three out of the window. At one point, Browne scraped the car against a tree while turning round in the fog. (This explained the damage to the wing and the leaves and bark found attached to the springs.) They drove on to Brixton, abandoned the car, and then took a tram back to the garage.

Two days later, Browne and Kennedy were charged with the murder of PC Gutteridge. On the same day, the firearms expert Robert Churchill was given the cartridge case found in the Morris Cowley, and the three bullets taken from the dead constable's skull, as well as the various revolvers found on Browne's premises and in the car.

Robert Churchill, whose evidence helped to convict so many criminals, had inherited the gunshop of his uncle Edward J. Churchill in 1910, as well as his uncle's position as one of the foremost ballistics experts in England. The science of ballistics had originated with the French forensic expert Alexandre Lacassagne in 1889, when Lacassagne examined a bullet under a microscope and recognized that the 'rifling' of each gunbarrel – the spiral grooves that cause the bullet to spin and give it greater accuracy – is as individual as a fingerprint. Provided the expert can fire another bullet from the same gun, he can identify the weapon with complete confidence. In 1923,

Philip Gravelle invented the comparison microscope, in which two bullets could be examined side by side, and two halves of the images joined together to show their continuity.

In the Browne and Kennedy case, Churchill's task was made easier by the 'blister' at the base of the cartridge, made by a flaw in the breech block. All Churchill had to do was to fire a bullet of the same type – an R.L.IV – from the Webley revolver found in the driver's door of Browne's car, to prove that this was the gun that had killed PC Gutteridge. Under the comparison microscope, his test bullet also showed identical grooves to those fired into the policeman's skull.

The forensic pathologist Dr Gerald Roche Lynch examined the brown spots on the running board of the car, and verified that they were human bloodstains.

In prison, Kennedy seems to have made a determined attempt to prove that he was insane, but a doctor who examined him declared that the inconsistent symptoms proved that he was feigning.

The trial of Browne and Kennedy opened at the Old Bailey on 23 April 1928 before Mr Justice Avory. Sir Boyd Merriman, the Solicitor General, led for the prosecution. Browne was defended by E.F. Lever, Kennedy by Frank Powell. Avory turned down Powell's request that the two men should be tried separately, after which the prosecution presented its case. Its most compelling evidence concerned the Webley revolvers, and the fact that the revolver that fired the fatal shots had been found in Browne's car. Merriman also underlined the fact that Kennedy had tried to shoot the policeman who had arrested him.

Kennedy's defence was based on the assertion that he had merely been present at the murder, but had no idea that Browne meant to kill Gutteridge – in fact, no idea even that Browne was armed. Powell ended his opening speech with the assertion that his client had no case to answer. Mr Justice Avory replied promptly that he disagreed, and the trial continued.

Browne's defence was based on his claim that he was simply not present at the murder – he was at home with his wife. This is what Browne had consistently maintained from the beginning. In court he called Kennedy's story about going to Billericay 'a horribly concocted statement.' Browne's wife supported his assertion that on the night of the murder they had just moved into new lodgings, and were unpacking. (In fact, their landlady also declared that she had heard them moving about and unpacking on that evening, but her statement was not read out in court.)

The task of the defence was impossible. Browne was implicated in the murder by Kennedy, and the Webley that fired the fatal shot was found in his car. Kennedy might have stood a chance of acquittal if he had not tried to kill the policeman who arrested him, but under the circumstances, he seemed to be as violent and desperate as Browne. On the fifth day of the trial, the jury found both men guilty of murder. Browne received the sentence impassively; Kennedy went pale and staggered in the dock. The judge then donned the black cap and sentenced both men to death.

After the failure of his appeal, Kennedy again tried to feign insanity, but a diet of bread and water caused the symptoms to disappear. Browne made three attempts at suicide, hanging himself with his braces, cutting his arm and leg with a safety-razor blade, and finally, trying to cut his throat with a broken button. He went on hunger strike, and had to be force-fed, and he also smashed every breakable object in his cell, after which he had to be subdued by several warders. On Thursday 31 May 1928, both men were hanged – Browne at Pentonville, Kennedy at Wandsworth. Browne went to his death quietly and unemotionally, still maintaining his innocence. Kennedy – who had become a Catholic convert in the condemned cell – was pale and gasping as he was led to the scaffold.

For 65 more years, no one doubted that the verdict was a just one, and that Browne and Kennedy deserved to hang. But in 1993, a book called *The Long Drop* by Christopher Berry-Dee and Robin Odell raised some serious doubts. Berry-Dee is the grandson of Kennedy's solicitor, Oscar Berry Tompkins, and he states that his grandfather often remarked that he believed Kennedy had lied about Browne's involvement, and that 'Browne was not responsible.' Since he was Kennedy's solicitor, he was unable to speak out at the time.

What is suggested, in *The Long Drop*, is that Browne was telling the truth when he claimed that he was in his new lodgings on the night of the murder, helping his wife unpack – in other words, that Kennedy was alone (or possibly with another accomplice) when he killed PC Gutteridge. The crucial piece of evidence lies in the two Webleys found in the car. What Berry-Dee and Odell argue, briefly, is that the murder weapon belonged to Kennedy, and was in Kennedy's possession until well after the murder, when Browne persuaded Kennedy to exchange it for the Savage with which Kennedy tried to shoot Mattinson. Because the two guns looked more-or-less identical, Browne failed to grasp, until too late, that he was accused of being the owner of the *other* Webley, the murder weapon. But all Browne's attempts to set things right were assumed to be the lies of an experienced villain trying to confuse the issue.

The evidence for this argument is briefly as follows. The first revolver to be found (by Detective Sergeant Frank Bevis) was a new Webley, oxidized to prevent rust; Churchill proved this to be the murder weapon. The next day, Bevis found another revolver – old and rather rusty – in a compartment behind the driver's seat. But when he had been asked about this first revolver – the new one found in the pocket of the driver's door – Browne replied that he had bought it from a sailor in Tilbury Docks the previous April, but that it began to go rusty, so he kept it well oiled. This undoubtedly sounds as if Browne thought they had found the *second* revolver – which was definitely not the murder weapon.

The murder weapon – the oxidized revolver – was stolen by Browne and Kennedy in a burglary in July, and Kennedy received it as part of the proceeds. Browne wanted it, and tried – unsuccessfully – to persuade Kennedy to part with it. But it was after a burglary in October – after the murder – that Kennedy finally agreed to part with the oxidized revolver, in exchange for the Savage with which he later tried to kill Mattinson. Berry-Dee and Odell argue that Browne did not know he was taking possession of the murder weapon – they point out, very persuasively, that if he *had* known, he would surely have got rid of it long before his arrest.

As to why Browne made the mistake – in assuming that it was the rusty revolver that had been found – he himself explained that the garage office was so crowded with policemen that he was only able to see the gun at a distance.

If this scenario is correct, then Kennedy, not Browne,

was the owner of the murder weapon at the time of the murder.

Another piece of evidence complicates this already complicated story. While Browne was in prison, he was visited by his wife Caroline, who brought a bottle of invisible ink. Browne wrote a letter to a little girl called Mabel Currie in Sheffield, and on the back of this, he wrote a message in invisible ink to her father, John Currie, asking if he could tell him the precise date when he (Browne) obtained the murder weapon from Kennedy. This letter was intercepted – as was a second letter – and the episode is generally taken to prove that Browne wanted to shift the ownership of the murder weapon to Kennedy. If Berry-Dee and Odell are correct, then Browne did *not* own the murder weapon at the time of the murder, and wanted Currie to help him prove it.

According to Berry-Dee, the police at the time knew that Browne was not present when Gutteridge was murdered, and notes made by his grandfather prove Browne's innocence – or at least, throw some doubt on his guilt. But these notes are confidential, and can only be released to some relative of Kennedy. So until some relative of Kennedy can be found to take possession of the notes, the reasons why Berry Tompkins was so certain of Browne's innocence must remain a mystery.

All this certainly sounds as if an appalling miscarriage of justice has taken place. Browne may have been a murderous ruffian who was prepared to shoot down the policemen who came to arrest him, but if Berry-Dee is correct, he was not the murderer of PC Gutteridge. Yet there are many objections to this version of events. First, why, if Browne was innocent, did he say: 'I'm done for now' when Bevis came into the office with the murder weapon (which, according to Berry-Dee, he thought to be the *other* revolver)? And above all, why did he not tell the story of exchanging the murder weapon with Kennedy, and make it the centre of his defence? He had many opportunities in court to make this statement. If he *was* innocent, and he knew that Kennedy was trying to get him hanged for a murder he had not committed, surely he would say so as emphatically as possible, not keep it quiet?

In any case, the murder weapon was kept in a pocket in the driver's door, while the 'rusty' Webley was locked in a compartment behind the driver's seat. Surely it would be obvious that the first weapon the police would find would be the one in the driver's door, not the one hidden behind the seat? So it seems possible that Browne's statement that he bought this Webley from a sailor, and that it began to go rusty, was an attempt to confuse the police rather than genuine confusion on his own part.

But even if we accept that the murder weapon belonged to Kennedy at the time of the murder, this is still no proof that Browne did not kill PC Gutteridge. If he and Kennedy went off on a car-stealing expedition, it is perfectly feasible that they carried both revolvers, and Browne used the oxidized Webley to kill the policeman. Both revolvers hung in the office in the garage, behind some coats, so although Kennedy may have been the owner of the murder weapon, it sounds as if Browne always had access to it.

In fact, Berrett always believed that it was Kennedy who shot PC Gutteridge. This may seem to support Berry-Dee's contention that Browne was innocent; but *if* Browne was present at the time, then he was equally guilty in law, and would have been sentenced to hang even if it had been proved that Kennedy fired the shots.

There are, nevertheless, two telling points in Browne's favour. Kennedy's first statement claimed that before Browne shot the policeman, he said: 'What are you looking at me like that for?', then went on to shoot him in both eyes. But the medical evidence cited by Berry-Dee claims that the bullets had passed through the policeman's *eyelids*. If so, then his eyes must have been closed, and Kennedy's statement was untrue. The point is hardly crucial, but suggests that Kennedy's account of the murder was designed to make sure that Browne was hanged. Which, in turn, suggests that Kennedy may have lied about other things in his attempt to clear himself.

But perhaps the most telling argument for Browne's innocence is the one advanced by Berry-Dee and Odell — that he kept the murder weapon. If he *knew* the oxidized revolver was the murder weapon, why did he not get rid of it? Without the murder weapon, there would have been no case against him. Yet even this objection may be countered by the suggestion that Browne had no idea that 'every bullet has a fingerprint', and that the oxidized Webley could be identified so positively as the gun that killed PC Gutteridge. Or, of course, he may simply have made the kind of stupid mistake that so many criminals make, and simply not bothered to get rid of his favourite revolver.

The Long Drop adds one interesting footnote to the case. It has often been suggested that whoever shot Gutteridge in both eyes was a victim of the superstition that the last thing seen by a victim is 'photographed' on the retina. In the Jack the Ripper case of 1888, photographs were taken of the victims' eyes in an attempt to discover the identity of the murderer. Surprisingly, according to Odell and Berry-Dee, the idea *did* have some scientific foundation. In 1881, Professor Willi Kuhne, of Heidelberg University, noticed in the eyes of a frog which had been killed for experimental purposes the image of a Bunsen burner. Further experiments with frogs and rabbits established that if the light source was strong enough, it *was* 'photographed' on the dying creature's retina. For a while, 'optography' (as it was called) was taken seriously by various police forces, including the Sûreté. It seems to have been dropped because the light in which most murders had taken place was not strong enough to 'photograph' the killer. Yet if Kuhne's experiments *were* successful, then it seems arguable that 'optography' may still be a useful addition to the arsenal of the forensic scientist.

6

The Burning Car Murderer

In the early hours of 6 November 1930, two cousins named William Bailey and Alfred Brown were returning from a dance in Northampton when the glow of a fire suddenly appeared above the hedgerow of the lane in front of them. At that moment, a hatless man suddenly clambered out of a ditch at the corner of the lane and hurried past them. 'What is that blaze?' one of the cousins asked the other, and the man called over his shoulder: 'It looks as if someone's had a bonfire.' He sounded as if he was out of breath. As they looked back at him in the moonlight, he reached the main London to Northampton road, seemed to hesitate, then turned towards London.

Meanwhile, the flames ahead of them were leaping 15 feet in the air. As they approached, they saw that it was a burning motorcar. As far as they could see, there was nobody inside. They ran on quickly to the village of Hardingstone, where they lived, and raised the alarm. William Bailey's father happened to be the village constable, and he summoned another constable named Copping. By the time they reached the blaze, the flames were only about six feet high. Now they could see that there was, in fact, a body lying across the front seat.

Buckets of water were hurled into the flames until the car was merely a steaming hulk. At 3.40 in the morning, the charred corpse – with one leg burnt off at the knee and one arm at the elbow – was removed to a nearby inn, and later to the Northampton General Hospital. In the rear seat of the car the police discovered a charred petrol can.

At this stage it looked like an accident. But who was the mysterious man who jumped out of the ditch? As the two cousins elaborated their evidence, the puzzle only deepened. Apparently a car had been driving past a split second before the man appeared, so that, dazzled by its headlights, he failed to see the cousins. This man, it seemed, had been carrying a briefcase, and was wearing a light mackintosh, and the cousins were able to say that he looked in his mid-thirties, was about 5 ft 10 ins tall, and had a round face and curly black hair. So he was obviously not a tramp. And if he was the driver of the car, going for help, then why did he try to mislead the cousins by implying that it was a Guy Fawkes bonfire?

The police visited every inn and hotel in Northampton, but were unable to trace the man. But the numberplate of the burnt-out car – MU 1468 – enabled them to learn that it had belonged to a man called Alfred Arthur Rouse, who lived at 14, Buxted Road, Finchley, in north London. Local police called at the house, and spoke to Mrs Lily Rouse, who told them that her husband was a commercial traveller. Mrs Rouse was taken to Northampton, where she was shown some brace buckles and a piece of charred clothing, which she thought *might* belong to her husband. The corpse was so badly burned that there would have been no point in allowing her to see it.

At this stage, police thought that the body might be

that of a woman — a heel had been found near the car, and it looked as if it came from a woman's shoe. The injuries caused by the fire meant that the sex was indeterminate.

Late that night, the Cardiff police contacted Scotland Yard, and told them that the commercial traveller they were looking for was at this moment on his way from Cardiff to London by coach. The result was that when the coach pulled up near Hammersmith Bridge at 9.20 a.m. on 7 November 1930, two plain clothes men were waiting to speak to Alfred Arthur Rouse. The round-faced man with the neat black moustache said: 'I am glad it is over. I have had no sleep.' His voice was rather high-pitched, and somehow conveyed an impression of untrustworthiness.

But his words were not a confession to murder. At Hammersmith Police Station, Rouse explained that the blaze had been an accident. He had, he said, been giving the man — whom he had picked up on the Great North Road — a lift to Leicester to look for work. Near Hardingstone, the engine of the car had begun to 'spit', and Rouse assumed he was running out of petrol. In any case, he wanted to relieve his bowels. So he asked the man to fill up the petrol tank from a can while he went some distance away from the car. He thought the man had tried to light a cigarette while pouring the petrol, for there was a surge of flame. He pulled up his trousers and ran back to the car. The man was inside; he tried to open the door, but was driven back by flames. 'I was all of a shake. I did not know what to do, and ran as hard as I could along the road where I saw the two men. I felt I was responsible for what had happened. I lost my head . . .'

Even this story contained obvious inconsistencies. If

the stranger had been pouring petrol when the car exploded, why was he *inside* it? And why had Rouse taken his briefcase when he went to relieve himself? Rouse answered this by claiming that he saw the stranger's hand on his briefcase at one point, and decided to take it with him.

He concluded this statement, which had taken four-and-a-half hours, at half past five in the morning. After that he was driven back to Northampton, to the Angel Lane Police Station. There he made things rather worse for himself by suddenly explaining that his wife – whom he was hoping to see – was too good for him, and that he had several mistresses. 'But it is a very expensive game.' He was, he explained, on his way to Wales when the accident had occurred. 'My harem takes me to several places.' Obviously, this admission provided a motive for murder: the desire to 'disappear'. The next day, the newspaper headlines were full of stories about Rouse's 'harem'.

Soon after these indiscreet remarks, Rouse's wife entered the room, and he leapt up and embraced her affectionately. He asked the police superintendent if his wife could have the 6s 3½d which he had on him. Having obtained permission to hand over the cash, he then asked her to buy two books and some tobacco, which left her with nothing more than her bus-fare to London; she had to walk home from the bus terminal.

Now, under police investigation, the whole story of Rouse's double life began to unravel. It made it perfectly clear that he had every motive for wanting to disappear.

Alfred Rouse was born in Herne Hill, London, on 6 April 1894, the son of a hosier, and his childhood seems to have been blameless. He was a regular churchgoer, a good tennis player, musical, intelligent, athletic, lively and clever with his hands, the kind of boy labelled 'most likely to succeed' by schoolmasters. He attended evening classes to study the piano and violin. The only shadow on his childhood was the separation of his parents when he was six years old; he was brought up by an aunt.

Educated at the local council school, the teenage Rouse was an office boy for a short time, until he found himself a job in a drapery store in the West End. He also became a sacristan at St Saviour's Church in Stoke Newington. At the outbreak of the First World War he enlisted in the 24th Queen's Territorial Regiment. Three months later, before he was posted to France, he married a clerk named Lily May Watkins, who, at 23, was three years his senior.

In Paris, some time between March and May 1915, he seems to have made the most of his time by fathering a child; little is known about this liaison. And on 25 May 1915, at Festubert, he was blown up by a mine and sustained a head injury that plunged him into unconsciousness for several days. He was also wounded in the thigh and lower leg.

It took him a long time to recover, and his head remained badly scarred, so that he was unable to wear a hat. A medical report also stated: 'memory very defective, sleeps badly, easily excited, talks and laughs immoderately at times.' He also suffered from nightmares about the bayonet charge in which he was blown up; he had just missed his man and was expecting to die from a bayonet thrust.

For many months Rouse was in a convalescent home in Yorkshire, slowly recovering. Finally, in 1916, he was invalided out of the army. He returned to his wife, and looked for an outdoor job that would enable him to

regain his health. The labour shortage meant that it
was easy to find work, and Rouse had no difficulty
in obtaining a position as a commercial traveller (in
braces and garters) with a Leicester firm. The job suited
him; he loved cars, and soon added 'skilled mechanic'
to his other qualifications. His manner was friendly and
pleasant, and his status as a war hero earned him respect.
Soon he was making £10 a week, which counted as a
middle-class income. About a quarter of this went on
his mortgage and the hire purchase on the car.

And, like the commercial traveller of legend, he
began to accumulate mistresses. Some commentators
have suggested that the injury to his head had caused
a change of character – and it is, indeed, possible to cite
a long list of criminals whose characters changed after
they sustained head wounds. Yet it is also necessary to
take into account that Rouse had fathered an illegitimate
child in Paris months before he was blown up. There
can be no doubt that Rouse was highly sexed from the
beginning. His job offered him boundless opportunities
– waitresses, chambermaids, shopgirls – every attractive
girl he saw aroused instant desire, and in 1917 the shortage of males meant that England was full of unattached
females. Rouse had a car – which was rare at the time;
few women could resist the invitation to go for a run –
particularly with a man who seemed a 'good catch' –
for Rouse never admitted he was married. Once alone
with a girl he found attractive, his imagination soared.
His parents were 'well off'. He had been to Eton, then to
Cambridge. In the army he had been a major. (In fact he
had remained a private.) His mother, from whom he had
been separated at the age of six, had reappeared during
his teens as a beautifully-dressed socialite . . .

Rouse was not an aggressive Casanova, out to take

advantage of the girl at the first opportunity. He preferred to exert all his charm, and to allow the girl to fall in love with him, so that at last she was as anxious to yield as he was to accept her surrender. Nowadays we would describe him as the master of the 'soft sell', but this may be unduly cynical. The truth seems to be that he was a romantic who enjoyed the courtship as much as the consummation. That he was no mere seducer is underlined by the fact that he always returned to his wife. Since they had no children – to his intense regret – there was no reason why he should not abandon her and devote his life to philandering. But she loved him – although Rouse complained that she never 'made a fuss of him' or sat on his knee – and Rouse was a man of tender feelings. His problem was that anything young and female aroused his tender feelings, as well as a desire to repeat the delightful ritual of courtship and conquest.

In addition to all this, he loved being a family man. In 1927, he and Lily purchased the house in Finchley on mortgage for £750, and he spent his weekends digging the garden and making home improvements.

All might have been well if it had not been for the problems involved in contraception at the beginning of the jazz age. In 1920, in the home of friends who believed him unmarried, he met a fourteen-year-old Edinburgh servant girl named Helen Campbell; she succumbed easily, and bore him a child in October 1921 in a home for unmarried mothers. The baby died when only five weeks old. Most men would have sighed with relief and vowed not to repeat unplanned parenthood a second time, but Rouse went back to Helen, and in October 1924 she found herself pregnant again. In the following month Rouse married her bigamously at

St Mary's Church, Islington, and then moved with her into lodgings in Liverpool Road, Islington, where a son was born in July 1925. As a commercial traveller, it was easy for Rouse to spend one night with his lawful wife and the next with his mistress, but it meant that he now had two households to support on £10 a week. Half of this was spent on his mortgage, car and Lily's housekeeping; the second household meant that he was spending another two or three pounds a week, and leaving himself very little for hotels, meals and other seductions. Admittedly, Helen also worked — as a waitress — but after a disagreement about one of her jobs, they separated, and a paternity order obliged him to pay her ten shillings a week. His payments were irregular, and his wife Lily finally agreed to foster the child. Rouse seems to have been a good father who often drove his son over to see his real mother.

The problem was that Helen was far from the only one. According to Browne and Tullett, the authors of *Bernard Spilsbury: His Life and Cases*: 'Several went through a form of marriage with him, and he had children all over southern England.' And Helena Normanton, in her introduction to the *Notable British Trials* volume, estimates that Rouse seduced about eighty women. Even before Helen Campbell had borne his son, he had made the acquaintance of another attractive servant girl in Hendon. Her name was Nellie Tucker and in 1925 she was seventeen. He told her he was unmarried, and had bachelor chambers in Victoria (where, in fact, he had a mailing address). Nellie often accompanied him to hotels, and in May 1928 she gave birth to a girl. The baby was fostered for 12s 6d a week. In October 1930, shortly before he ran away from the burning car, she gave birth to a second child, a daughter, in the London Maternity Hospital.

For Lily, Nellie Tucker seems to have been the last straw, and they discussed separation. But Lily was only partly informed of the worst complication so far. She had found in her husband's pocket a photograph of yet another pretty teenager. This was a probational nurse named Ivy Jenkins, whom Rouse had met in London and who had swiftly yielded to his courtship. Unlike Helen and Nellie, Ivy came of a respectable, middle-class background; her father was a retired colliery manager, and they lived at Gellygaer, in Monmouthshire. As usual, Rouse told her he was single, and offered to marry her as soon as things improved. He even persuaded her to tell her family that they *were* married, and went to stay in their home for long weekends once a fortnight. Soon, Ivy was pregnant, and fell ill. She returned home to be nursed, and Rouse told her parents that he had bought a luxurious house in Kingston-on-Thames costing £1,250 (which would have represented two-and-a-half years wages), which he had also furnished. He invited her sister Phyllis to come and stay with them for a few months after they moved in.

Ivy was safely at home at the moment, but Rouse had set 6 November as the date when they would move to Kingston. Meanwhile, Nellie was in hospital giving birth to yet another child, and Lily was talking about separating from him and demanding an allowance. It was becoming impossible. No matter how much he loved his wife and illegitimate son, and Nellie and her daughter, and the pregnant Ivy Jenkins, it would surely be sensible to vanish and let them all think he was dead.

Now whatever Rouse's faults – a liar, a boaster, a

philanderer – he was undoubtedly not a violent man, and it is a sign of his desperation, his sense of being trapped and ruined, that he began to see murder as his only solution. Merely to disappear would not serve his purpose; he wanted to make sure he left his wife and son provided for with insurance money. In the July before his attempted disappearance he had insured his car for £1,000, in respect of the death of a passenger or the owner.

And now, a few days before Guy Fawkes night, an opportunity suddenly presented itself to put his plan into operation. Outside a public house in Whetstone called the Swan and Pyramid, he was accosted by an unemployed man, and bought him a drink. The man said he had been hitchhiking around the country looking for work – Peterborough, Hull, Norwich and other places. And then he threw in the fatal remark: 'I have no relations.' Suddenly, Rouse felt that fate was beckoning him; this was the opportunity he had dreamed about. He told the man he was driving to Leicester on Guy Fawkes night and offered him a lift. They agreed to meet at the same pub at eight o'clock in the evening.

Early that evening, Rouse went to visit Nellie Tucker and her week-old daughter in the City of London Maternity Hospital. She noticed that he seemed abstracted, with his eye on the clock, and asked if he was meeting someone. Rouse stared vacantly for a moment, then said no. He went on to explain his abstraction by saying that he had so many things to pay that he had no idea where to turn.

What happened next would emerge in two confessions that Rouse wrote after he was sentenced to death.

Rouse picked up his passenger shortly after eight, as arranged. He had also bought the man a present – a bottle of whisky. (Rouse himself did not smoke or drink.) The stranger (whose name Rouse never learned) drank it straight from the bottle. By the time they reached St Albans, he was drunk enough to turn off the lights by accident, and a policeman stopped them. Rouse explained what had happened, and they drove on.

They reached Hardingstone, a village close to Northampton, shortly before 2 a.m. It would obviously have been dangerous to put the plan into operation earlier, while most people were still awake; but in the early hours of the morning, in a quiet village off the main road, it seemed perfectly safe. In all probability, it was the passenger who asked if they could stop while he went to empty his bladder. They got out of the car, but Rouse was carrying a wooden mallet, and before his fuddled passenger had time to move far, he hit him with all his force on the head. The man collapsed without a sound. Rouse lifted his body and heaved it into the driver's seat; the man fell sideways, but that hardly seemed to matter. Rouse now emptied the petrol can over him, then made a trail of petrol from the front of the car to a spot ten yards away. He also took the top off the carburettor and loosened a joint in the petrol pipe, so that the car itself would burn after the petrol he had poured on the body had burnt itself out; after that he replaced the can in the back of the car, took his attaché case, then ran to the end of the petrol trail and ignited it with a match. Within seconds, the car was blazing; inside it, a man was being burnt to death.

Rouse had committed the perfect murder. There was no way of proving that the fire had not started accidentally. All he had to do now was 'disappear' and start a new life. His wife and child would be provided for by the car insurance.

But he had made one major mistake – choosing Guy Fawkes night for the murder. It meant that many people were still about. Within a minute, Rouse had bumped into two of them on their way back from a dance . . .

Even now he could have saved his neck by quick thinking. All he had to do was to say: 'Help me! There's been a terrible accident', and return with them. But the sight of the flames had produced a totally unexpected effect. In France, a few seconds before he was blown up, he had seen an aeroplane burst into flame in the sky and crash. Now the sight of the blazing car revived that memory and threw him into panic and confusion. Any chance of collecting himself and behaving with calculation vanished in that moment. So he did the worst thing he could possibly do: tried to run away.

Under the circumstances – and allowing for the fact that his plan had gone awry – it is true that escape must have seemed the most sensible course. If he had stuck to his plan and 'vanished', he might have been able to make his way to Scotland – as he had originally intended – and then sailed for New Zealand or the South Seas under a false name. With luck, the mystery of the man who jumped out of the ditch would have been forgotten and the body would have been identified as his own.

Instead, Rouse hitched a lift on a lorry back to London, dropped off in Finchley, and made his way home to 'tell his wife not to be worried.' He arrived at 6.20, and was on his way again before 7 a.m. This curious statement is bound to arouse some doubts about his wife's role in the affair. If he really told her that he was about to disappear, and not to be worried, presumably she asked him what it was all about. Yet she later claimed that, although she heard him come in, she had no idea what time it was (she thought it was about 1 a.m.) – so that when the police came to tell her about the 'accident', she jumped to the conclusion that it had happened after he left home.

To create a consistent theory from this version of events, we have to assume that his wife knew – at some stage – about the murder plan, and was willing to allow him to disappear. On the whole, this seems unlikely. Certainly, every writer on the case has given her the benefit of the doubt.

Rouse now compounded his problems by making his way to the home of Ivy Jenkins in Gellygaer – he had received a telegram saying she was ill. He booked on a motorcoach in the Strand, joking with the clerk and telling him that his car had been stolen on the Great North Road while he was drinking coffee at a roadside stall. On the journey to Cardiff he sat beside the driver, and told him that his car had been stolen at St Albans, and that he was on his way to see his wife in Cardiff. When he arrived in Gellygaer – fourteen miles north of Cardiff – at about 8.15, he told Ivy's father, William Jenkins, and a visitor called Tom Reakes, that his car had been stolen in Northampton while he was in a restaurant.

When he was upstairs visiting his 'wife', Tom Reakes went home and saw the account of the burnt-out car at Hardingstone; he returned to the Jenkins and showed them the item, asking Rouse: 'Is this your car?' Rouse denied it.

Worse was to come the next morning. Ivy's sister Phyllis produced a copy of the *Daily Sketch* with a photograph of the burnt-out car and a headline: 'Body Found in a Blazing Car.' The car's registration number was given, as well as the fact that it belonged to a Mr A.A. Rouse of Buxted Road, Finchley. Fortunately for Rouse, it did not mention that his wife also lived there. He took the paper and went upstairs to show it to Ivy, probably mopping his brow at his close shave.

A visitor named Hendell Brownhill – a motor salesman – had called on Mr Jenkins that morning, and Rouse asked him for a lift back to Cardiff. Mr Brownhill also wanted to hear how the accident happened, and Rouse again explained that his car had been stolen while he was eating in a Northampton restaurant. But when they stopped briefly at the Cooper's Arms Hotel – where the motor salesman had business – Brownhill heard Rouse telling the proprietor that his car had disappeared after he had gone into a London pub for a meal. When a butcher's assistant came in and told them that a woman's body had been found in the burnt-out car, Rouse said: 'Oh dear, dear, I can't bear to hear about it.'

But when Rouse had climbed on to the London coach, Mr Brownhill decided that his story was suspicious. And since the police station was only a few yards from the bus station, he went and communicated his suspicions to the police. So when Rouse arrived in Hammersmith that evening, he found two policemen waiting for him. It was now that he told the story of how his passenger had set fire to the car while filling the petrol tank.

The mallet had been found, with human hairs adhering to it, some distance from the car. Rouse produced the preposterous explanation that he must have been rubbing the mallet over his own hair.

In Northampton a few hours later, he made his worst error so far – by mentioning his 'harem', and the fact that having several mistresses was an 'expensive game'. It was fatal because in the preliminary police court hearings, the solicitor who appeared for the Director of Public

Prosecutions – G.R. Paling – mentioned Rouse's 'harem' speech, which in turn meant it was reported in the press. In England, evidence about the character of the accused is not permitted at his trial, and without the evidence to blacken his character, Rouse might have been acquitted. But Rouse's loquacity meant that his 'harem' speech was widely reported, so that all the jurors knew about it.

Yet in spite of this, Rouse felt he stood a good chance of acquittal. It would be extremely difficult to actually disprove his story of the accident.

The trial of Alfred Arthur Rouse on a charge of murdering an unknown man opened at Northampton Assizes before Mr Justice Talbot on 26 January 1931. Rouse was defended by Donald Finnemore, while Norman Birkett and Richard Elwes appeared for the prosecution. Birkett had no difficulty making out a strong case against Rouse. The removal of the carburettor cap and the loosening of the petrol joint must have been deliberate, to ensure that the car would go on burning.

Birkett decided against using the 'harem' evidence – although the jurors had certainly read it in the newspapers. In any case, Birkett had two witnesses who would leave very little doubt in the minds of the jury that the fire had been started deliberately.

The first was Cuthbert Buckle, the managing director of a firm of fire-loss assessors. He explained how the loosening of the petrol joint meant a continual flow of petrol into the car, near the feet of the passenger. Since the car would lose a gallon of petrol every twenty minutes if the union joint had been loose since the car left London, and hence would never have reached Hardingstone, it followed that the joint must have been loosened soon before the fire.

But the most formidable witness for the prosecution

was Sir Bernard Spilsbury. He had examined the body, and had concluded that the victim was a male of about 30, and that he had probably been a coal miner. Soot in the bronchial tubes revealed that he had been alive when the fire broke out. The man had died of shock from burns.

The most damning part of Spilsbury's evidence was based upon a tiny piece of rag which had been trapped in the dead man's leg when intense heat had caused the leg to bend; this rag smelt of petrol. So did a fragment of the trouser fly which had also survived by being trapped between the thigh and the stomach. These made it quite clear that the man had been soaked in petrol before he died.

Spilsbury also described how the right foot of the dead man had been extended beyond the door of the car, which seemed to indicate that he had left the car – and so given Rouse a chance to hit him with the mallet. Rouse had denied that the man had left the car. (It would, of course, have been virtually impossible to knock him unconscious with a mallet within the confines of the car.) When asked whether it was not possible that the man, in his agony, had kicked the burnt door open, Spilsbury replied that he would have been dead long before that.

The defence called Harvey Whyatt, a pathologist, to rebut Spilsbury's evidence. He argued that the position of the body proved nothing – he might well have been sitting up and smoking in the passenger seat when the explosion occurred, and then fallen sideways as the fire caused his limbs to contort and the roof to fall in. Whyatt denied that the fact that the victim had not tried to escape proved that he was unconscious when the fire started. But he found it hard to refute Birkett's suggestion that the position of the body indicated that the man had been flung into the car when unconscious.

Another fire assessor who argued that the petrol joint was invariably loosened by fire had an equally hard time at Birkett's hands, and his qualifications as an engineer were called into question when he admitted that he not only had no idea of the coefficient of expansion of brass, but did not even know what that meant.

Rouse's story – when he was called into the witness box – was that his passenger must have opened the petrol can in the car while striking a match to light a cigar; understandably, this notion aroused incredulity. To explain his many lies during the twenty-four hours that followed the fire, Rouse explained that he was embarrassed by the fact that he had left the car to relieve his bowels, and that he was unwilling to admit this 'with ladies present.'

The judge's summing up was highly unfavourable to Rouse. 'There is no doubt that he is by his own confession a most facile liar.' From the moment of the fire to the moment of his arrest he had told a whole series of absurd and incompatible lies. Why lie at all if he was really an innocent man who had just witnessed a terrible accident?

The jury agreed; they took only a quarter of an hour to find Rouse guilty of murder. On 31 January 1931, Mr Justice Talbot sentenced Rouse to death. His appeal was dismissed. On 10 March 1931, he was hanged at Bedford Jail. Ironically, Bedford had been the first place he had seen when he recovered consciousness after being invalided back from France.

Rouse's wife claimed that she remained convinced of his innocence to the end. She had sold the house and moved to Northampton so that she could be near him in prison. Yet here again there are some matters that raise doubts. Three weeks before his execution, she telephoned the wife of the Home Secretary, asserting that she was sure of her husband's innocence; on the day before his execution she told a *Daily Express* reporter that she had been seeing him constantly and that he had never ceased to deny his innocence.

Yet on the day after Rouse's execution, the *Daily Sketch* published his confession to the murder – although it still deviated from the truth in his assertion that he had strangled the passenger in his car. Mrs Rouse then published – in the following Sunday's *News of the World* – another confession that Rouse had written on 7 March, two days before she told the *Express* that he had never ceased to deny his innocence.

Looking back over the evidence, it is hard to decide whether the deterioration of Rouse's character was due to shell-shock, or whether – as another writer has suggested – the childhood trauma of separation from his mother made him dependent on women for a sense of emotional security. There is another possible explanation – that brain-damage due to the war accident had the effect of filling him with insatiable sexual desires that led him to devote his life to seduction.

What seems undoubtedly clear is that Rouse simply lacked the qualifications to be a successful murderer. Compared, for example, to 'Brides in the Bath' Smith, he completely lacked foresight. Helena Normanton offers an example in her *Notable British Trials* introduction: Four days before the murder, Rouse went to St Mary's Church, Islington – where he had bigamously married Helen Campbell – and posed as his own brother in order to get a copy of his marriage certificate. He explained to the clerk that his brother, Alfred Arthur Rouse, had just been burnt to death in a terrible motor accident, and that he needed the marriage certificate for legal formalities. In fact, he wanted it in order to get Nellie Tucker admitted to the maternity hospital. But why tell the absurd story about the accident? Plainly, because he wanted to be able to pose as his own brother after his 'disappearance', and wanted a witness to be able to state, if necessary, that he bore a startling resemblance to his 'dead brother'. Yet it never seems to have struck him that when the clerk heard of the accident that destroyed his car, he would wonder why Rouse's 'brother' had reported his death four days before it happened. Compared to the shrewdly calculating Smith, Rouse was a childish incompetent.

In conclusion, a personal note. In 1930, the grandmother of the present writer(s), a 19-year-old girl named Hattie Jones, worked in Leicester in a garment factory called Rudkin and Laundon, where Rouse called as a commercial traveller. Rouse saw her there, and one day in the spring of 1930, happened to see her looking in a shop window and invited her for a meal. My grandmother had already eaten, and said that her father would probably object. When he learned that her father was on the telephone, Rouse rang him and secured permission to take her out – promising to bring her straight back home.

My grandmother told him she would prefer to wait in the car while he had a meal, and Rouse brought her a box of chocolates. After his meal, he took her for a drive. She said he 'behaved like a gentleman', and drove her home afterwards. She never saw him again.

This seems to demonstrate that Rouse's technique was fairly leisurely. If his personal affairs had been less tangled, he would probably have asked Hattie Jones out for a drive and a meal on his subsequent visits to Leicester, and in due course suggested that she might like to take a longer trip with him and spend the night in a hotel.

In fact, my grandmother was already 'keeping company' with a man named Arthur Wilson, and in the following September became pregnant by him. They were married at Christmas and my father was born the following June.

It is an odd thought that, under different circumstances, I might have been the grandson of the burning car murderer.

The Human Jigsaw Puzzle

Red stains on the carpet,
Red stains on the Knife;
Oh, Dr Buck Ruxton,
You cut up your wife.
The nursemaid, she saw you,
And threatened to tell,
So, Dr Buck Ruxton,
You killed her as well.

1935, schoolyard rhyme (to *Red Sails in the Sunset*)

On 19 September 1935, a young woman named Susan Johnstone left her hotel in the Scottish town of Moffat and took a walk along the Edinburgh road to enjoy the unseasonably fine weather. As she stood on the Gardenholme Linn Bridge to watch the stream splashing by beneath her, she noticed, down among the jutting rocks and boulders, what appeared to be a bundle of clothes. She leaned a little further over the parapet to get a closer look, and saw something that sent her hurrying back to town – sticking out of the bundle was what appeared to be a human arm.

Miss Johnstone was frightened, and by no means sure that her eyes had not been deceiving her. On arriving at her hotel she found her brother and told him the story. Rather than call out the police on what might be a false alarm, he decided to return with his sister to the bridge. There he climbed down to inspect the package. He soon confirmed that there was indeed a human arm poking out of the cloth wrappings. Further investigation revealed that the bundle also concealed a head and other butchered pieces of human flesh. He hurried to the police, and they were soon combing the area for the rest of the body.

Four other bundles wrapped in old clothes and newspapers were found by the stream. They contained parts of arms, legs, a torso and various lumps of flesh. At this stage it became evident that the authorities had at least two victims to identify, because one of the parcels, found directly under the bridge, contained a second head.

Whoever had disposed of the packages had done so in the reasonable hope that they would never be found. Until recently the Gardenholme Linn had been swollen by autumnal rains, and the remains had only to float a few hundred yards downstream to be swept into the River Annan. From there it was likely that they would be washed into the Solway Firth, never to be seen again. However, the Gardenholme Linn was a very rocky stream, and most of the bundles had become snagged. Then, with the coming of the spate of warm weather, the stream had shrunk and the remains had been beached.

Two local doctors made the initial examination, but they soon concluded that the case demanded specialist handling. Although dismemberment is a not uncommon method of disposing of unwanted bodies, the murderer is frequently unskilled, and leaves behind clues to his victim's identity. In this case, the bodies had clearly been dissected by somebody with a cool head and extensive surgical or butchering skills. It was obvious that this person had been determined to destroy all evidence useful to the authorities.

The heads had been carefully flayed of skin. (One had some scalp and facial tissue left, but the other was virtually bare.) The eyes and some teeth had been removed, and what hair was left had been hacked short. The finger-ends on two of the hands had also been cut off. This may have been done to confound efforts to take fingerprints, but since the other two hands were left undamaged, this seemed unlikely. It was also noted that a substantial portion of flesh had been removed from one of the arms, as had an area from one of the feet. It looked as if the mutilator had set out to remove all identifying marks from the victims.

Dr John Glaister, Regius Professor of Forensic Medicine at Glasgow University and author of the classic *Medical Jurisprudence and Toxicology*, was called in to head an investigative team on the case. At first they had little enough to go on. Although the remains had been treated with ether and 'pickled' in a formalin solution immediately after discovery, the victims were estimated to have been dead for over a fortnight before that and decomposition had already done much damage. The fact that the bundles had been immersed in running water, even for only a short time, meant that many clues such as hairs and house-fluff had been washed away.

Out of the 70 body parts found – those in the four parcels and others discovered around the Gardenholme Linn area over the following weeks – Glaister assembled two corpses. One consisted of only a head, arms and legs, while the other, the taller of the two, was almost complete. This body was clearly a woman, but Glaister could not yet hazard a guess as to the sex of the smaller victim.

Assuming, for the sake of a good story, that the victims were a man and a woman, the press speculated that they were lovers who had been murdered by a jealous spouse. This notion had to be abandoned when Glaister's team found a portion of a third breast among the many unidentified pieces of flesh.

To further confuse the issue, a mutated eye, matching neither skull, was also found. It was a huge 'cyclops eye' – or rather, two eyes that had grown together like Siamese twins. Glaister's team could have taken this to indicate a bizarre third victim, but since they could not determine whether the eye was human or animal in origin, they decided to treat it as a red herring.

Deducing the ages of the victims was a relatively straightforward matter. While a person is still growing, fracture-like 'joining lines,' called sutures, run across the dome of the skull to allow development. Between 35 and 40 years of age, when the body has stopped growing, they close up. In the case of the taller woman this process had already begun, indicating that she was approaching middle age. This was not the case with the smaller woman, therefore she was almost certainly under 30. Indeed, X-rays of her jaw showed that her wisdom teeth had not yet begun to grow through, placing her age tentatively in the early twenties.

The study of the victims' joints confirmed these estimates. Cartilage gradually forms into 'caps' or 'epiphyses', and since the process is uniform for everyone, the age of a person can be judged by the extent to which the process has taken place. The taller victim was finally estimated as being in her mid-thirties, possibly approaching 40, while the smaller one was probably about 20.

In examining the skulls, Glaister also made a note of

the unusual length of face of the older woman. Before she was mutilated, she would have had an unusually 'horsey' appearance. This simple observation was to have enormous importance later in the investigation.

In both cases, the causes of death were clear. Glaister found that the small hyoid bone in the throat of the older victim had been broken – a sign of strangulation. She had also sustained much bruising, several broken bones and five stab wounds to the chest. Examination of the skull of the younger woman indicated that she had been battered to death with a blunt instrument. The dismemberment and mutilation had been done post mortem.

Glaister guessed that the older woman had been killed first since the savagery of the attack was mostly directed at her. She had been strangled, beaten and stabbed by the murderer – evidence of a jealous rage perhaps? On the other hand, the lack of violence in the case of the younger woman suggested that she might have been a witness who was silenced.

For Glaister, the evidence suggested that the killer had once received medical training. The dismemberment had been carried out with a sharp knife or a scalpel, including the removal of the limbs – a tricky job, even for a trained surgeon. (Unskilled murderers tend to resort to saws or axes.) Likewise, the removal of the teeth suggested someone who knew about dental records. Finally, the expert flaying of the heads and removal of the eyes pointed to a surgeon rather than a butcher.

The first major problem faced by the investigating officers was to discover the identity of the victims. There was a possibility that the killings had taken place locally, but the care taken by the murderer up to that point suggested that he or she would have travelled a long distance from home to dispose of the bodies. At this point, the police had an unusual stroke of luck.

The dissected bodies had been wrapped-up in old clothes – including two sets of baby's rompers – straw and newspapers. One would have expected the newsprint to have dissolved into mush, but much was still legible. The newspapers dated from August, with the most recent being part of a *Sunday Graphic and News* for 15 September 1935. This was on, or around the probable time of death. The most interesting point about this sheet was a photo of a young woman and a damaged headline reading: '. . . ambe's Carnival Queen Crowned.'

The *Sunday Graphic* was contacted and confirmed what the police had hoped; the issue carrying the carnival queen story had been a special 'slip' or local edition. Only 3,700 had been printed to be circulated in the Morecambe and Lancaster areas. It was of course possible that the murderer had bought a paper away from home, but since it was dated so close to the estimated time of the killing it seemed unlikely.

In fact, the Lancaster police already had a likely suspect. They had been investigating the death of a Morecambe woman called Smalley, whose body had been found a year earlier. In the course of their investigations they had routinely interviewed a woman called Curwen. Shortly afterwards, on 24 September, a doctor named Buck Ruxton burst into the office of Detective Inspector John Moffat. In obviously high emotion, he accused the inspector of prying into his personal affairs. Mrs Curwen, it transpired, was a part-time servant of the doctor's, and Ruxton felt that the police were implying that he was involved in the death of Mrs Smalley.

Inspector Moffat tried to calm him down, but Ruxton continued to rage on about seemingly unconnected matters. He complained that his wife had left him, taking their maid up to Edinburgh. Then he showed Moffat a bandaged hand and told him that he had given himself a bad cut opening a can of peaches for his children. Finally, he insisted that any rumours that he had been involved in the death of Mrs Smalley were the inventions of other doctors – who were jealous of his large practice and modern methods – then he stormed out. Moffat was amazed; there had been absolutely no rumours to connect Dr Ruxton with the Smalley case. It had been five days later when the bodies were found in the Gardenholme Linn.

With hindsight, it is easy to see that Ruxton's behaviour seemed to suggest guilt; but the Lancaster police were used to his emotional outbursts, and did not pay much attention to the episode. Dr Buck Ruxton – who had changed his name by deed poll from Bukhtyar Hakim – was a short, handsome, 36-year-old Asian with a profitable practice. He and his Scottish wife, Isabella, had moved to Lancaster in 1930, and their frequent rows were a regular source of local gossip.

In fact, in 1933, Isabella Ruxton had complained to the police that her husband had brutally beaten her. Dr Ruxton was interviewed and proceeded to rave at his wife and the police. She was an adulteress, he insisted, she deserved beating and if she continued to see other men he would kill her. Then he suddenly calmed down, apologized, and gave her money to go to stay with her sister in Edinburgh. In fact, they made-up immediately and apparently went on as before. Their relationship was obviously a stormy one; Isabella had left Ruxton several times, but had always returned. There seemed no reason to suspect anything sinister in this latest disappearance.

*   *   *

Bukhtyar Hakim was born in Bombay in 1899, during the period of the British Raj. After qualifying at Bombay University as a Bachelor of Medicine and Surgery in 1922, he served for a while in the Indian Medical Corps and achieved the rank of captain. He came to Britain in the mid-1920s to study for his medical doctorate at Edinburgh University. There he met Isabella Kerr, a Scots restaurant manageress two years his junior. Isabella was not conventionally pretty – her face was too horsey – but Ruxton, as he now called himself, found her immensely attractive. For her part, Isabella was equally drawn to the dashing Captain Ruxton. He was extravagant in romance, as in most of his emotions. They hurled themselves into a passionate affair and when Ruxton went to study in London, then later to practice in Lancaster, Isabella followed him.

In due course they had three children. Although they lived as man and wife, they never actually married. There seems no particular reason for this; Isabella's previous marriage to a Dutch doctor called Van Ess had been annulled. It is likely that they enjoyed the thrill of 'living in sin'; there seems to have been a headlong, possibly masochistic element in their relationship. They would have explosive rows, followed by reconciliation and passionate love-making. The beating episode in 1933 does not appear to have been an isolated incident, yet in spite of his violence, Isabella seemed to enjoy baiting her husband. He is reported to have said that she would often interrupt him in his surgery, saying with a smile: 'I'm wondering how I can pick a quarrel with you.'

One of the frequent causes of these fights was Buck Ruxton's suspicions about Isabella's fidelity. He had become convinced that she was having an affair with a mutual friend called Robert Edmondson. A week before she disappeared, Ruxton had secretly followed Edmondson and Isabella to Edinburgh, where they spent a night in the same hotel. The fact that Edmondson had also taken his whole family on the trip, which was not in the least clandestine, did not dissuade Ruxton that the two had slept together. In fact, by most standards, Dr Ruxton was showing signs of a jealousy that amounted to insanity.

On 9 October 1935, eleven days after the bodies had been found, the stepmother of Mary Rogerson, the Ruxton's maid, gave the girl's description to the police. She had been missing since the middle of September, but, on Ruxton's insistence, she had not been reported missing until the beginning of October. The description was issued to the other regional police forces and to the newspapers. Three days later, on the evening of 11 October, the Lancaster police received another dramatic visit from Buck Ruxton.

He was shown into the office of Captain Vann, Lancaster's chief constable, and although he seemed calm enough, soon became increasingly emotional. He told Vann that his wife was still missing and that the police must find her. He also asked that the police publish a statement declaring that the disappearances of Isabella and Mary were totally unconnected with the bodies found in the Gardenholme Linn. For evidence he offered a newspaper report which stated (incorrectly, as it turned out) that both skulls had full sets of teeth in their lower jaws – Mary had four teeth missing from hers. His practice, he claimed, was being ruined by rumours that his wife and maid were the victims. Captain Vann calmed him as best he could, and drew-up a non-committal statement which he promised to release to the press. This seemed to mollify Ruxton, and he left.

In fact, the doctor had been the main suspect in the double-murder investigation since that morning. The chief constable of Dumfriesshire had seen the description of the missing Mary Rogerson in the Glasgow *Daily Record* and had immediately contacted his colleagues in Lancaster. A 20-year-old girl vanishing with the middle-aged wife of her doctor-employer fitted the case perfectly. The Scottish police hurried to Morecambe to question Mary's parents. They brought with them the clothes in which the body parts had been wrapped. When Mary's stepmother saw a blouse with a patch under one arm, she told the officers that she was certain that her stepdaughter was one of the victims. She had bought the blouse in a jumble sale, patched it herself and had given it to Mary the previous Christmas.

Ruxton had explained Mary's disappearance to her parents by telling them that she had become pregnant by a laundry-boy. Mrs Ruxton had taken her away for an abortion and he was therefore keen to keep the whole thing hushed-up. Abortion was still a serious crime and he could be struck-off if his involvement were discovered. However, Mary's parents had not been fully convinced. She was a plain, home-loving girl, not the type to become involved with laundry-boys.

The baby's rompers, which had also been used to wrap the remains, were unfamiliar to Mrs Rogerson, but she suggested that a Mrs Holmes, with whom Mary and the Ruxton children had stayed earlier that year, might recognize them. Mrs Holmes gave a positive identification when she saw them – she recognized a particular knot she had tied in the elastic. The circumstantial evidence was rapidly mounting against Dr Ruxton.

The police then decided to question the Ruxton's charladies – they had no less than three. One of them, a Mrs Oxley, had the early shift, and usually arrived at the Ruxton house at 2, Dalton Square, around 7 a.m. On the morning of Sunday 15 September, however, a most unusual thing had occurred. An agitated Dr Ruxton appeared at her door at 6.30 a.m. and told her husband that she needn't come that day. The reason he gave was that Mrs Ruxton had gone to Edinburgh, and he was taking the children to Morecambe. When Mrs Oxley arrived the following morning, she had found the house in a state of chaos. The stair carpets had been taken up and removed, the bath had been stained yellow and wisps of straw had been strewn about the floor.

In fact, Ruxton did take his children to Morecambe that Sunday, but, after leaving them with a friend, he returned to Lancaster immediately. Police inquiries showed that he then called on one of his patients, a Mrs Hampshire. He told her that his wife and maid were away and that he had to get his house ready for some decorators who were arriving the next day. As he had given himself a severe cut opening a tin of fruit, he begged her to come and help him. She and her husband both agreed to help and followed the doctor back to 2, Dalton Square.

The carpets had already been taken up from the stairs and landing. The carpets and stairs themselves, were stained with rather a lot of blood which Ruxton said was his own. In the lounge stood two cold, untouched meals. In the backyard was a pile of bloodstained towels that had been partially burned with petrol. Ruxton then left, leaving the whole house open to the Hampshires, except his and Isabella's bedrooms; these were locked. While Mr Hampshire scrubbed the stairs, his wife tried to get the odd yellow stain out of the bath. She made some headway, but the stain proved highly resistant. In fact, when Mrs Oxley called the next morning, it had mysteriously renewed itself.

Dr Ruxton thanked the Hampshires by giving them the bloodstained carpets and a bloodstained blue suit, which he said he had been wearing when he had the accident with the tin of peaches. His generosity even stretched to coming round to the Hampshire's house a few days later to offer to have the suit cleaned. Oddly enough, when Mrs Hampshire insisted on doing it herself, Dr Ruxton demanded that she take his name tag out of the suit and burn it before he would leave. Later, when Mrs Hampshire tried to wash the dried blood out of the carpet, she was surprised by how much seemed to have soaked into it; 'I . . . threw about twenty or thirty buckets of water on it to try to wash the blood off, and the colour of the water that came off was like blood.'

When the newspapers reported the discovery of the dismembered bodies in the Gardenholme Linn, Dr Ruxton seemed oddly pleased. He showed the article to the charlady and said; 'So you see, Mrs Oxley, it is a man and a woman. It is not our two.'

The police were now certain that Ruxton had killed his wife and maid. He had made several trips north to Scotland during the last weeks of September. He had claimed that he was searching for his wife, but it now seemed clear that he was, in fact, disposing of her. Glaister's team had managed to take a set of fingerprints from the undamaged hands, and these were matched with prints found in Mary Rogerson's bedroom.

Even the careful mutilation of certain body parts now worked against Dr Ruxton. A large proportion of one of the forearms had been removed. This was exactly the area where Mary had a large birthmark. She also had a cataract, or 'wall-eye,' which would explain the removal of the eyes. Even the piece of flesh removed from the older victim's foot corresponded with a corn on Isabella Ruxton's foot.

Buck Ruxton was called to the police station on the evening of 12 October. After all-night questioning, he was arrested the following morning. The doctor indignantly denied the charge, and at the subsequent trial entered a plea of not guilty, but his defence counsel could have had little hope for his client. Although there was no positive evidence against Ruxton, the circumstantial evidence was overwhelming. Their only real chance of acquittal lay in convincing the jury that the bodies found in the Gardenholme Linn might not be Mary Rogerson and Isabella Ruxton.

It was the expert witnesses for the prosecution who demolished any such hope. Glaister pointed out the correspondence between the known, identifying marks on Isabella Ruxton and Mary Rogerson, and the mutilations found on the victim's corpses. He showed the jury a photograph of Isabella, superimposed over the skull of the older victim, her long, horsey features fitted it perfectly. The jury were even shown photographs of the victims' feet, gruesomely fitting into the shoes of Mary and Isabella. The cumulative effect of the medical evidence was overwhelming.

The prosecution's argument was that on the night of Saturday 14 September, Isabella Ruxton had returned after midnight from visiting her sisters in Blackpool. Ruxton had expected her back in time for dinner – thus the two untouched meals seen by the Hampshires. During the long wait he had worked himself into a jealous fury. When she returned they quarrelled, and he killed her. Mary had either gone to her mistress' aid, or Ruxton killed her to prevent her discovering what he had done. He had then dismembered one of them, probably Isabella, in the bath, discolouring it with blood. During this operation the scalpel had slipped and cut him badly. An expert was called to state that it would not be possible to receive such a cut from opening a tin, only from a very sharp knife.

The next morning he had taken his children (who had spent what must have been a disturbing night in their mother's room) to friends in Morecambe. He returned and tricked the Hampshires into helping him cover his tracks. That night, he had dissected his second victim, staining the bath yellow once again. He wrapped the remains in clothes, newspaper and straw; the last being scattered about and later picked up by Mrs Oxley. Over the following days he had made several trips over the Scottish border to dispose of the body parts in the Gardenholme Linn.

To support this theory, the prosecution produced numerous witnesses, some of whom claimed that Ruxton had come to them and asked them to make false statements to correspond to his version of events.

The defence had only one witness to counter these; Ruxton himself. He gave a very poor showing on the stand, doing little more than contradict the statements of the other witnesses.

In a last ditch attempt to save Ruxton, the defence argued that even if the jury was convinced that the victims found in the Gardenholme Linn were Mary and Isabella, it was not impossible that they *had* gone on a trip to Edinburgh, as Ruxton claimed. Was it not conceivable, the jury was asked, that some third party had killed the women, dissected them and wrapped them in whatever they had been travelling with before disposing of them? The prosecution disdainfully countered this argument by pointing-out that the ladies would have hardly packed two sets of baby's rompers for a trip to an abortionist.

It was undoubtedly a mistake for Ruxton to plead not guilty. Perhaps before, but certainly after the murders, he was showing distinct signs of paranoid dementia. If he had risked a guilty plea, he might have escaped the rope by a defence of insanity. As it was, he appeared to be a man who was addicted to violence, and who schemed and lied to escape the consequences of his brutality.

It took the jury only an hour to find Buck Ruxton guilty of first degree murder. A subsequent appeal also failed and he went calmly to the gallows on 12 May 1936.

8

The Body in the Trunk

The Derby Day rush hour – 6 June 1934 – saw Brighton railway station crammed with people. It was therefore hardly surprising that when a large trunk was deposited in the left-luggage office, the attendants later failed to remember anything about the owner. Eleven days later, when a nauseous smell filtered out of the trunk, they decided to call in the police to break the locks. Inside, wrapped in brown paper, was the rotting, disarticulated torso of a woman. Her legs were found the next day in a suitcase in the left-luggage office at King's Cross station, but her arms and head were never recovered.

The police faced a difficult problem in identifying the victim. Without a head, they couldn't check their photo files, and without the hands there was no chance of fingerprinting. Their main hope was that evidence of the presumed murder might be found in the Brighton area – only the coolest of killers would have travelled far with a heavy trunk containing human remains.

It was decided to conduct a door-to-door investigation in the area surrounding the station – it was possible that the killer, or killers, might have been observed if they had arrived on foot. Unfortunately, no one remembered seeing anything unusual that day. Nevertheless, the police did turn-up a possible lead. A prostitute called Violette Kaye had disappeared early the previous month without a word to anybody, and had not been seen since.

Over forty women had been reported missing from Brighton that summer, so it took the police until mid-July to get around to interviewing Violette's pimp, a small-time crook called Tony Mancini. In his statement, Mancini insisted that, as far as he knew, Violette was alive and working in France. They had quarrelled on 10 May, and Violette had left for Paris. The last he had heard of her, he said, was a telegram sent to her sister-in-law saying: 'Good job sail Sunday will write – Vi.'

The police were initially satisfied with this version of events, but on 15 July, called at Mancini's lodgings at 52, Kemp Street for a second interview. The landlady told them that he was not at home, but invited them in to wait in his flat. As they entered the room the officers became aware of a foul smell. It seemed to be coming from a large trunk and, thinking grimly about the missing head and arms, the officers forced it open. Inside was Violette Kaye – over two months dead, but otherwise complete and unmutilated.

Mancini had left that same morning on a train for London. The worry about the disposal of the body, the police interview and the increasing smell had driven him to bolt to the metropolis. He may have intended to seek help from his gangland connections, but his fears had got the better of him and he changed his mind and hitch-hiked into Kent. A police patrol picked him up trudging along the Maidstone road. When they told him that he fitted the description of the suspected murderer of Violette Kaye, he replied wearily: 'I'm the man, but I didn't murder her.'

Under interrogation, he admitted that he had concealed Violette's death, but he denied the charge of murder. He had come home from work on 10 May and found her lying dead. He had known his bad record would make him a prime suspect as the murderer, he said, so he had covered-up the death as best he could.

He gave his name as Jack Notyre, but, like Tony Mancini, this was a pseudonym; he was actually called Cecil Lois England. (He had presumably chosen the name Mancini because he was very Italian in looks.) He was 26 years old and tended to speak in a working-class London accent, but this was also a front. His father was a Whitehall civil servant and Mancini's background was typical middle-class.

His criminal career had started when he deserted from the RAF as a teenager. While hiding from the military police he had become mixed-up in London's underworld, eventually working as a strong-arm man for the gangster 'Harry Boy' Sabini. A scar to his upper lip gave him a sinister look, and he had a reputation for brutality. However, his only actual convictions were two counts of burglary and one of loitering with intent to commit a felony.

He and Violette Kaye had met in 1932. Mancini was working in a restaurant just off Leicester Square at the time, but his real job was that of a 'collection agent' in Sabini's protection racket. Violette, whose real surname was Saunders, was an attractive showgirl, but, at 42, work was increasingly hard to find. She turned to prostitution to support her alcohol and morphine habits, and needed a pimp for protection. Mancini, 17 years her junior, was glad to oblige, but he was jailed in March 1933 for petty theft. When he was released the following September, he and Violette decided to move to

Brighton – 'the place it was all happening in those days,' he said later.

Violette was by no means a common prostitute; her good looks and show business connections had earned her a well-to-do clientele. Many of these gentlemen were quite prepared to make the drive from London to see her; so money, despite her addictions, was not in short supply. Her trade brought other problems though. Landlords soon guessed what the stream of visitors meant and the couple had to move home about once a fortnight. Eventually, after twelve other addresses, she and Mancini moved into 44, Park Crescent, an unfurnished basement flat, down a narrow flight of steps.

Violette seems to have been quite dependent on Mancini. He did all the cooking and housework, and may well have obtained her morphine for her. Several times, Violette dissuaded Mancini from taking a job, because it would take him out of the flat all day. Of course, when she was entertaining, he had to make himself scarce, and it was probably boredom that prompted him to ignore her wishes and take a job as waiter and cook in the Skylark Cafe, under the promenade.

Five days after he had started work, on Thursday 10 May 1934, Violette arrived at the Skylark in a fairly drunken state. It was a slack period, so Mancini made her a meal and sat talking to her. After a while, he got up to make tea for the rest of the staff. As he handed a cup to a young waitress called Florence Attrell, he made the mistake of saying: 'Here you are, mate.' Violette, overhearing the remark, shouted: 'I won't have it. Don't call her mate.' A shocked silence fell over the cafe, and Mancini told her to pull herself together. Violette burst into angry tears, but an ugly scene was averted when she stormed out instead. She sat on a public bench outside the cafe for a while, Mancini told the police, then went away. He also claimed that the incident cost him his job. However, this did not stop him going to the cafe the next morning to tell everyone that Vi had left him and gone to Paris. It was at this time also, that Violette's sister-in-law, planning to come down to visit the following Monday, received the telegram about a job offer. In fact, Violette was already dead, her body wrapped in a blanket and propped in a cupboard at 44, Park Crescent.

Mancini seems to have kept his cool, even though he was obviously at a loss as to what to do with Violette's corpse. He and Florence Attrell, the waitress he had called 'mate', went dancing twice the following weekend and he even gave her some of Violette's clothes, explaining that he couldn't be bothered to send them on. About a week later he told Mr Snuggs, his landlord, that since Vi had left him he couldn't afford to keep the flat on himself. Snuggs – who seems to have believed that they were a perfectly ordinary married couple – was sympathetic. As they talked, he noticed a large trunk in the middle of the room, apparently waiting to be packed. When Mancini had gone, Snuggs inspected the flat and noticed that the internal tray to the trunk, which would have reduced its internal capacity, had been left behind. He also found a dark stain on the floor of the cupboard.

Mancini moved into 52, Kemp Street with Violette's body still in the trunk. He seems to have been unable to shake off a sense of indecision about what to do next, and made no attempt to dispose of the body. It was a hot summer, and as the smell got worse a friend asked him if he was keeping rabbits in his room. The ruthless strong-arm man was obviously going to pieces.

Now that he was in custody, the case against Mancini

seemed overwhelming. The newspapers were of one mind in portraying him as a vicious thug, and possibly a foreigner as well. The general opinion was that only a monster could have lived for two months, without apparent guilt, sleeping a few feet from the rotting body of his girlfriend. Public feeling was so aroused that after his initial hearing at Lewes Magistrate's Court, Mancini had to be smuggled out of a backdoor, while an angry mob booed and threw things at the unfortunate decoy being helped into a Black Maria at the front of the building.

The prosecution's case seemed water-tight. The Home Office forensics laboratory had found traces of blood on Mancini's clothes. The telegram slip, on which the false message sent to Violette's sister-in-law had originally been written, was in the same handwriting as the menus Mancini had written-out in the Skylark Cafe. Witnesses came forward to give evidence that Mancini and Violette often quarrelled. Several even claimed that they had heard him say: 'What's the good of knocking a woman about with your fists? You should use a hammer, same as I did . . .' In fact, a partially burned hammer was one of the objects found at 44, Park Crescent.

Mancini had at least one piece of good fortune: he was defended by Norman Birkett, KC, one of the most brilliant advocates of his time. Birkett – who confided to friends that he found Mancini a 'despicable and worthless creature' – saw that his main task was to convince the jury that the prosecution's case was based heavily on supposition. The fact that his client had covered-up Violette's death did not necessarily mean that he had killed her. It was a slim chance, but it was Mancini's only hope.

Cecil England was tried under the name he had given

the police when arrested, Jack Notyre, on 10 December 1934. The prosecution's line of attack was predictably devastating. The Recorder of Brighton, J.D. Cassels, acting as counsel for the Crown, delivered a 40 minute opening address in which he listed the known facts of the case, which in themselves, seemed to make it impossible that Mancini could be innocent.

Violette and Mancini had been seen quarrelling the day before she went missing, said Cassels. The false telegram, aimed at covering-up that disappearance, was clearly Mancini's work. Violette's skull had received multiple blows and somebody had tried to destroy a hammer at 44, Park Crescent – the tool Mancini had bragged he had used on a woman. Finally, there was the damning fact that the defendant had lived with the rotting corpse for over two months. If he was not guilty, why had he concealed Violette's death and lived under such revolting conditions through the hottest part of the summer?

The prosecution called fifty witnesses in all. Birkett cross-examined each in his characteristically quiet, polite style; never badgering or raising his voice. The result was that juries saw him as a man of complete integrity – an effect that might well have coloured their view of his clients. Yet, despite his kindly demeanour, Birkett was as sharp as a razor. No witness left the stand without, in some way, aiding the defence of his client.

A chauffeur called Kerslake was called as the last person who admitted to seeing Violette alive. He had visited her on the afternoon of 10 May, to tell her that his employer, one of her regulars, had been certified insane. Even before he told her the news, she had seemed shaken and upset. Birkett asked him if Violette seemed drunk or on drugs. Kerslake admitted that she had looked that way, but added that she was obviously frightened as well. He also mentioned that he had heard voices coming from another room of the flat, the implication being that it was these other guests who had done the frightening. This was an important point for the defence; Mancini claimed he was still at the Skylark Cafe at the time of Kerslake's visit.

When Henry Snuggs, the landlord of 44, Park Crescent, was called, he gave evidence about the stain in the cupboard and identified the trunk he had seen in Mancini's room as the one that had contained Violette's body. Then, Birkett questioned him on quite different matters. He elicited the admission that the landlord had never seen or heard the couple quarrel – in fact, he admitted, they had seemed noticeably affectionate. Snuggs even told the court that he had always found Mancini a 'perfect gentleman', a far cry from the heartless gangster portrayed by the prosecution.

Birkett continued to attack the prosecution's claim that Mancini and Violette had often quarrelled. This may best be seen in his cross-examination of a witness called Joyce Golding, who had given evidence that she had seen the couple fight several times.

First of all, he undermined her credibility in the eyes of the court by coaxing her to admit she was a prostitute. Then he asked her how long she had been acquainted with the man who had called himself Tony Mancini. When she replied five or six years, he asked her if she had read a great deal about the present case. To this she made the mistake of answering that she had read nothing. This, of course, sounded ridiculous, and while she was still off-balance, Birkett told her that he believed her to be lying on this and the matter of the quarrels. She replied that she could offer other witnesses to back

her statement, and when pressed named a Mrs Phyllis
Summers.

However, what she could not have known, was that
Phyllis Summers had given evidence the previous day and
had said that Mancini and Violette had always seemed
'on very friendly terms'. Birkett did not press this point,
he did not need to – Joyce Golding had destroyed herself
as a credible witness.

He used a similar approach when questioning the
three witnesses who claimed that Mancini had bragged
about hitting a woman with a hammer. By simply leading them in the right direction, he let them contradict
each other and blacken each other's characters. The
first, a stall-keeper, admitted that he had sacked his
assistant, the second witness, for theft. The third witness
refused to admit that he had heard Mancini mention a
hammer at all.

In taking this line of argument, Birkett was demonstrating that the prosecution's version of events only held
together if one took an overview of the evidence. As soon
as you looked closely, you could see numerous faults in
their interpretation of the case. A logician will point
out that this is true for *any* proposition, but this does
not necessarily mean it is incorrect. However, Birkett
only needed to sow seeds of doubt on the circumstantial matters. His major line of attack was aimed
at undermining the prosecution's physical evidence and
expert witnesses.

A charred hammer had been found in the fire-grate of
44, Park Crescent. The prosecution called the previous
tenant, who claimed that he had left a hammer behind
when he moved out. This implied that a hammer had
been in the flat when Violette had received her injuries,
and afterwards had been burned. Birkett showed this to

be pure supposition when he persuaded the witness to admit that he could not be sure if the charred hammer was the one he had left behind. The prosecution could no more prove that there had been a hammer in the flat at the time of Violette's death than Birkett could prove that there had not been. The piece of evidence was effectively neutralized.

When the prosecution called Dr Roche Lynch, the Home Office pathologist, to give evidence about the battering Violette's skull had received before she died, Birkett again started his cross-examination on a slight tangent. He asked Dr Lynch if he had found morphine in the body. Lynch agreed that an amount 'distinctly greater than a medicinal dose,' was present in Violette's corpse. Birkett asked him if this might have been the actual cause of death, and Lynch acknowledged that he could not be sure. In admitting this he opened a large hole in the prosecution's case; the corpse in the trunk had been so decomposed, it had proved impossible to ascertain the cause of death. It was only a supposition that she had been beaten to death, and this was now plain to the jury.

Birkett went on to question Dr Lynch about the blood-spotted shirt and trousers found in Mancini's possession. He began by asking several technical questions about the type of blood-splashing. In his answers the doctor made it plain that he believed that Mancini had worn the clothes while attacking someone. Birkett then asked if the doctor could be certain that the blood was Violette Saunders'? 'No,' was the reply; her corpse had been too decayed to allow the grouping of her blood. Then, Birkett struck his decisive blow. He told the court that he would be calling the tailor from whom the shirt and trousers had been ordered that May. Neither he said, had been delivered until June, a month after the murder. They were thus irrelevant to the case. Dr Lynch had to leave the stand looking at best a fool, at worst, a biased tool of the prosecution.

Cassels attempted to rally the Crown's case the next day when he called Doris Saville; a meek looking, 17-year-old orphan who claimed that Mancini had tried to bully her into providing him with an alibi.

She told the court that on Sunday 15 July, she had been introduced to Mancini and they had gone for a walk, during which Mancini had told her that he had killed somebody and that if he was caught she had to go to the police. She was to tell them that sometime around the end of May, she and Mancini had gone to tea with a woman at 44, Park Crescent. This woman had sent them away because she was expecting three men. When they had returned the woman was dead. Doris said that she had been so frightened of the menacing, scar-faced man that she had agreed. Mancini had set up another meeting for 11.30 that night, but, although she had kept the appointment, he had not.

Throughout her testimony Doris had been frightened and tearful. Birkett cross-examined her in a kindly, gentle manner, but demolished her statement all the same. He asked how she had been dressed when she met Mancini that first time. Doris had to admit that she had been dressed as an adult woman; the implication being that she was trying to pick-up men. Birkett then read out the deposition she had made when she was first interviewed by the police: 'He said that a murder had been done and that he was innocent of it and that I was supposed to have met him.' This contradiction of statements and the implication that she was a prostitute, destroyed any value she might have for the prosecution.

On the first day of the trial, Birkett had cross-examined a police inspector who had given simple, technical evidence as to the lay-out of the basement flat at 44, Park Crescent. Birkett had asked him if the stairs down to the flat were narrow and worn, and the inspector replied that they were. He was then asked what the floor at their foot was made from. The inspector replied it was made of stone.

The reason for this apparently pointless line of questioning became clear later, when Sir Bernard Spilsbury, a legend in the field of criminal pathology, took the stand. It was Spilsbury's unreserved opinion that Violette Saunders had been killed by repeated blows to her head from a blunt instrument; quite possibly a hammer. Prompted by Cassels, he demonstrated on a human skull just where, and with what effect, the blows were administered. He even presented a piece of Violette's skull into the evidence which, he said, proved his view of the case.

Birkett started his cross-examination with an apparently philosophical question. Was it not true, he asked Sir Bernard, that his views were not equivalent to facts? Indeed, could Sir Bernard describe these views as anything other than *theories*? The respected pathologist had to admit that, even with his vast experience, he could never claim his views to be the same as absolute fact. In the light of Dr Lynch's testimony as to the advanced decomposition of the body, the jury now had some reason to doubt Spilsbury's certainty.

The question of the piece of Violette's skull was now brought up. Why, asked Birkett, if the autopsy had taken place five months earlier, had the bone fragment only just been brought to the attention of the defence? In a similar vein, why had there been no doctor for the

defence at that autopsy? Spilsbury could answer neither
question satisfactorily. Like Dr Lynch before him, he had
been made to look biased towards the prosecution and
not, as he claimed, a neutral man of science.

Birkett then returned to the question of the high dose
of morphine found in the body. Spilsbury was forced
to admit that he had no definite evidence that Violette
had not been killed by the drug. Birkett then turned
to another possible cause of death. Could Violette,
in a drunken or drugged state, have fallen down the
narrow flight of stairs, described earlier in the trial,
and sustained the possibly fatal head injuries on the
stone floor beneath? Spilsbury had to agree that it was
quite possible. Thus, Birkett had, in effect, neutralized
the prosecution's star witness.

The defence still had one brilliant move to make
before starting their own case. Cassels had called a
Chief Inspector Donaldson to answer some routine
questions on police procedure. Birkett, cross-examining,
asked him to tell the court of the defendant's previous
criminal record – something defending counsels are
usually desperate to conceal. The Chief Inspector had
to read the rather mild list of convictions: two for petty
theft and one for loitering with intent. The prosecution's
claim that Mancini was a brutal, professional criminal
now seemed rather thin.

In fact, Birkett was misleading the court over this
matter of his client's past. Tony Mancini had been
an extremely vicious criminal, but he had never been
caught. While working for 'Harry Boy' Sabini, he had
been ordered to mark a man for life for informing to
the police. Mancini had walked up to him as he leaned
on the bar of his local pub and had lopped off his
left hand with a hatchet, then walked casually out of

the bar leaving the axe embedded in the counter. On another occasion he had gleefully turned the handle of a meat mincer as the hand of a fellow crook was forced into the grinders. He later admitted that the violence 'was like a drug addiction'. It was therefore ironic that many of the prosecution witnesses had their characters blackened during the trial for quite petty moral or criminal misdemeanours, while Mancini's past was thoroughly whitewashed.

Birkett opened the case for the defence with an impassioned attack on the newspapers' biased reporting. The jury had yet to decide on the matter, he said, but the press had already found his client guilty. This prejudice seemed to have spread even to such respected members of the medical profession as Sir Bernard Spilsbury and Dr Lynch. He had already shown that some of the witnesses had given contradictory and inaccurate testimony concerning the relationship between Violette and Mancini. Even the prosecution's hammer theory had proved to be nothing but supposition. Put together, it amounted to a virtual conspiracy against the defendant, yet the Crown could offer no solid evidence that Mancini had killed Violette Saunders.

Having thus prepared the court, Birkett called his chief witness; Tony Mancini himself. On the stand, he appeared chastened and unsure of himself; more a penitent than a monster. As he answered Birkett's gentle questioning he became increasingly emotional, and occasionally wept. This behaviour clearly made a strong impression on the jury.

He told the court that he and Violette had loved each other and never quarrelled. If there had been any stress in the relationship, he said, it was purely due to her profession. The constant moves from one flat to another and the fear of arrest had caused her to drink excessively and use morphine to help her sleep. He went on to tell the court about the events of 10 May. Violette had clearly been drunk when she arrived at the Skylark Cafe, so he was not surprised to find her lying on the bed when he eventually got home. It was only when he tried to wake her, and saw blood on the pillow, that he became alarmed. It was at this point that the defence scored one of its most telling points. When Birkett asked Mancini why he had not informed the police he responded incredulously: 'With my record?'

His reply sounded both spontaneous and candid, which moved the jury in a way Birkett knew he never could. The fact that Mancini belonged to the criminal underclass meant that he would never expect fair treatment at the hands of the law. Even the least experienced members of the jury were bound to have seen the stereotyped mistrust of the police portrayed by crooks in numerous gangster movies. Realizing this, made it easy to see why Mancini had kept Violette's corpse for so long. After his initial hesitation, each day that passed increased the necessity of concealment as it increased his chances of hanging. Mancini had become trapped, and dared do nothing for fear of discovery.

After the defendant's statement, Birkett called the tailor, who testified that he had delivered the shirt and trousers too late for them to have been worn at the time of Violette's death. After that, Mancini's mother appeared as a character witness. But the major work of the defence had been done.

In his final summing-up, Birkett reminded the jury that it was their duty to release his client if there was so much as a shadow of a doubt as to his guilt. He went on to shrewdly point out that the 'voices' that

Kerslake had heard in Violette's flat had never come forward. If one was to accept supposition as evidence of guilt – as the prosecution appeared to wish them to do – then surely these people were just as suspect as the present defendant? He ended on a ringing note: 'People are not tried by newspapers, not tried by rumour, not tried by statements born of a love of notoriety, but tried by British juries, called to do justice and decide upon the evidence.'

On 14 December, after two-and-a-half hours' deliberation, the jury found Mancini Not Guilty and the judge ordered him freed. Over the next year he actually lived off the case. He joined a travelling fair and, billed as 'The Infamous Brighton Trunk Murder Man', performed a stunt in which he appeared to cut off a young lady's head with a trick guillotine.

The Violette Saunders case went down as one of the most brilliant defences in legal history, but it is now known that the verdict was wrong.

On 28 November 1976, the *News of the World* had a scoop. Under the headline I'VE GOT AWAY WITH MURDER, Tony Mancini was interviewed by Alan Hart. Hart began:

A man acquitted of killing his mistress, after one of the most famous murder trials in British history, has now confessed to me that he was guilty. Ex-gangster Tony Mancini has lived 42 years with the secret that he was responsible for what became known as the Brighton Trunk Murder.

Mancini told a very different story to the one he had given to the court in 1934. When he and Violette had argued in the Skylark Cafe, he said, he had been sacked on the spot. They had then taken a taxi back to 44, Park Crescent – so that it was Mancini who was in the other room at the time of the chauffeur, Kerslake's visit.

During their on-going argument, Violette had complained of being cold. As Mancini knelt to make a fire she stepped up behind him and hit his head a glancing blow with a hammer. He leapt up, took the hammer from her and started to walk away. She screamed, 'Give me that hammer' and he, in a fury, turned and threw it at her head. It knocked her to the ground and he grabbed her shoulders and started to bang her head down shouting, 'You stupid bitch, look what you made me do!' It was only when he saw blood trickling from her mouth that he realized that her head was hitting the brass fender, not the carpeted floor. 'I honestly didn't mean to kill her,' he said, 'I had just lost control of myself in the heat of the moment.'

About the trial he said: 'When I gave evidence I had carefully rehearsed my lines like an actor. I had practised how I should hold my hands and when to let the tears run down my cheeks. It might sound cold and calculating now, but you have to remember that my life was at stake. I was charged with murder, and in those days the penalty was death.'

As to the first body found in a trunk in Brighton station, it remains one of the unsolved crimes of the period. Despite a massive police investigation, which eventually extended over four countries, the identities of the victim and her murderer were never discovered.

9

The Killing of Percy Casserley

At ten minutes past nine, on the evening of Wednesday 23 March 1938, a hysterical woman rushed out of 35, Lindisfarne Road, in Wimbledon, and hammered on the nearest front door. She was Mrs Georgina May Casserley, wife of the managing director of a local brewery. She told her neighbours, the Burchells, that she had just returned from a walk to find the house burgled and her husband bleeding on the floor.

Mr Burchell and his son hurried next door to investigate, and found Percy Casserley dying on the floor of the disordered lounge. He had been shot twice in the head and neck. The police arrived at 9.30 p.m. but Mr Casserley died moments later

Surveying the crime scene, detectives found obvious signs of a break-in. The burglars appeared to have entered the house through the French windows in the dining-room; breaking the glass from the outside to reach the catch. The coat-stand in the hall had been upset and silverware was scattered across the dining-room floor. Other items of silverware were lying on the blood-spattered lounge floor. By the door to the lounge was the fawn button of a mackintosh that had been ripped off the coat so fiercely, it had taken a patch of cloth with it.

At first sight, it seemed to be a straightforward case of a burglary that had gone wrong. But investigation into the Casserleys' background soon raised serious doubts.

Percy Arthur Casserley had married Georgina, nicknamed 'Ena', some eleven years previously. She was twenty years his junior and there had apparently been some marital difficulties of late. Percy, due to retire in a year's time, was becoming increasingly alcoholic, drinking an average of a bottle-and-a-half of whisky every evening. As a result, he was becoming irritable, moody and anti-social. Moreover, Ena Casserley, now in her thirty-eighth year, was known to be keen to start a family, but her husband apparently vetoed the idea.

Percy had spent a month of the previous winter in a nursing home for alcoholics. On his return, Ena told him she was pregnant. Since they had not had marital relations since he had undergone an operation in 1936, he took the news badly.

He confided his troubles to his brother-in-law, naming his wife's lover as a tea-planter of their acquaintance, home from Ceylon on six-months' leave. In fact, the truth was less exotic. Questioning the couple's maid, Lydia Scott, the police discovered that the father was a builder's foreman called Edward Royal Chaplin.

Chaplin, a muscular, handsome man of 35 was undoubtedly more attractive than lanky, 58-year-old Casserley. Ted, as Chaplin was known, had been working on a house being erected on a neighbouring plot of land. One day, while Percy was at the clinic, Ena had asked him in for a cup of tea. The relationship had quickly developed to the point where he had stayed overnight at Lindisfarne Road in Casserley's absence, and she had visited him at his flat in Morden – an appalling risk for a married woman to take with her reputation in the 1930s.

Following his wife's announcement of her pregnancy, Percy Casserley had a nervous break-down, and returned to the nursing home for a fortnight, from 8 to 22 March. During this time, Ted and Ena saw each other regularly. The pair appear to have been genuinely in love. As soon as Chaplin heard of Ena's condition, he insisted that she should divorce her husband and marry him. Ena was by no means averse to the idea. Compared to the aging, cantankerous Percy, Ted Chaplin must have seemed an ideal mate. Unfortunately, nothing was less likely than that Casserley would give them his blessing.

On the night following Percy Casserley's return, Ena and the maid Lydia had planned to go to the cinema. At the last minute, Ena was forced to drop the plan. She told the maid that when she had told her husband she was going out, he had become enraged and threatened to shoot her. Lydia later told the police that Mrs Casserley had seemed genuinely frightened and upset.

As the maid was leaving, Ena had asked her to pass a message on to Ted. If he came to the back door, she said, she would be able to see him for a couple of minutes, but no more. Lydia gave him the message, and also told him about the shooting threat. What effect such information had on him is a matter for conjecture.

The police investigation had by now turned up several pieces of evidence that did not concur with Ena Casserley's burglary story. Microscopic examination of the pane of glass broken out of the French window showed that it had been smashed from *inside* the house, and the autopsy conducted by Sir Bernard Spilsbury, revealed that Casserley had been beaten about the head and back, and that the killing shot to the head had been fired from point blank range. Why, wondered investigators, would burglars have beaten then executed a householder they had surprised?

On 29 March, detectives visited Ted Chaplin on a building site in Epsom. They asked him to accompany them to the police station. He asked if he might get his coat first. On his return he was wearing a fawn coloured raincoat with a missing button.

Chaplin initially denied being at Lindisfarne Road on the night Casserley had been shot. Then, after being told that his denial might further implicate Ena Casserley, he decided to confess.

He admitted going to the Casserley house that evening, after having spoken to Lydia Scott. He had arrived just after 7.30 p.m. and met Ena coming out of the front door in tears. They had walked to an off-licence together to buy a bottle of whisky, which was Ena's excuse for leaving the house. Chaplin said that she had plainly been terrified by her husband's threats, and he had decided to settle matters there and then.

On their return to number 35, they conferred in the scullery for a few moments. Chaplin, still in his raincoat and hat had said: 'You had better leave this to me,' and after sending Ena upstairs, went into the lounge to confront his lover's husband.

According to Chaplin's statement, Casserley was dozing in an armchair by the fire when he entered. 'Good evening,' said the younger man, pulling off his gloves and offering his hand to shake. Casserley, surprised, got to his feet, dropping his spectacles on the floor. 'I've called to see what the trouble is between you and Mrs Casserley,' Chaplin continued, 'I've just left her and she's terribly upset. You know about her condition. I'm responsible for it. I want to suggest to you that either she comes away with me tonight or I'll phone and get her police protection, as I understand you've threatened Mrs Casserley.'

Percy Casserley looked stunned. 'Oh, so it's you, you swine,' he exclaimed, then appeared to be overcome with grief. Chaplin, pulled his gloves back on. Meanwhile, Casserley, head in hands, staggered, drunkenly to the writing-bureau and slumped into a chair.

According to Chaplin, he had suddenly whipped open a drawer and pulled out a .25 automatic pistol. Chaplin, taken off guard, made a leap and grabbed Casserley's right forearm, twisting it until he dropped the gun. The older man then leant against him heavily, as if passing-out, then unexpectedly dropped to one side and grabbed the gun in his *left* hand. Chaplin caught the other man's wrists and the two engaged in a face-to-face struggle, both trying to force the gun away from themselves. Then the gun went off.

The bullet entered and exited Casserley's neck, making a superficial wound. Chaplin was shocked, and let go of the other's right wrist. He then tried to grab Casserley around the waist to throw him to the floor. The older man half-turned, doubled-up and grabbed Chaplin's testicles. In agony, Chaplin snatched an electric torch from the top of the bureau and belaboured the stooped man on the back and head. Casserley let go of Chaplin's testicles, but maintained his desperate grip on the automatic. Chaplin, still holding the other's left wrist, tried to throw him again. Casserley fell backwards, dragging the young man down on top of him. They lay face pressed against face, Casserley, now with both hands on the weapon, trying to level the gun at his assailant. Chaplin heard two clicks from the automatic, then Casserley went limp and said: 'All right, I give in.'

Chaplin let go and began to stand up, then he heard another click and saw that Casserley was aiming the gun at him with both hands. He leaped forward, forcing the older man's arms upwards. Then the automatic went off a second time. The shot entered Casserley's head, just in front of the left ear. He collapsed and lay still.

Chaplin's first impulse was to call for medical aid. Then, realizing that this would compromise Ena, he decided to make it look like a bungled burglary. Ena Casserley was horrified when he went upstairs and told her what had happened, but fell in with his plan.

Following the signing of his statement, Edward Chaplin was formally arrested. He gave every appearance of wanting to assist the authorities, even offering to lead them to the half-completed house in which he had hidden Casserley's automatic and cartridges, saying: 'I'll show you where the gun is, you'll never find it on your own.'

Searching Chaplin's flat in Morden, the police found Percy Casserley's diamond ring, and a life-preserver (a long handled cosh). Chaplin said the cosh was a gift for his aged father, but freely admitted that he had washed blood off it recently. It had been in the drawer in which he had temporarily stored the automatic pistol, he said, and some of the blood had rubbed off on it.

Percy Casserley was buried the same day that Chaplin was arrested. Three days later, on 1 April, Georgina Casserley was also arrested and charged with being an accessory after the fact. She was initially held on remand in the hospital at Holloway prison. So virulent was the prejudice against 'fallen women' at the time, that she was forced to scrub floors, and forbidden to bathe. Fortunately, her lawyer protested that such treatment was inappropriate for a woman of her respectability, and she was released on bail.

Edward Chaplin's trial opened at the Old Bailey on Tuesday 24 May 1938. The prosecution's case, put by G.B. McClure, KC, was that Chaplin had deliberately murdered Percy Casserley, and had made-up his 'confession' afterwards to fit the facts. Chaplin, he said, had stayed in the Casserleys' house while Percy was at the clinic. During that period he would have had ample time to discover where the automatic pistol was kept. Indeed, it might have been as early as this that Chaplin hatched his plan to kill his lover's husband.

Specifically, the Crown believed that Chaplin had gone to Lindisfarne Road on the evening of 23 March, armed with the cosh and a murderous intent. He had attacked and beaten the older man, then cold-bloodedly shot him. If there had been any fight at all, Casserley had only been trying to protect himself, not attack a younger and fitter man. Chaplin had then, by his own admission, faked the burglary to throw the authorities off the track.

McClure asked why, if his story of accidental shooting were true, had Chaplin not called a doctor? He knew perfectly well that there was a telephone in the house. Chaplin claimed that he had panicked, and had only thought of protecting Mrs Casserley. However, Percy Casserley's diamond ring had been found in Chaplin's flat. If he was in a panic, why had he paused to acquire this memento?

The Crown's main witness was Sir Bernard Spilsbury, who had conducted the autopsy on Casserley. He told the court that he had found 17 separate bruises on the victim's head and back. All of these might easily have been caused by a cosh. By comparison, the court was told, Edward Chaplin had been totally unmarked when he was examined following his arrest, less than a week later.

Spilsbury went on to state that the shot which had caused the neck wound, since there were no powder burns to the skin, had been fired from more than 12 inches away. This was quite a distance, considering the two men were struggling hand-to-hand at the time. A pistol, pointing upwards and forced more than a foot from the body tends to point *away* from the combatants. On the other hand, the shot to the head had been fired with the weapon pressed against Casserley's temple; execution style.

McClure went on to point out that Percy Casserley was right-handed; as indeed was his assailant. Yet, according to Chaplin's statement, he had picked up the weapon with his left hand and, despite several opportunities to change hands during the fight, had never done so. Chaplin claimed that the gun had been in Casserley's left hand each time it went off, thus causing the wounds to the left side of his neck and head. Did this not seem more like a concocted story to explain away difficult facts, than the realistic truth, asked the prosecutor?

The most unlikely aspect of Chaplin's story, said McClure, was the length of the fight. Percy Casserley was 58 and sickly. Edward Chaplin was 35 and, as the court could see, strongly built and at the peak of physical fitness. Was it conceivable, the prosecutor asked, that the younger man could have had so much trouble overcoming his infirm rival? After disarming Casserley's stronger hand in a matter of seconds, why had Chaplin had so much trouble with his left arm?

Finally, there was the matter of the fatal shot to

the temple. At the end of his summing-up, McClure confronted the jury: 'Chaplin was holding the hand that was holding the pistol. Whose was the force that was pressing that pistol against the skin? The man [Casserley] was flat on his back . . .'

Chaplin was defended by the masterful Norman Birkett, arguably one of the best advocates of the twentieth century (see the Tony Mancini case, Chapter 8). He pointed out that his client had freely admitted to beating Casserley's back with the torch while the latter gripped 'a portion of his body.' However, Sir Bernard Spilsbury had found no bruises to the front of the corpse. Surely, he said, if Chaplin had launched an unprovoked attack, he would have struck at Casserley's face? In fact, McClure had said as much himself. In trying to undermine Chaplin's testimony on the stand, he had asked him: 'Why didn't you hit him in the face with that large hand of yours?' Chaplin had replied simply: 'I had no intention of harming Mr Casserley.'

Chaplin had another stroke of luck, in that Casserley's .25 Webley and Scott automatic was found to have a defective reloading mechanism. Weapons expert Robert Churchill, told the court that after the first shot, the pistol would invariably jam. This tied in with Chaplin's description of the clicks the automatic had made as Casserley tried to shoot him.

In his summing-up, Mr Justice Humphreys told the jury that if they believed that Casserley had been shot 'in the heat of passion in the course of a quarrel so serious that the accused lost complete control of himself' they might convict Chaplin of manslaughter, but not murder.

'Considering the largely circumstantial nature of the Crown's evidence, it was not surprising that the jury took this course. Edward Chaplin was convicted of manslaughter and sentenced to 12 years' imprisonment.

Sitting outside, the six-months pregnant Georgina Casserley fainted when she was told the sentence. Her trial, as an accessory after the fact, took place just half-an-hour later. She wept uncontrollably throughout.

Judge Humphreys was clearly unsympathetic towards the tearful widow. When her counsel, Mr Hutchinson, pleaded for leniency on the grounds of her condition, the judge replied: 'We know she is pregnant, as hundreds of other women are pregnant. But there is nothing the matter with her, no disease or anything like that?' Hutchinson said that there was not, but she was suffering from nervous strain. 'She can pull herself together if she wants to,' snapped Humphreys.

Before passing sentence, the judge chose to speak his mind candidly. 'The less said about your part in this case the better,' he pronounced, 'I am not going to treat you with lenience because I think there is nothing in particular in your condition that calls for it. Your case has aroused the most ridiculous nonsense. A great many people have treated you as though you were some sort of heroine. You were a participator in a vulgar and sordid intrigue.' He then condemned her to eleven days' imprisonment, a fate she probably felt to be less severe than her public humiliation in the courtroom.

Edward Chaplin was released after eight years, on 17 May 1946. Ena Casserley was waiting by the prison gate as he was set free. They were married the same day.

10

The Widow Killer

In the 1930s, there were seven Chief Detective Inspectors at Scotland Yard. They were organized in a rota system – whoever was at the top of the list was on 24-hour call to any police force in the country that asked for the Yard's expert assistance. At 10 p.m. on 3 August 1931, Chief Inspector John Horwell was relaxing at home when Scotland Yard rang to tell him he was needed in Oxford. A woman had been brutally murdered, and the local police were having problems.

Catching the midnight train, Horwell and his team arrived in Oxford in the dead of night. They were met at the station by Chief Constable Fox, and taken to a small, semi-detached villa in the St Clement's district of the town. In his memoirs, Horwell recalls heavy rain falling as they arrived at the murder site, lowering their spirits and adding a sinister touch to the proceedings. They entered the house and were ushered into the dining-room to view the victim.

Lying on the floor was a middle-aged woman, in apron and curlers. She had a round hole in her forehead, penetrating to the brain, and a similar wound in the back of the head. She had also been stabbed clean through the neck, just below the ear. Judging by the amount of bleeding, all three wounds had been inflicted on her while she was still alive.

Chief Constable Fox told Horwell that the victim was Mrs Anna Louisa Kempson, a 54-year-old widow who lived alone, although she had numerous relatives in the city. She had inherited several shops and houses from her husband, and was quite well-off. Unfortunately, her affluence appeared to have been the indirect cause of her death. The house had been ransacked by the murderer, and the police had found several empty purses scattered about. The motive for the killing was obviously theft.

Looking at the mutilated woman, Horwell wondered why the assailant had gone to the trouble of stabbing her through the neck as well as beating her head in. Was he particularly keen that Mrs Kempson should not survive to give evidence to the police? If so, it would suggest that the murderer was someone the victim knew well enough to identify.

The body had been discovered earlier that day by a relative. Mrs Kempson had been due to visit friends in London on Saturday night, but had not appeared on the pre-arranged train. They had telephoned her house, but there had been no reply. Two days later they called her relatives in Oxford to ask them to check she was all right. When there had been no reply to their knocks, one of them had borrowed a ladder from her neighbour, and clambered in through the bedroom window. He found her downstairs, already cold.

The autopsy was performed by the Home Office pathologist, Sir Bernard Spilsbury. It showed that Mrs Kempson had been dead since the Saturday, 1 August. He judged that the holes in her head were caused by extremely violent blows with a heavy, blunt weapon; probably a hammer. The throat wound was made by a sharpened instrument, like a slim-bladed knife or a chisel. There was no bruising on the body to indicate a struggle, so he guessed that one of the head blows, probably the one to the back of the skull, had been struck first, knocking her insensible.

Horwell inspected the dead woman's home. He had been told that Mrs Kempson was an extremely house-proud woman. Yet, in the kitchen, he found her dirty breakfast crockery still on the table. Since she was unlikely to have left things in such an untidy state, he guessed that she had been interrupted by her attacker during her meal.

His opinion that she had been killed on Saturday morning was reinforced by the discovery of a pair of new shoes, found wrapped in brown paper, standing on a Chesterfield in the room where she was discovered. Mrs Kempson had bought the shoes while shopping with a relative on Friday. On returning home, the relative had found the shoes among her packages, and had come calling on the Saturday afternoon. She got no reply after knocking for some while, so had popped them through the dining-room window. Although the relative had not looked inside, Horwell was reasonably sure that Mrs Kempson had not been out that day, and that her failure to answer meant that she was already dead . . .

The investigators searched the house with painstaking thoroughness. In Mrs Kempson's bedroom they found a large china crucifix apparently fixed to a wooden base. On closer inspection, the base was found to be a secret cash-box. Inside was a collection of gold £5 coins – no doubt the widow's emergency fund. The killer had turned the house upside-down searching for money, but had missed the prize. Horwell, judging by the size of the emptied purses, estimated that the murderer could not have found more than £3 in them. It was small return for such a brutal crime.

Another important discovery, although it was not realized at the time, was made in the dining-room. It was a written receipt for an electric cleaner. The vacuum cleaner was found upstairs, so Horwell put the slip of paper out of his mind for the time being.

Having run out of leads, and finding no forensic evidence to aid them, the police were forced to employ the old-fashioned, needle-in-a-haystack approach to the case. Horwell ordered the questioning of every house-holder within a half-mile radius of Mrs Kempson's villa, on the off-chance that they had seen something unusual. For this purpose, he was assigned a number of uniformed officers, who were told to wear everyday clothes to put local residents at their ease. Horwell had to coach these officers in interview technique, and the correct method of taking a statement – not because the Oxford police were untrained in their duties, but because crimes of that magnitude were almost unknown in the city, and the local officers had little or no experience in dealing with a murder investigation.

As the days passed, with no breakthrough, Horwell and Chief Constable Fox extended the radius of the house-to-house inquiry from half-a-mile to three-quarters-of-a-mile from the murder site.

In the meantime, Horwell and his team went over Mrs Kempson's house with a fine-tooth comb, but found nothing that seemed linked to the killer. In desperation, he ordered the search of all the gardens and fields in the immediate area, in case the murder weapon had been thrown there, but once again, results were negative. Finally, as a last effort before giving it up, Horwell extended the house-to-house search to a one-mile radius from the murder site. The area being covered by the investigation was now enormous, and the strain on the investigating officers was beginning to tell. Then, at last, they had the break they were looking for.

A widow named Andrews, living almost a mile from Mrs Kempson, told an officer that she had put-up a house guest on Friday 31 July, a door-to-door salesman called Henry Daniel Seymour, who had been down on his luck. She had known him since he sold her a vacuum cleaner. He had been friendly and helpful, and had called back several times to check that the machine was working properly.

On the day before the murder, he had appeared at her door in a sorry state. His money had been stolen, he said, while he was swimming in the Thames. She had lent him 4s 6d, and he had gone away. However, that evening he had returned, and told her that he had missed the last bus. Her son was staying with her, so Mrs Andrews felt safe in inviting him to spend the night.

The next morning, as she was cleaning the hall, the widow had noticed a paper bag on the floor. Inside was a new hammer and chisel. When Seymour left later that morning, he took the bag with him. At the time, Mrs Andrews had thought it odd that he should be buying tools with borrowed emergency money, but had said nothing to him.

Horwell now remembered the receipt for the electric cleaner found in the murder room. Checks with Mrs Kempson's neighbours revealed that Seymour had sold several vacuum cleaners in the area, one of them to the murdered woman. As with Mrs Andrews, he had made a point of returning several times to make sure that the machines were working properly. Was he just a conscientious salesman, Horwell wondered, or was he casing the homes of potential victims?

Scotland Yard reported that Henry Seymour had a criminal record. The son of an English doctor, he had drifted to South Africa when he was 20, apparently financing his travels by crime. Since then, he had been in and out of prison at home and abroad. He was known to be an ambitious thief – at one point he was reputed to have hatched a plan to rob the jewel room of the British Museum in broad daylight. He had even managed to obtain copies of the keys to the gem cabinets, but his confederates backed-out at the last minute, fearing the massive police hunt that would follow such a robbery.

It was Seymour's last conviction, however, that interested Horwell the most. Almost a year to the day, before the Oxford murder, Seymour had been charged with attempting to strangle a helpless old widow. In fact, the charge was eventually reduced to one of assault. He was bound over for two years and told to pay the lady £10 in damages within a year. That period had expired on the very day Mrs Kempson had been murdered. Had Seymour killed one widow in order to pay a legal debt to another?

Now that the police had a suspect, the case gained momentum. One of Seymour's local customers told investigators that she had met him on the morning of the day Mrs Kempson died. It was around eleven o'clock, and he had been waiting for a bus. They had chatted, and he had told her that he was going to London. She noticed, however, that he seemed so nervous and agitated that, in her opinion, he had not been fit to be alone.

In answer to a general request for information, police in Aylesbury reported that Seymour had stayed in a local hotel, but had left without paying the bill on the same day he had visited Mrs Andrews. The next day, the hotel's landlord had seen the door to the vacated room standing open, and had investigated. Inside, Seymour was standing by the bed fiddling with something over his open suitcase.

When the landlord demanded to know what he was doing, Seymour jammed the unseen item into the case, and made some excuse about needing his washing-bag. After promising to pay the bill after lunch, Seymour left, but was forced to leave his suitcase and its contents behind as collateral. When he failed to return, it had been handed to the local police. Inside were some clothes, a washing-kit and a hammer.

An ironmonger, not far from Mrs Andrews' house, had reported a man of Seymour's description buying a hammer and chisel on the day before the murder. But the hammer in question had a bright-red label on the handle, while the one found in Seymour's case did not. When Chief Inspector Horwell examined the suitcase, he found a number of rolled-up crumbs of paper, which when immersed in warm water, opened out like Japanese paper flowers, revealing themselves to be pieces of a red label like the one described by the shopkeeper. Seymour had clearly been scraping the label off when the landlord surprised him, failing to realize that the flakes of paper were falling into his open case.

Inspecting a blotting-pad in Seymour's hotel room, Horwell found the impression of an address in Brighton. It turned out to be a boarding house, kept by a widow, in which Seymour had lived since the time of the murder. There he was finally arrested.

Detectives now inspected Seymour's room. Under the carpet, close to the mantelpiece, two small peepholes had been made into the room below – his landlady's bedroom. Was he simply a voyeur, or had he been watching to see where she kept her money?

When questioned by the police, Seymour – a dapper man in his forties – denied any knowledge of the murder. He admitted buying the hammer, but claimed it had been a screwdriver, not a chisel, he had bought at the same time. (A screwdriver would have been too blunt to make Mrs Kempson's neck wound.) He explained that he had bought the tools to apply for a carpentry job. The screwdriver had been lost when he moved to Brighton.

As to his whereabouts during the morning of Saturday 1 August, he gave the police the names of a number of householders who he claimed to have visited, following up vacuum sales. When checked, all these people denied seeing him that day.

His trial was held at the Oxford Assizes on 20 October 1931. The prosecution's case, based entirely on circumstantial evidence, was that Seymour had originally meant to kill and rob Mrs Andrews, but the presence of her son prevented him doing this. He had then gone to Mrs Kempson's house, interrupting her in the middle of breakfast. Since she was still in her house-apron and curlers – and being a woman who would not like to be seen in this dishevelled state by the neighbours – she had asked him inside. As she walked into the dining-room he had struck her violently on the back of the head with the hammer. She had fallen to the floor and he had struck her again, this time on the forehead. Fearing that she might survive the head-blows, he had then stabbed her through the neck with the chisel.

To counter this, the defence produced no less than nine witnesses who claimed to have seen Mrs Kempson on the evening of the day she died. These people, all of whom knew the murdered woman, believed they had seen her walking about the local shops. One even claimed to have served her with a loaf of bread, another with half-a-pound of butter. Since it was certain that Seymour had left the city by eleven o'clock that morning, said the defence counsel, he could not have committed the crime.

The Crown argued that these witnesses must be mistaken. To support their claim, they offered two further pieces of circumstantial evidence. Firstly, Mrs Kempson had been due to go to London that day; why would she buy food if she were about to go away? Secondly, she had not gone to place flowers on her husband's grave – an act of devotion which she had performed each and every Saturday afternoon for the past ten years.

In the end though, it was Seymour's inability to provide a supportable alibi for the morning of 1 August, that told most heavily against him. The jury took only a short time to return a guilty verdict, after which Judge Rigby Swift passed the death sentence. Seymour's subsequent appeal failed, and he was hanged three weeks later.

In his book *The Life of Mr Justice Swift*, E.S. Fay notes the importance of this verdict: 'Seymour, and his trial may pass into legal history not only as one of the neatest examples of a circumstantial case but also as an outstanding instance of the efficacy of such a case. Offered the choice of the prosecution's circumstantial evidence and the defence's direct evidence, the jury chose the former.'

11

The Murder of Walter Dinivan

On the night of 21 May 1939, the Dorset police were called to a villa off the Poole Road, in Branksome, Bournemouth. The house appeared to have been burgled, and the owner, 64-year-old Walter Dinivan, had been savagely attacked. He was still alive, but it seemed unlikely he would survive the night.

Dinivan was a well-to-do garage owner who lived with his adult granddaughter, Hilda. He also owned several rental houses, and had converted his home into two spacious apartments. Two elderly spinsters, Miss Young and Miss Lancefield, lived in the upper part of the building, while he and Hilda occupied the lower. The only other resident of the house at the time of the attack was Hilda's brother, a telegrapher in the Royal Navy.

Earlier that evening, the grandchildren had gone to a dance. Returning shortly after 11 p.m. they were surprised to see that the lights were extinguished, as their grandfather had promised to wait up for them. After knocking for some time, they peered into the living-room window to see if he had dozed off. They saw, by the light of the electric fire, Walter Dinivan collapsed, face-down on the floor with a dark pool about his head.

Fearing that he had fainted and perhaps vomited, the young man broke the window panel in the front door and reached in to turn the key. To his surprise, it was not in the lock. He climbed through the broken window and hurried into the living-room. His grandfather's head was a bloody, battered mess, but he was still breathing faintly. The police and an ambulance were called, and Dinivan was rushed to Boscombe Hospital. His condition continued to worsen, and he died at 3 a.m. without regaining consciousness.

The next day, the pathologist, Sir Bernard Spilsbury, arrived from Scotland Yard to conduct the autopsy. He reported that the attacker had first tried to strangle Dinivan. Then, failing to kill him in that way, he had beaten him about the head with a weighty, blunt object like a hammer. There were no bruises or cuts to suggest that Dinivan had tried to defend himself, so it might be supposed that he had either been taken by surprise, or he had been attacked suddenly by somebody he knew. The two old ladies upstairs told the police that they had heard odd noises just before eleven o'clock, and Sir Bernard concurred that this was about the time the attack had taken place.

The police examined the scene of the crime, and found evidence that pointed to theft as the motive. The small safe in the wall of the living-room had been opened with the key from Dinivan's pocket, and emptied. The killer had also taken his victim's rings, watch and gold chain, and had emptied his pockets of money. Hilda told the police that her grandfather had been carrying about £19 – he had given her money to go to the dance, and she had seen what he had left.

Other clues found at the scene seemed to shed some light on events leading up to the attack. Dinivan was known to be a spirit drinker, but on the table beside his whisky bottle was also an empty beer bottle and glass. He was also a non-smoker, but a number of cigarette-ends were found on the rug beside the sofa, as well as – oddly enough – a woman's hair-curler. Finally, a brown paper-bag was found on the floor, crumpled in such a way as to suggest it had been tightly wrapped around a hammer.

When asked if she recognized the curler, Hilda Dinivan coloured with embarrassment. Her brother explained that Walter Dinivan was in the habit of occasionally entertaining 'women visitors' when he had the flat to himself. Although reluctant to say it directly, it was clear that they believed their grandfather had been with a prostitute before he died.

Superintendent Swann, heading the investigation, decided that the case was fairly clear-cut. A prostitute had been with Dinivan that night, and while she distracted the old man – or perhaps tried to strangle him – her male accomplice had attacked him with a hammer. He told his men to concentrate their inquiries on the local prostitutes.

When Superintendent Fred Cherrill, of the Scotland Yard fingerprint division, arrived, he confirmed that there was a clear thumbprint on the beer glass. He took comparison prints from Hilda and her brother, as well as from the dead man, but none of these matched the thumbprint.

Superintendent Swann had also asked for additional detective assistance from Scotland Yard. Chief Inspector Leonard Burt and a Sergeant Dyke, were sent to Bournemouth and examined the crime scene. Almost immediately they found evidence that seemed to contradict Swann's theory.

To begin with, they observed that the cigarettes had not been stubbed-out, but simply dropped. A burning cigarette should obviously have damaged the rug, yet there was no sign of burn-marks. Further examination revealed another butt which had been dropped down between the sofa-back and a silk covered cushion; once again, neither were burnt. If the stub had been lit when it was dropped, it would have probably started a fire. It therefore seemed clear that the cigarettes had been brought to the scene cold, and dropped to give the impression of a long conversation.

Sergeant Dyke, examining the hair-curler, discovered another discrepancy. It was of a very old-fashioned French design – the sort that would be used by an old lady rather than a prostitute. Had this item also been a plant, designed to put the police on the wrong track?

Chief Inspector Burt remembered that Dr Roche Lynch, director of the Department of Pathological Chemistry at St Mary's Hospital, had recently devised a method of distinguishing blood groups from spittle. Eighty-six per cent of the human race are 'secretors' – that is, they secrete blood cells in their spittle and semen. These could now be detected and grouped thanks to new blood-typing methods.

Dr Lynch had, in a recent case, managed to obtain a result from a cigarette-end. Wrapping the stubs in tissue paper, Burt dispatched Sergeant Dyke to St Mary's to beg the doctor's assistance. Dyke returned that afternoon with a promise of help from Dr Lynch – who was fascinated by the case – but explained that, due to mounting work, it would take him several days to produce results.

In the meantime, Burt and Dyke took a different tack. The killer had been admitted late at night and was offered a beer. If it was not a prostitute, it might well be a friend or acquaintance of the murdered man. Hilda gave them a list of her grandfather's regular friends, and the two inspectors paid visits to the most likely sounding ones. After about a dozen interviews, they still had no lead.

Superintendent Swann's investigation was faring little better. Many of the local prostitutes knew Dinivan, or 'old Dinny' as he was known, but none of them admitted to knowing anything about the murder and burglary. As Dyke had predicted, they laughed when asked if they used curlers like the one found at the scene – they said it was the sort their grandmothers used to wear. But one of them was able to provide an interesting piece of information.

Joseph Williams, an old soldier and friend of Dinivan's, had recently come into money. He was usually as poor as a church mouse, the prostitute reported, but now he seemed to be rolling in cash. Burt and Dyke had his name on their list, but had not bothered to interview him, since Williams was over 70 and was reportedly too frail to lift a hammer.

Before going to interview him, the policemen checked into the old man's background. He was a veteran of the Indian Army, and had known Dinivan for decades. He was now separated from his wife and was living alone in a house on Ingworth Road, ten minutes walk from Dinivan's villa. Williams' house, the detectives also discovered, was mortgaged to the hilt, and he had been, up until recently, behind with his mortgage payments. Shortly after the murder, he had paid the first instalment for some time.

On 25 May, Burt and Dyke called on Joseph Williams. They found him living in a single, sparsely furnished room. His whole house was in a filthy state and the stench was appalling. Williams himself seemed to be hardly more than skin and bones as he glared at them through his thick spectacles. As they entered, he snatched an old sword from the table, and waved it menacingly. 'Busybody Burt,' he yelled toothlessly, 'I'll show you the way to go home!'

As the officers stared in amazement, he went on: 'I know you. I know what you're after. But you shan't bloody get it.' Dropping into a chair he calmed a little; 'Oh yes, Inspector, I can account for every minute of the day poor Dinivan was murdered. Queer thing, you know, I saw him . . . on the seventeenth. We met on the street outside, and he insisted on taking me in and giving me a drink. But he wouldn't lend me all the money I needed. Oh no – only £5. And that he got out of his safe . . .' Williams ceased suddenly, perhaps realizing he was meandering into dangerous territory. After that he refused to discuss the murder and became abusive again when asked for his fingerprints. Burt and Dyke left with little accomplished, but much to think about.

By this time, Dr Lynch had completed his tests on the cigarette-butts. The smoker had been a secretor, he said, and best of all, he or she was AB blood-type. This is the rarest blood group of all, found in only 3 per cent of the population. What Burt really needed now was a sample of Williams' saliva. However, the difficulty he had faced in trying to get the old man's fingerprints persuaded him that a little deception was necessary.

An officer was told to follow Williams, and report the moment he entered a pub. When, several days later, Williams dropped into his local, Burt and Dyke hurried there and feigned surprise at meeting him. They pretended that their investigation had cleared him of suspicion, and offered to buy him a pint to make peace. He was only too glad to accept the offer and relieved Burt of a cigarette as well. The policeman watched with interest as he finished the cigarette and tossed it away. Burt offered Williams another then started a heated argument about horses to distract his attention. Meanwhile Dyke surreptitiously retrieved the dog-end. They continued this farcical act until Sergeant Dyke had a pocket full of cigarette-butts.

The stubs were, once again, packed off to Dr Lynch, and he eventually sent back his report. Williams was a secretor with type AB blood. Burt was now sure that the irascible old man was the murderer, but he needed his fingerprints, at the very least, to have any hope of a conviction.

Biting the bullet, they revisited his malodorous house. He was, predictably, unhappy to see them. On opening the door he snarled: 'What the hell do you want?' When they told him he protested: 'Me kill old Dinny? I couldn't kill a cat.'

Carrying on in a self-righteous vein he added: 'Oh, if you like; take a dekko around the place.' To his consternation they gratefully accepted his offer. In the coal shed they found a pile of brown paper-bags, identical to the one found at the murder scene.

Having got the address of Williams' wife from one of his neighbours, they went to visit her. The old woman had left her husband some time before under bitter circumstances. She immediately recognized the curler found at the scene as identical to her own. Subsequent tests revealed that hers were indeed produced by the same French manufacturer. She confirmed that she may well have left a few at her husband's house.

At that point, the case ground to a halt. Weeks

passed, but no new evidence came to light. What Burt really needed, he realized, were Williams' fingerprints, but he still had too little evidence to justify an arrest. On 20 June, in desperation, he and Dyke visited Williams again.

The long delay had clearly improved the old man's confidence. He smirked at them and said 'Innocent, that's what I am. Innocent. And even you can't pin it on me.' He gleefully answered their questions, delighting in their gloomy faces. When Burt glumly asked for his fingerprints again, Williams, revelling in their discomfort, agreed. 'How's that for confidence mate?' he chuckled.

Once again he had fallen neatly into their trap. The police lab found that his thumbprint was a perfect match with the one found on the beer glass. Burt and Dyke made one more call to the disgusting house on Ingworth Road; this time to arrest the owner. He was amazed that his luck seemed to have run out. 'Arrest me? You're not going to arrest me, are you?' he demanded. 'The whole thing's ridiculous.'

At his initial hearing at the magistrate's court, Williams was typically rumbustious. He called to the press: 'Take a pretty picture, lads,' and when questioned by the magistrate he joked: 'There'll be a sensation when I don't go to the whist drive tonight ... I am just as innocent as you are, sir, that's all. Of course I don't know whether you did it or not ...'

He behaved with similar jauntiness when his trial opened at Dorset Assizes the following October. As he was led into the courtroom he shouted: 'Here we are. Keep on smiling.' As the trial continued, he regularly interrupted the proceedings with cries of 'I'm innocent!' The Crown prosecutor was interrupted several times by

Williams yelling: 'That's a lie!' and 'I hate people who tell lies!' Each time, his counsel, Norman King, KC, persuaded him, with some difficulty, to quieten down and apologize to the court. King, despite his difficult task seemed quietly confident when he addressed the court. His main line of argument soon became clear.

He insisted that the Crown had only four pieces of evidence, and one of those was based on questionable scientific methods. The prosecution, he went on, had presented no eye-witnesses to support their version of events; they had only offered a few circumstantial pieces of evidence to satisfy the court.

Going on to criticize the Crown's assertion that the hair-curler and the paper-bags linked Joseph Williams with the killing, he pointed out that these were perfectly common household items that might be found in any-one's home. Their inclusion as major items of evidence by the Crown merely showed how thin their case was.

Quietly skirting the question of the thumbprint, he saved his main attack for the saliva tests on the cigarette-butts. This, he said, was the prosecution's main piece of evidence. The proof with which they hoped to convince the jury that his client should hang. If there was a 'reasonable doubt' in the minds of the jurors that this new test was not completely infallible, they could not convict Joseph Williams.

There clearly was such a doubt, as the jury acquitted Williams of all charges. The old man left the courtroom with the air of a triumphant gladiator, under the embittered eyes of Burt and Dyke.

Another person who watched Williams leave with professional interest was Norman Rea; a reporter who believed that the old man's story of police harassment might constitute a scoop. He approached Williams, and asked if he would like to chat about his adventures at a local hotel. Williams immediately accepted, and they made their way to the hotel's bar. Downing a double whisky, Williams gave the toast 'To the hangman! The hangman who has been cheated of his victim.' A little later, on an impulse, Williams asked to be taken back home to Poole: 'I want to see their faces when I walk down the street,' he explained. Having enjoyed this victory, Williams decided he would rather spend the night in the hotel in Dorchester, so the pair returned there and booked-in.

In the middle of the night, Rea was awakened by hysterical banging on the door to his room. Standing, spectre-like in the hall was the terror-stricken Williams. 'I couldn't sleep,' he moaned. 'Christ I couldn't sleep at all. I've got to tell somebody. You see the jury was wrong . . . The jury was wrong,' he cried, 'It was me.'

Rea calmed him and led him back to bed. The next morning, the old man seemed to have forgotten the whole incident.

The reporter did not write-up the story for his newspaper. He waited until 1951, some years after Williams' death, to publish the old man's confession.

12

The Body in the Church

On 17 July 1942, workmen were demolishing the Baptist Chapel on Vauxhall Road, south London. The building had been hit by a German bomb during the Battle of Britain in 1940, and was considered too unstable to be salvaged. One of the men, digging through the rubble and earth that had seeped down into the vestry cellar, hooked his pick under a heavy stone slab and hauled it up. Underneath he found a scorched human body; now little more than a skeleton hung with a few rags of flesh.

He was not as shocked as he might have been. The blitz had reduced much of the city to rubble and there were many victims of the bombing yet to be unearthed. He gently slid the blade of his shovel under the corpse's rib-cage and lifted it out of the shallow grave. To his surprise the head, which he had assumed was still attached to the neck, stayed on the ground.

Despite the havoc caused by the bombing, official procedure was still adhered to when a body was discovered. The police were informed, and Inspectors Keeling and Hatton duly arrived to examine the corpse. The remains consisted of a torso and the severed head. The arms were missing from the elbow and the legs from the knee. The skull was bare of flesh and the lower jaw was also missing. The inspectors knew that the chapel had been built on an old cemetery some 50 years before. Yet, the body did not look old enough to be left over from that period. On the other hand, if this was a bomb victim, how had he or she come to be buried under a stone slab in a cellar some distance from the nearest bomb crater?

The remains were wrapped in brown paper and taken to Southwark public mortuary. The next morning, the Home Office Pathologist Dr Keith Simpson, arrived to inspect them. Simpson's work had increased dramatically since the start of the blitz; he had to examine many hundreds of bomb-victims in addition to his normal, crime-related work. In a state of chronic overwork, it would not have been surprising if he had simply concluded that the burned skeleton was yet another casualty of the war. But, on close examination, he remarked several interesting anomalies. The head had not been broken-off when the workman lifted the torso out of the grave; it had been neatly severed. The same was true of the missing forearms and legs. Whoever the victim was, he or she had not been blown apart, but dissected. Studying the skull, he noted that the face and scalp had neither rotted away nor been burned off; the head had been flayed. All the evidence pointed to murder.

He was able to tell the police that the victim was a woman – the remains of the womb were still visible in the decayed trunk. She had been dead about a year to 18 months, judging by the deterioration of the soft tissue. This ruled out the possibility that she was a leftover from the old graveyard, and it also ruled out the possibility that she had been killed when the chapel was bombed, since that had taken place almost two years previously.

Simpson had the remains removed to his laboratory at Guy's Hospital. On close examination, it seemed clear that the murderer had gone to great effort to conceal the identity of his victim. Some attempts had been made to incinerate the body, although fortunately, not much damage had been done. The flaying of the head and the removal of the eyes was obviously intended to prevent facial identification. The arms had plainly been removed to confound attempts at fingerprint identification. Finally, the removal of the lower jaw could be a half-hearted attempt to confound dental identification; fortunately, four of the upper set of teeth had survived.

None of this gruesome work showed any evidence of surgical expertise, so Simpson assumed that the killer was an amateur at dissection. Whoever he was, he might have saved himself the trouble. The corpse was in such a state of decay that most of these points of identification would have been lost anyway.

In fact, what the pathologist needed most was one or both of the missing legs. Even to start to narrow down the list of possible victims, he would need an accurate height. Without the legs this would be a matter of guess work. Simpson spent two afternoons with the police, sifting about three tons of earth from the vestry cellar. No sign of the missing limbs or jaw were found; the murderer had clearly disposed of them elsewhere.

Nevertheless, they discovered two additional clues. The first was a yellowish powder which was found on the earth where the body had been buried. The second was a wooden chest, just under 5-feet-long. Since the box did not belong to the chapel, it was guessed that it had been used by the murderer to transport the body to the cellar. The yellow powder, Simpson recognized as corresponding to a yellow stain to the victim's head and neck. When analysed at Guy's Hospital, the substance proved to be slaked lime.

This proved to be important for two reasons. Firstly, it showed that the murderer was ignorant of elementary chemistry. If he hoped for decomposition he had chosen the wrong substance – it is quicklime, not slaked lime that generates heat in the presence of moisture and causes flesh to dissolve. The stuff had actually discouraged maggots from eating the flesh, and so had acted as a preservative.

The second interesting point was why the killer had chosen to coat the neck as well as the head. Was it especially important to him to eradicate this area as well? When Simpson dissected the victim's voice box he found that the right horn of the thyroid cartilage had been broken. A blood-clot around it showed that the injury had been sustained while the woman was still alive. It was a sure sign of strangulation, since that form of injury occurs in no other way. A bruise on the back of the head suggested that the woman might have been throttled while having her head beaten against some hard surface.

Simpson now began to piece together a physical description of the victim. Despite the removal of the scalp, he managed to find a small piece of skin the killer had missed. Under a microscope the hairs from this area proved to be dark brown, turning to grey.

This supported his estimate of her age. The sutures of the skull – the joins between the skull plates – gradually seal up as a person ages. Judging from the victim's skull, Dr Simpson guessed that she was between 40 and 50.

As to the tricky question of her height, Simpson made

an educated guess. Taking into account the missing
leg-bones and soft tissues, he estimated that she had been
about 5 feet tall. There were also two 'fixed' methods
of obtaining a person's height from measurement of
the long bones of the limbs; Pearson's formulae and
Rollet's tables. Since the left humerus was undamaged,
Dr Simpson applied both of these. The results were
slightly different, but the average between the two was
5 feet ½ inch.

He noticed that the woman's neck was curved at a
fairly sharp angle to the trunk. If this had been a feature
of her posture when she was alive, she would have been
obviously deformed. However, an X-ray revealed no
evidence of disease to cause such a disfigurement, so
Simpson inferred that the twisting of the neck had been
done after she had died. His guess was that it had been
caused by her transport in the wooden chest, which was
several inches shorter than she was.

Now he had a general description, he turned to more
specific features. He had noticed immediately that the
victim's uterus was enlarged. His first thought was that
she might have been pregnant when she died, so he
had her stomach area X-rayed. This revealed that the
swelling had been caused by a fibroid tumour, about
3 or 4 inches in length and which must have caused
some discomfort. It was likely that she had sought
medical attention, in which case records of her condition
would exist.

Even more revealing was the victim's mouth. Despite
the absence of the lower jaw, Simpson found several
identifying features in what remained. Three of the four
molars had been capped, there were marks showing that
a denture had replaced the front teeth, the palate was
high, and there was a marked thickening of the bone in

the region of the back teeth. If the victim's dentist had kept accurate records, these details could be as revealing as a set of fingerprints.

Inspector Keeling was delighted with these findings. He had learned that the wife of a fire-watcher in the Baptist Chapel had gone missing at about the right time, and Simpson's description fitted her perfectly. Her name was Rachel Dobkin, aged 47, and she had not been seen since 11 April 1942.

Mrs Dobkin had not been living with her husband at the time – in fact they had been separated for over 20 years. Harry Dobkin was a short, balding, heavy-set man with a bullish demeanour. Born of Jewish parents in Russia in 1891, he had been taken to England when he was only a few months old. Rachel and he had been introduced, in the traditional Jewish fashion, via a marriage-broker. Following the wedding, in September 1920, they took such an intense dislike to each other that they separated after only three days. However, this had been long enough for them to conceive a son.

In 1923, Rachel obtained a maintenance order of £1 per week, but Dobkin proved reluctant to meet the obligation. He made a precarious living by alternating work as a ship's steward and cook with minor jobs in the tailoring trade, and his payments were both irregular and infrequent. On several occasions, the courts imprisoned him for defaulting, but the experience left him just as unreliable as before. Rachel was reduced to badgering him in the street for money, and the ensuing rows tended to be explosive. She had him summoned for assault on four separate occasions, but each time the magistrate had dismissed the charge.

On the afternoon of 11 April 1941, the pair had tea in a cafe in Dalston. Harry had just landed a job as

fire-warden – a special blitz night-watchman whose job
was to spot any fires starting in a set area – and Rachel
was doubtless keen to share his good fortune. They left at
6.30 p.m. and this was the last time Rachel Dobkin was
ever seen alive. Rachel's sister, Polly Dubinski, became
alarmed when she failed to reappear by the following
afternoon and reported her disappearance to the police.
However, with so many unrecorded deaths due to the
blitz, the authorities were sceptical of Polly's assurance
that Rachel had been murdered by her husband.

Harry Dobkin was eventually interviewed on 16 April
1941, but denied knowing anything about his wife's
disappearance or her present whereabouts. He told the
police that when they had parted company, Rachel had
told him that she was not feeling well and was going to
her mother's to listen to the wireless. That was the last
he had seen of her.

The police might have left it at that, if Rachel's handbag, complete with her identification papers, had not
turned up in a Guildford post office on 12 April. Without
identification, no one could travel far in wartime Britain,
and since Mrs Dobkin had not appeared to collect them,
this seemed to confirm that she was no longer alive.

The police decided to dig up the floor of the crypt of
the bombed Baptist Chapel, one of the buildings in Harry
Dobkin's fire-watch area. They found a freshly dug hole
6 feet by 2 feet, but it was empty. But, when the skeleton
was found in the cellar of the neighbouring vestry the
following year, this discovery was at first forgotten.

Re-investigating the events of the previous year,
Inspectors Hatton and Keeling discovered another interesting report. On 14 April 1941, three days after Rachel
had disappeared, a policeman noticed smoke and flames
coming out of the cellar of the Baptist Chapel vestry. As

he ran to investigate, he bumped into Harry Dobkin. The fire-warden said sheepishly: 'I'm glad you've come. It's a terrible blaze isn't it?' But he did not explain why he had failed to raise the alarm. Questioned by another officer after the blaze was extinguished, Dobkin exclaimed 'I didn't do it,' although nobody had suggested he was responsible for the fire. Since the skeleton in the vestry cellar had been partially burned, this report assumed a new significance.

On 26 August 1942, Inspector Hatton asked Dobkin to accompany him to the Baptist Chapel 'to assist the police with their enquiries.' Since no reports had yet appeared in the press it should have been impossible for Dobkin to know how the victim had died. Yet, on being shown the grave in the cellar, he protested: 'I wouldn't strangle a woman! I wouldn't hit a woman! Some men might, but I wouldn't. I didn't know the cellar was here, and I've certainly never been down here in my life.'

In fact, Hatton had evidence from a PC Wakeley that on the previous 4 August, he had spotted Dobkin entering the vestry. In view of the half-demolished state of the building, he must have noticed the cellar. Yet, when confronted with PC Wakeley, Dobkin offered no explanation, but vociferously insisted that he was lying. The inspector formally charged him with the murder of his wife, and took him into custody.

The trial took place in the Old Bailey on 17 November 1942. Dobkin's only real hope was that the defence counsel, F.H. Lawton, could undermine the medical identification of the victim as his wife. However, as the trial continued, this hope dwindled away.

Lawton cross-examined the prosecution's witnesses with great expertise, but argument was all but useless against the fact that Rachel Dobkin's dental records

matched the skeleton's mouth exactly. Likewise, there
was little he could do when the Crown presented medical
records showing that Mrs Dobkin, like the body found
in the cellar, had a fibroid tumour of the uterus which
had not been treated. (Rachel had refused to have an
operation.)

The most memorable moment of the trial came when
a snapshot of Rachel Dobkin's face was shown, superimposed on a photograph of the skull, a technique used
by Professor John Glaister in the Ruxton case (see
Chapter 7). The match was striking. Lawton countered
by reading a passage from Glaister's own book on the
case, in which he stated that 'a positive identification
of the skulls, no matter how close a correspondence of
skulls and portraits was obtained, would have been open
to very grave objection.' Did this not, he asked Simpson,
undermine the validity of the process? The pathologist
replied that he was not offering the superimposed photograph as 'positive identification,' merely as 'scientific
evidence' that tended to support his identification of the
body. That identification, it was now clear, was virtually
water-tight.

Nevertheless, the defence still had one card to play.
Lawton re-called Polly Dubinski, Rachel's sister, to ask
her about a missing-person advertisement she had run
in the *News of the World*, on 4 May 1941. The ad
described Rachel's height as '5 feet 3 inches,' not 5 feet
1 inch, as Polly had previously stated.

In his evidence, Simpson had stated that the margin
of error on his height calculations was only 1 inch either
way. When pressed by Lawton, Simpson agreed that if
Rachel could be proved to be more than an inch taller
than the estimate, she could not have been the victim.
Thus, if the defence could prove she was more than

5 feet 2 inches tall, they would have all but won the case.

However, Polly Dubinski seemed unruffled when confronted with the advertisement. She reiterated that she and Rachel had been roughly the same height, and that the newspaper had printed a mistake. After she left the stand, the prosecution had Polly measured by a doctor and returned, triumphantly with the results: 'height without shoes, 4 feet 11¾ inches; height with shoes 5 feet 1 inch.'

Dobkin himself made a poor impression in the witness stand. He seemed confused by the technical evidence and was evasive when cross-examined by the prosecution. His basic misunderstanding of the legal system was revealed when he repeatedly insisted that, following his arrest, detectives had tried to force him to sign a confession. He said that violence and intimidatory methods had been used on him, including the reading of a poem, ominously titled 'The Wheels of Justice'. In fact, even if this was true, such actions by the police had no bearing on the case, since he had signed no confession.

The jury took only 20 minutes to find Harry Dobkin guilty, after which Judge Wrottesley sentenced him to death.

Shortly before he was hanged, Dobkin confessed to the murder of his wife. In his book *Forty Years of Murder*, Dr Simpson mentions, with perhaps justified smugness, that it was his duty to carry-out the post mortem following the execution.

13

The Wigwam Murder

On 7 October 1942, a unit of marines was engaged in battle training on the beautiful but windy slopes of Hankley Common, near Godalming in Surrey. The area was thick with blank shell-cases and tripwires attached to false bombs, as well as nervous soldiers practising their skills for the real conflict that they would soon be seeing. In this haven of imaginary battle, no one was expecting to find a real corpse. Yet early on that bright October day, two marines climbing to the summit of a heather-covered ridge noticed something strange sticking from a mound of sandy earth. It was brown and desiccated yet looked disturbingly like a human hand. Closer inspection revealed that it was a decomposed human forearm, including hand, with the thumb and two fingers missing. Protruding from the mound there was a second lump of desiccated flesh. By its shape and position the marines guessed that it was part of the leg. Abandoning their exercise the men alerted the rest of their unit, and the Surrey police were called by field telephone.

When Superintendent Richard Webb arrived on the scene later that day he saw that this investigation was going to need medical expertise. The body had obviously been on the ridge for weeks. It would require something akin to an archaeological excavation to preserve whatever clues might remain. Webb had the mound covered with a waterproof sheet and posted a guard around the site. He then called for the specialists.

Acting for the coroner, Dr Eric Gardner was the first medical man to arrive, at around noon the next day. While awaiting the arrival of Dr Keith Simpson, medico-legal adviser to the Surrey police, Gardner made a preliminary inspection of the surface details. The missing thumb and fingers of the hand seemed to have been gnawed off by vermin, probably rats. Carefully examining the texture of the earth, Gardner found that there was an inverted piece of turf near the top. Turning this over revealed a clump of heather that, although shrivelled, had evidently still been green and flowering when the sod was cut. Gardner knew that in this region heather finished flowering at the beginning of September, so the corpse must have been buried about a month before. Without even examining the body a likely time of death had been established.

By the time that Keith Simpson arrived with his secretary Molly Lefebure, the site was crowded with senior police officers. An official photographer was at work recording the scene. Detective Inspector Ted Greeno of Scotland Yard had been called in, and was on his way. Despite the police presence, military exercises continued as normal with mortar-fire and shells exploding frequently on the plain below them. As the two pathologists began their difficult task, it began to drizzle.

With the earth removed from the corpse, a thick smell of putrefaction filled the air, causing those standing around to rapidly move upwind. The doctors worked on unperturbed. It soon became clear that the body was that of a woman. She was buried shallowly, lying face downward in the earth with arms and legs outstretched. The right arm in particular stuck straight out, as though pointing. She had been wearing a green and white summer dress with a lace collar, a head-scarf knotted around her neck, a slip, bra and panties. The underwear was neatly in place, showing no signs of the tearing normally associated with a sexual assault. The scarf was knotted tightly but was loose on the neck, and so was unlikely to have been used as a ligature. Moreover, the cause of death seemed to be obvious: the back of the skull was smashed in, evidently from a heavy blow from a blunt instrument, perhaps a large tree-branch or an iron bar. Her right arm seemed to show some signs of wounding, but because the body was badly decomposed it was impossible to judge clearly. Due to the extensive damage to the skull and the action of vermin, the head was on the point of losing its shape completely.

The pathologists' job was made doubly difficult by the fact that the body was infested with maggots. Despite the freezing cold and drizzle, that kept the policemen and others present huddled into their coats, the two doctors found that the heat generated by the decomposition of the body and the action of maggots made it necessary to remove their jackets. As they worked they passed specimens of tissue, earth and maggots to Molly Lefebure, who stored them in buff envelopes.

Although the infestation of blowfly larvae hindered the pathologists' investigation of the body's wounds, and made the job of excavation even more unpleasant, it did reveal one thing: the body had remained uncovered and in the open before its burial, possibly up to two days. This would have allowed time for the extensive laying of blowfly eggs that had led to the corpse's present condition.

The victim had been wearing socks, but no shoes. Examining her feet, Dr Simpson found that one of the socks was torn, and that both feet had suffered grazing and lacerations. This seemed to point to the body having been dragged some distance, with the heels scraping along the ground. The pointing gesture of the right arm could mean that this was the limb by which she was dragged.

Simpson and Gardner realized that no proper medical examination of the corpse could take place until the blowfly larvae and other beetles were killed off. This is normally achieved by leaving an infested body in a vat of lysol until the creatures have died, a process that takes about two days. The two pathologists applied to Dr Wills Taylor, the coroner in the case, to allow them to take the corpse to Guy's Hospital where they could soak and de-infest it. The decomposed corpse was carefully moved, wrapped in the mackintosh sheet that Webb had used to cover the mound the previous day.

Meanwhile, Detective Inspector Greeno had ordered his men to search the common for the murder weapon, and also the dead woman's shoes or other personal effects that might have been lost either during the attack or in the body's journey to its eventual make-shift grave.

At the end of two days, Dr Gardner joined Simpson at Guy's to conduct a full autopsy. Superintendent Webb was also present. The woman's face had all but disappeared, so a description for identification purposes would have to be built up from other details. She was aged about 19 or 20, 5 feet 4 inches tall, with small hands and feet. Although her two front teeth seemed to have been knocked out, they had evidently been very prominent and overlapping in life. Her hair was sandy-brown, cut into a bob and had been bleached shortly before death.

She had suffered three stab wounds to the front of the head and another single wound under the right elbow, as Simpson had noted at the scene. The flesh of the right arm showed 'vital reaction' to the wound, meaning that from the shape of the puncture it could be seen that it had been sustained during life. Although it was not possible to conclusively say the same about the head wounds, the two pathologists felt that they could infer that the wound to the arm came about as a result of the victim trying to shield her head from the attack. The weapon used to make the stab wounds seemed to have been hooked at the end, Simpson observed, because when it had been pulled from the victim's right arm it had drawn out the ends of some severed tendons. Furthermore the stab wounds to the skull seemed bevelled, as though a blade with a slightly hooked end had been twisted there.

As to the time of death, the original estimate of about a month before the discovery seemed to be thrown into doubt by the advanced state of decomposition. Much of the corpse's fat had turned to adipocere, a greasy, white substance that usually takes at least five weeks to form in the outdoor British climate. That anomaly could be resolved however by taking into account the raised temperature created by the larvae infestation. Under those conditions the original estimate could easily be correct. With a description and supposed time of death established, Simpson and Gardner set about reconstructing the back of the victim's skull, riveting and wiring the 38 fragments that they had recovered.

These physical details were enough to nudge Superintendent Webb's memory. Something about the green and white dress had seemed familiar to him at the excavation, and now, combined with the other particulars determined by the pathologists, he had completed the picture. The woman's name was Joan Pearl Wolfe. Webb had met her six or seven weeks before the discovery of her body, a fortnight before her death. The police in the area knew her well because they were concerned about her lifestyle: she lived in the woods in a makeshift hut made from leaves and branches. She was friendly with the soldiers stationed nearby, and common wisdom had it that she lived rough because she had run away from home.

For days Greeno's men continued to painstakingly search Hankley Common. Their care was rewarded periodically: Pearl Wolfe's shoes were found, separately, both some distance from her grave on the ridge. Lying near one of the shoes, police found a bag containing a rosary. This very probably belonged to Wolfe; she was Roman Catholic. In the same area, by a small stream, there was also a military tripwire. Could she have run on to the wire while being pursued, knocking out her two front teeth as she fell? This seemed to become a more likely scenario when police located a heavy birch stake near the stream. Stuck on its surface were brown, bleached hairs.

Meanwhile, other officers were making enquiries about Joan Pearl Wolfe among the local community. Several people reported seeing her with a Canadian private named August Sangret. It was this soldier who, according to locals, had built the wigwam-like home for her in the woods. When she had been admitted to hospital earlier that year, she had kept a photo of the Canadian by her bed. Wolfe had apparently been seen knitting baby-clothes early in September. An abandoned cricket pavilion was said to be one of the couple's meeting places, and when police examined the building they found it covered in their graffiti, including Sangret's home address in Canada, and the address of Joan Pearl Wolfe's mother. Also pencilled on the wall was a prayer: 'O holy Virgin in the midst of all thy glory we implore thee not to forget the sorrows of this world.'

Greeno's priorities were to question Sangret and to find the hook-tipped knife. It was now fairly certain that it was the stake that had delivered the killing blow. Simpson found that the hairs clinging to it belonged to Joan Pearl Wolfe. There was little else that the stake could tell police: it bore no bloodstains and its bark would not retain fingerprints. As the search of Hankley Common continued, this time looking specifically for the knife, Greeno headed for the Canadian army base, Witley Camp.

From Sangret's commanding officer, Greeno's men discovered that Sangret had asked for a marriage request form, but had never returned it completed. It transpired that Sangret had reported Pearl Wolfe missing to his provost sergeant, telling him that if she was found and anything had happened to her, he did not want anything to do with it. To his fellow soldiers Sangret had apparently explained her disappearance in a number of ways: to one he had said that she was in hospital, to another that she had run out of clothes and thus gone home.

Greeno telephoned the base and asked them to confine Sangret until his arrival. Then he took him to Godalming Police Station. Sangret a good-looking man, of medium height, was half French-Canadian and half Cree Indian. His native American ancestry was evident in his face, straight features and bronze-coloured skin. As Greeno laid out the victim's clothes before him, he looked grim.

These clothes, Sangret admitted calmly, belonged to Joan Pearl Wolfe, and the last time that he had seen her had been on 14 September. He had no idea where she might have been since then. Sangret did not ask if anything had happened to her, and Greeno decided not to announce that she was dead. If Sangret knew anything of the crime, he might incriminate himself. Asked to make a statement, he launched into such a lengthy and detailed account of his association with Pearl Wolfe that it exhausted a string of note-taking sergeants and a rota had to be drawn up.

As Greeno listened to these unremarkable details, his officers were making other discoveries on Hankley Common. In and around a small dell on the ridge-side, above the stream where the stake had been found, the searchers unearthed a number of interesting items. Wolfe's identity card, revealing her to have been 19 years old, was found in the undergrowth together with a green purse, a white elephant good-luck charm, a crucifix and the marriage request form that Sangret's CO had issued to him. Even more revealingly, police discovered a letter, written by Wolfe and addressed to Sangret. It was a love-letter written from hospital and dated 25 August. In it she explained to Sangret, whom she addressed as 'my darling', that she was pregnant and looking forward to their coming marriage.

Meanwhile officers sent to examine Sangret's possessions found what seemed to be faint bloodstains on his battle dress and on a blanket belonging to him. Simpson was soon at work on this new evidence. The marks on the blanket, he observed, corresponded roughly with the wounds sustained by Pearl Wolfe. If her body had been under the blanket, her head, right arm and right foot would have made just such stains. The marks tested positive to a benzidine test. This however only proved that the substance *could* be blood; other substances also give a positive result. The more specific but less sensitive tests for blood carried out by Dr Roche Lynch of the Home Office analysis team failed to come up positive, perhaps because the blankets and battle dress had been washed.

When Sangret finished his statement it was 17,000 words long. He admitted knowing Pearl Wolfe but denied all knowledge of her beyond 14 September, when he had, apparently, left her safe and well. He was shown all the articles found around the dell near Hankley Common. As with the clothes he immediately identified them as Pearl Wolfe's. After signing the statement, Sangret asked the police if they had found her, and when they said that they had, remarked sullenly that he was certain to get the blame. Sangret was tantalizingly close to admitting guilt, but he had not yet done so. Greeno had no choice but to let him go free. As he left Sangret suggested that perhaps Pearl Wolfe had killed herself.

While no one doubted that Sangret had murdered Pearl Wolfe there was not enough evidence for Greeno to arrest him, and the slow work of enquiry continued. A friend of Sangret's on the army base told police that he wrote letters for him because Sangret himself was illiterate. As well as writing letters to Pearl Wolfe for Sangret, he had also transcribed love-letters to a woman in Glasgow. Sangret was evidently an enthusiastic lover.

More significantly, a Private Crowle told police that

while out blackberrying one day he had seen a knife like the one described by Simpson stuck into a tree near the wigwam in the woods. He had taken it to the provost back at camp, who had in turn given the knife to Sangret via a corporal named Harding. According to both Crowle and Harding, the knife was British Army issue, black handled with a hooked point. Yet it was not among Sangret's possessions when the police searched them. Where had it gone?

The answer soon presented itself. One of the toilets in the wash-house attached to the Witley Camp guardroom was found to be blocked, and private named Brown was detailed to clear the obstruction. After grabbing two handfuls of damp paper and cigarette butts, Brown felt something hard. Pulling the object free, he found that it was a black-handled knife, with a hook point.

How had the knife ended up stuck in a U-bend? Sangret had been locked in the guardroom on Greeno's request when he was on his way to question him. The soldiers guarding him remembered that just before Greeno had arrived, Sangret had requested to go to the toilet. If Sangret had done this in order to dispose of the knife, as seemed very likely, it could only be because he knew about its connection to Greeno's visit. This was certainly incriminating.

Sangret was once again called in for questioning. Beginning with a few casual enquiries, Greeno then matter-of-factly asked Sangret why he had not mentioned the hook-point knife before. Foolishly Sangret admitted knowledge of the knife, saying that it had belonged to Pearl Wolfe's previous boyfriend. He explained that he had not seen it after the provost had got hold of it, denying that it had been returned to him. This statement was enough for Greeno, and he asked the Surrey police to arrest August Sangret and charge him with the murder of Joan Pearl Wolfe.

Sangret was in custody for five months before his trial was held at Kingston Assizes. The Crown's accusation centred around a possible reconstructed version of events agreed upon originally by Simpson and Greeno. The scenario was this: Sangret, unwilling to marry Pearl Wolfe, argues violently with her at the dell near Hankley Common. Sangret becomes so angry that he pulls out the black-handled knife and stabs at her head. She shields herself from the blows with her crooked right arm, then runs away from her attacker, spilling the contents of her handbag as she flees. Pursued by Sangret, and probably screaming for help, she runs over the tripwire by the stream and crashes down, knocking out her front teeth. Sangret, perhaps in an effort to silence her, beats-in her head with a stake. The body is concealed in a blanket for one or two days in the open, before Sangret returns and drags it to the ridge-top, where he buries her shallowly in a mound of sandy earth. (This was the only point at which the story did not seem to adequately explain the facts. Why would someone drag a body out of secluded woodland where it would be relatively easy to hide, and onto a bare hilltop, where it was almost certain to be found. Could it perhaps be a native American burial ritual?)

It was the knife that formed the centrepiece of the prosecution's evidence. The police had Sangret's statement admitting that at one time he had owned it. They also had further circumstantial evidence that Sangret had tried to hide it when he thought he was suspected of the crime. This is why the defence decided to concentrate upon Dr Simpson's medical evidence, trying to introduce an element of uncertainty.

It was during this trial that, for the first time in a British court, a forensic scientist brought the skull of a murder-victim into court to demonstrate his findings. With the knife and the heavily wired and riveted skull, Simpson showed how he believed the wounds were made. Linton Thorpe, defence counsel, demanded to know whether the black-handled knife was the only implement that could have caused such holes, and whether indeed the wounds might not have been made by any knife. Dr Simpson stuck to his findings, repeating them again and again. During this evidence the defendant remained totally impassive.

Taking the knife and the skull with them, the jury retired. In two hours they were back. Their verdict was that August Sangret was guilty of murder. They accompanied their finding with a strong recommendation for mercy..

But in spite of this recommendation, Sangret was hanged at Wandsworth jail about a week later. When Dr Simpson performed the routine autopsy upon him, he found that the soldier had a tattoo on his arm: the name 'Pearl'.

14

The Body in the Sack Case

Chief Superintendent Fred Cherrill – 'Cherrill of the Yard' – described it as 'the perfect murder – nearly.' That is perhaps an exaggeration; a perfect murder would demand careful planning. The crime that has become known as 'the body in the sack case' was undoubtedly unplanned. But the subsequent attempt to conceal the murder was – either by luck or design – one of the most successful in the history of British crime.

Friday, 19 November 1943, began as a foggy day in Luton, Bedfordshire, but by midday the mists over the River Lea, which flows around the outskirts of the town, had cleared. Several people who walked along the footpath by the Osborne Road allotments noticed a bundle wrapped in sacks and tied with string, lying in the shallow water at the foot of a steep bank. None of them paused to look closer – it would have involved scrambling down the slippery bank. But at 2.15 that afternoon, two sewage workers who were testing the level of the river approached the bundle, and recognized – from the naked flesh protruding through the sacking – that the bulky object was a human body. They immediately notified the police.

When the sacks – four of them – were stripped away,

the police found themselves looking at the naked body of a fairly young woman, with the legs doubled-up and held in place by a cord; the ankles were also tied together. The face was so battered as to be unrecognizable. Whoever killed her had given her a violent beating; a blow on the left side of the face had split the flesh, and another blow had fractured both the lower and upper jawbones, splitting the tongue. Her false teeth were missing. The face was swollen and black with bruises, and there were more bruises on the throat, caused by a right hand. The cause of death, according to the first doctor who saw the body, was a shotgun-wound in the head.

The woman had, apparently, been dumped there overnight; the sewage workers had been past the spot at four o'clock the previous afternoon and were certain it had not been there then.

Detective Inspector Finch, of the Luton CID, saw that it was going to be a difficult case. The battering of the face meant that the woman would be hard to identify. The four sacks in which the body was wrapped provided no obvious clue. Unless her fingerprints could be identified, the police were going to have to rely on missing persons reports.

After the body had been photographed, and moved to the mortuary of the Luton Hospital, the chief constable decided to ask for help from Scotland Yard. Chief Inspector William Chapman and his assistant Sergeant Judge were assigned to the case and arrived the next day. The well-known London pathologist, Dr Keith Simpson of Guy's Hospital, and his assistant Molly Lefebure, travelled down with them.

After looking at the place where the body had been found – and noting that the river was really a stream, about 6 inches deep – they went to the morgue at the

Luton and Dunstable Hospital. It took Simpson very little time to determine that the dead woman – who was in her mid-thirties – had not died of a gunshot-wound, but of a very heavy blow to the head. This had knocked her unconscious, and her assailant probably assumed she was dead, for he went on to undress her and tie her up. But bruises underneath the cord around her legs showed that she had, in fact, been alive at the time, probably dying about 40 minutes later. Rigor mortis had set in, revealing that she had been killed some time around the afternoon of 18 November. She had an old appendix scar, had borne at least one child, and was five months pregnant with another. There was no sign of forcible rape, ruling out one more possibility – that she had been the victim of a sex-attack. The cause of death was later revealed to be a brain haemorrhage.

Keith Simpson and his assistant returned to London in a pea-soup fog; Chief Inspector Chapman – known as 'the cherub' because of his baby-like round face – stayed on in Luton to grope around in a fog of mystery as all attempts to identify the victim failed.

The mortuary did some excellent work in cleaning up the dead woman's face until it was more-or-less recognizable, and a photograph was taken, which was shown in local cinemas, with a notice: 'Police are still anxious to establish the identity of this unfortunate woman . . .' It was discovered later that the dead woman's 17-year-old daughter had seen the photograph, and had failed to recognize it. Her two sons, aged 14 and 15, *did* tell their father that a photograph they had seen in a shop-window resembled their mother, but he told them that was impossible.

Chapman and Judge spent unproductive weeks in pursuing every possible lead. Tyre marks found on the

Osborne Road bridge, not far from the body, proved to be a local milk-van. They took a plaster-cast of the woman's jaws, published it in a dental journal, and showed it to every dental surgeon in the area; the victim's dentist actually saw it, but failed to identify it. A search was instituted for every missing woman in the Luton area – an astounding 404 – and all were accounted for. Another 681 women whose addresses were unknown were traced. Thirty-nine members of the public went to view the body in the mortuary, and four of them thought they knew the dead woman's identity, but proved to be mistaken.

One of the main factories in Luton – then as now – was the Vauxhall works; 250 lorry drivers who had called there were interviewed. None could help the police.

Since the woman's clothes were missing, the detectives checked all cleaners. If the clothes were bloodstained, it was just possible that the murderer had taken them to be cleaned – or that he had taken his own. This idea also led nowhere. The police conducted thousands of door-to-door interviews, and they actually spoke to the two boys who had seen the photograph in the shop-window; the boys thought it unnecessary to mention that their mother had left home. In any case, they failed to recognize the photograph – with the swollen face – as their mother. One neighbour did, in fact, think that he recognized it, and wanted to go to the police, but his wife told him 'not to be a damned fool.'

Rubbish dumps were searched for discarded items of women's clothing, and dozens were found. Most were unidentified; those that were had nothing to do with a missing woman.

The months dragged on – December, January, February – and the enquiry seemed to have reached a dead-end. Unable to think of any new possibilities, the detectives decided – on 21 February – on a thorough review of the evidence they already had. Among this was a black coat which had been cut up – a fact which, in days of clothes rationing, aroused suspicion. But the coat had been unidentifiable, until the 'review', when a dyer's tag was found inside it. The shop was traced, and the records showed that the coat had belonged to a Mrs Rene Manton, who lived at 14, Regent Street, Luton.

Chapman went to the house, and the door was opened by a ten-year-old girl who identified herself as Sheila Manton. For the first time in weeks, Chapman experienced a flash of optimism. Sheila undoubtedly bore a resemblance to the dead woman. She explained that her mother had left home some time ago, and had gone to stay with *her* mother, then her brother in Grantham. He asked if she had a photograph of her mother. The photograph confirmed his belief that he had found the victim's identity.

Chapman also learned that Rene Manton's mother, Mrs Bavister, lived nearby in Luton. He went to visit her, and discovered that she was a half-blind old lady, who flatly denied that her daughter had come to stay with her after leaving her husband. She had received four letters from her daughter since last November, all sent from an address in Hampstead. Chapman noticed that the letters had a number of spelling mistakes, which included 'Hampstead' spelt without the 'p'.

Rene Manton's husband Bertie proved to be a member of the National Fire Service; he had once been a light-weight boxer. Chapman went to see him at the station. Manton admitted that he and his wife – whom he married in 1926 – often had violent quarrels. She had left him once before, and he suspected that she was unfaithful to him with soldiers, although Manton also admitted that she objected to a certain barmaid of his acquaintance. Mrs Manton, said her husband, had 'slung her hook' after a quarrel last November – he gave the date as 25 November, six days after the finding of the body – and had gone to stay with her mother. He remembered the date she left home because it was the last day of his annual leave. He said that his wife had been home since then to collect her clothes, and identified the letters received by her mother as being in his wife's handwriting. When shown the photograph of the body he said: 'That's nothing like her. I wouldn't do a thing like that.'

Manton provided the name of Mrs Manton's dentist. When shown the photograph of his patient in life, he instantly recognized it. He had removed all the dead woman's teeth – except for three roots which she refused to have extracted – and provided her with false teeth. His records showed the exact position of the roots. A check with the plaster-cast of the victim's jaws left no doubt that this was Mrs Manton.

Further enquiries revealed that Manton's annual leave had ended on the eighteenth – the day of the murder – not, as he said, 25 November.

Asked to note down various addresses for the police, Manton spelled Hampstead without the 'p'. And when he copied one of the letters sent to his mother-in-law, it was obvious that the handwriting was his, not his wife's.

One more thing was needed to confirm that Mrs Manton was indeed the dead woman. The Yard's chief fingerprint expert Fred Cherrill was called to Luton to try to find a fingerprint that matched those of the corpse. After searching for hours, he had to admit that it seemed hopeless; someone had polished every cup, plate, cupboard-door and shelf. But finally, under the stairs, he saw a cellar-like cupboard, with a shelf of jamjars and bottles. Cherrill tested them one after another, and again had to admit that whoever had cleaned them had been thorough. Finally, only one bottle was left, lurking in a dark corner – a pickle jar. The layer of dust on its sloping neck revealed that it had not been cleaned. It was this jar that yielded a thumbprint which proved to be that of the dead woman.

Chapman went to Manton and charged him with the murder. Manton immediately broke down and admitted it. 'I killed her, but it was only because I lost my temper. I didn't intend to.'

His story was that he and Rene had quarrelled around midday on 18 November. She had flung a cup of hot tea in his face with the words: 'I hope it blinds you.' He had grabbed a heavy wooden stool and hit her several times with it. She fell backwards on the floor.

After this, he said, he decided he had to get rid of the body. He undressed her, tied her knees, then cut open four sacks from the cellar, wrapped her in them, then hid the body in the cellar. When the children had gone to bed that night, he laid the sack on his bicycle and wheeled it to the river.

The next day he had burned her clothes and false teeth. For some reason, he overlooked the black coat, and later made a partial attempt to cut it up, and then threw it on a rubbish dump. This was his one mistake in the 'nearly perfect murder.'

But was it murder, or simply manslaughter? It was the medical evidence that finally condemned him. If he had simply struck his wife with the stool, it would probably have been accepted as manslaughter. But the marks on the throat showed that her husband had throttled her after knocking her down. In court, he admitted to Richard O'Sullivan, the Crown counsel, that he had 'grabbed her twice.' That admission made it clear that he had intended to kill her.

Manton was found guilty of the murder of his wife and sentenced to death. His appeal was turned down, but a petition organized by his children and fellow workers collected over 26,000 signatures, and he was finally reprieved. Broken in health, he died of cancer in Parkhurst prison three years later.

15

The Fingerless Strangler

On the afternoon of 21 December 1943, two plain clothes policemen arrested a man whom they suspected of trying to sell stolen goods on London's Waterloo Road. The offence was relatively minor – the man was only trying to sell a pair of shoes that he had probably taken from a tramp or a drunk. As soon as the officers laid hands on the suspect however, he began spouting confessions to other, considerably more violent crimes. 'I am wanted for other things far more serious than this . . . I have been a bastard all my life, and I will finish as I have lived.' He handed a silver cigarette case to one of the officers: 'This is a Christmas box for you. I know this will be my last Christmas.' By the time he was safely at Kennington Road Police Station, he had confessed to robbery, assault, and murder.

Harold Loughans was the man's name, and he evidently believed that Scotland Yard was hotly pursuing him. Indeed, checking their records, the officers found that Loughans had an appalling criminal record – not only was he clearly a habitual criminal, but he was always getting caught. He had spent 28 of his 47 years in prison. Robbery was his main area of activity, often involving assault. He had never been charged with murder. Yet here before them the guilt-ridden Loughans was admitting to doing 'the murder job in Hampshire.' The London police had no idea what he was talking about. Scotland Yard was unaware of any such case at the moment. They were inclined to suspect Loughans of being one of the false informants that plague police stations throughout the country. Yet, something in his manner told them that he could be telling the truth. They took a statement and contacted the Hampshire police.

The statement described a murderous attack on a Portsmouth pub landlady. Loughans explained that he had heard that his victim was in the habit of keeping the night's takings in her bedroom, ready to be taken to the bank the next morning. This would be a temptingly large sum, amounting to hundreds of pounds. Loughans told how, on a night late in November, he had crept over the wall of the pub and gained entry to the building through the kitchen window. Just as he had found the bedroom and was about to grab the money, the landlady woke up and screamed. He had clutched her throat to silence her. They had landed in a heap on the floor – but when the landlady made no attempt to struggle, it dawned on Loughans that she must have had a heart attack. Disgusted by her fixed grimace, he had covered her face with a cloth, collected the money and escaped.

The story sounded genuine, and the Portsmouth police soon confirmed that they were investigating the murder of a Mrs Rose Ada Robinson, landlady of the 'John Barleycorn' in Portsmouth, and the theft of the pub's takings. Some of the details that Loughans had furnished were not only accurate, but had not appeared in the rather vague newspaper coverage that had followed the crime. Loughans was held and asked to make a further statement in the presence of the Portsmouth officers.

Back in the previous November, police investigating the crime scene had found little to point them towards a possible suspect. A sleepless neighbour had told them that she had heard noises in the 'John Barleycorn' at around three in the morning. In Mrs Robinson's bedroom the blackout curtain had been pulled off the window; it lay on the floor by the victim's body. Searching the room, police only located one small clue, a jacket button with a short length of thread attached to it, lying on the windowsill. Most of the evidence was turned over to Dr Walls at the forensic laboratory in Hendon. Despite extensive testing of the bedclothes, floor mats and the handbags that had contained the money, no more information on the crime had emerged.

With no further leads to aid them in their search, Portsmouth police had eventually dropped the investigation. Now it seemed that luck had delivered a suspect to them. Loughans made statement after statement, adding more details every time. The sum stolen, the fact that it was contained in two handbags placed upon a glass-topped dresser and the fact that the victim had worn no rings, were all mentioned in the confessions. He had not meant to kill the woman, said Loughans, and remorse had driven him to confess. Police could hardly believe their luck. There was however one small problem.

Dr Keith Simpson, the forensic pathologist who had examined Mrs Robinson's body on the morning of 29 November, had noted that the throat was bruised in two places, one on either side of the voice box, altogether spanning about 4 inches. This suggested to him that a single hand had been applied to the throat. The mark on the right of the throat was the largest and most livid, making it seem likely that the murderer had used his right hand. Harold Loughans' right hand was severely damaged, each of the four fingers having been sheared off halfway by an accident in a brickyard when he was a child. His thumb was intact however. Could the mangled fingers have made the marks upon the left side of Mrs Robinson's throat?

The person to ask would clearly be Dr Simpson himself, but this proved to be a problem. Simpson seemed dubious about the notion of a pathologist examining a living suspect. Nevertheless, he agreed instead to study life-size photographs of Harold Loughans' hand.

In the event, Simpson's conclusions supported Loughan's claims. The bruise on the right-hand side of Mrs Robinson's throat, made by the murderer's thumb, ended in a small cut, caused by the thumbnail. The left-hand marks did not end in similar cuts, just as Loughans' four fingers had no nails. As for the question of whether the damaged hand could have made those bruises, Simpson concluded that there was no reason why not. Loughans hand still spanned the 4 inches between the two marks. Also, Simpson reasoned, according to the principle of leverage, smaller fingers should be able to exert a greater pressure than longer ones.

Loughans' clothing and specimens of his hair were sent to the police laboratory. Some of the thread used to repair his jacket was similar to that found attached to the button on the windowsill of Mrs Robinson's bedroom. This evidence would almost certainly be inadmissible at any trial because the thread had come from Parkhurst Prison tailor's shop, Loughans' last government residence. Previous convictions cannot be brought up in a trial unless it is at the specific request of the defence. The only other clue the scientists had, a hair found in one of the handbags, proved as they suspected, not to belong to the suspect but to Mrs Robinson herself.

So the forensic evidence was at best equivocal. Yet there were still the numerous confessions of guilt from Loughans, the details of which suggested an inside knowledge of the crime. These alone would go a long way towards convicting him. Which explains why the police were distressed and annoyed when, at the committal hearing at Hampshire Assizes, Loughans' representative announced that his client was withdrawing all confessions.

The hearing began in March 1944, with J.D. Casswell, KC prosecuting and John Maude, KC defending.

Loughans, Maude said, had confessed in order to annoy the police, and had got his original knowledge of the case from a piece in the *News of the World* of 5 December 1943. After he had started a vague confession, Maude said, Loughans had been provided with details by the interrogating officers, in the form of leading questions. Maude pointed out that in the statement given to the Metropolitan police, who knew nothing of the case, Loughans had made several mistakes. These errors were corrected progressively in the series of statements given to the Portsmouth police, who of course knew all the details of the crime.

It did seem that there may have been some police prompting. For example in Loughans' first statement to Scotland Yard, he had said: 'I was looking through a room when the woman came in ... I just put my hands around her throat ... I think I got the money out of a little desk ...' This is vague and inaccurate. A later statement given to the Portsmouth police was nearer the facts: 'In the back-room I saw a woman ... I grabbed her by the throat with my right hand . . . There were two large handbags full of money . . .'

Loughans could, of course, have just remembered more as the interrogation went on. Yet the defence's argument sounded plausible. On the other hand, it was also true that Loughans had got some unpublished details correct even in his first statement. The jury was going to have to make a difficult decision.

In questioning Keith Simpson on his medical evidence, Maude almost succeeded in trapping the renowned pathologist. The defence was evidently very unhappy that the Crown's medical evidence had been deduced from photographs rather than from a genuine medical examination. Maude had seen this as a weakness in the Crown case and duly attacked.

He began his questioning by producing *Gray's Anatomy*, the standard textbook on the subject. He asked Simpson if he was familiar with the book, then proceeded to more specific questions giving page references. Maude was evidently about to produce a contradiction between Simpson's procedure and the textbook method. Faced with the prospect of this kind of humiliation Simpson responded with some trickery of his own. Before Maude could produce his killer question, Simpson asked which edition of *Gray's Anatomy* he was using. Maude replied that it was the twenty-eighth. That edition, Simpson regretted to inform the counsel, was out of date. Simpson knew this because, as a young man, he had performed some of the dissections that were photographed to illustrate the book. Thus he always received a pre-release complimentary copy of each new edition. The day before he was called to give evidence, the twenty-ninth edition had landed on his doormat. The judge, loathe to allow facts from antiquated

textbooks to cloud the issue, disallowed the line of
questioning.

This setback did not trouble Maude at all, for he had
yet to reveal his most convincing piece of evidence. A
firm of private investigators engaged by the defence had
succeeded in finding five people who had seen Loughans
sheltering from the bombings in Warren Street tube
station on the night of the murder. Among these were
two London Transport officials. Each witness was called
before the court by Maude and performed well under
questioning, insisting they had seen Loughans on that
particular night. His crippled hand made him easy to
remember.

The jury retired, and were presumably very confused
by the strong evidence upon both sides. They were
unable to reach a verdict. A date for a re-trial was set
for the Old Bailey.

In the intervening time Maude and Casswell set
to work destroying each other's cases. The medical
evidence still troubled Maude, and he looked into the
possibility of getting a second opinion on Loughans'
ability to commit the murder. Casswell attacked the
Warren Street alibi, tracking down the people who had
seen Loughans and trying to find discrepancies.

Two weeks after the indecisive verdict at Hampshire
Assizes, the Loughans case re-opened at the Old Bailey.
Both counsels seemed to have achieved little in terms
of improving and refining their evidence; the pattern
of witnesses and questions was virtually identical. This
changed however, when Simpson returned to the stand.
This time he was subjected to a thorough interrogation on Loughans' injury and its effects. Simpson
maintained that his previous assessment from photographs was sound and accurate, and that the marks on

Mrs Robinson's throat could have been produced by the hands of the accused.

Maude's next witness was Sir Bernard Spilsbury. Spilsbury was the most respected authority on forensic medicine in the country. He had been Simpson's predecessor and in that capacity had appeared as an expert witness in hundreds of criminal trials. Maude had engaged Spilsbury to test the extent of Loughans' hand injury while visiting him in prison. Before the court, Spilsbury testified that when he had asked Loughans to grip his hand as hard as he could, he found the resulting pressure in no way sufficient to strangle anyone. Such was Spilsbury's reputation that this rather suspect opinion was greeted as important evidence. On cross-examination Casswell brought up the obvious objection to Spilsbury's testimony. Loughans knew very well that he *had* to show his grip to be weak. Any other result would almost certainly have seen him hanged. Could there not, Casswell asked Spilsbury, have been some element of deception in Loughans' test results? None, Spilsbury believed. He also testified that he found Simpson's 'blind' assumption that shorter fingers can exert greater pressure, overly academic. Sir Bernard was a convincing witness, and his evidence, combined with that of the witnesses from Warren Street tube station, certainly undermined the case against Loughans. The Crown's medical evidence was in tatters. In his autobiography, Dr Simpson speculates that Spilsbury was in some way expressing jealousy of his celebrated successor by offering such weak evidence. Certainly, to anyone who accepted Spilsbury's assessment, Simpson's decision not to physically examine Loughans looked exceedingly irresponsible. The Crown was losing ground rapidly.

Casswell had planned to challenge the defence with

a new piece of evidence. Unfortunately, the judge ruled against it, on the grounds that it had come too late. This was true, but it was not Casswell's fault. He had been obliged to wait until he was certain that Loughans would be presenting the alibi involving Warren Street tube station, for the new evidence was intended to undermine the alibi. By the time the Warren Street witnesses had repeated their evidence, the judge ruled it too late.

So no one was surprised when the jury returned finding Loughans innocent of the murder of Rose Ada Robinson. Maude had done an excellent job of demolishing the Crown's case. On the steps of the Old Bailey, as he paused to savour his triumph, Loughans was arrested on a charge of aggravated robbery committed in St Albans. For this crime he eventually received seven years in prison, to be followed by seven years preventive detention. So in fact his acquittal of the murder charge proved to be a phantom victory.

Oddly enough, the case was far from over – two trials for the same crime were not enough for Harold Loughans. Sixteen years after the end of the Old Bailey trial, he instituted a libel action against the publishers of *The People* newspaper, and also against the newspaper's editor, and Mr J.D. Casswell, KC, his old prosecutor.

Casswell had eventually retired and written his autobiography, entitled *A Lance For Liberty*. As is common with books that contain anything at all sensational, the work was being serialized before publication in a Sunday newspaper. The previous four instalments of the barrister's story, partially re-written for *The People* by a sub-editor, had been well received. The fifth concerned the two Loughans trials. Casswell was evidently still very angry that his rebuttal evidence had never seen the light of day, and used his memoirs to finally reveal what he had discovered.

Back in 1944, between the Hampshire and Old Bailey trials, Casswell had tried to interview all the five witnesses that said they had seen Harold Loughans sheltering in Warren Street tube station on the night of 28/29 November. Looking back through their evidence, Casswell noted that only one of the witnesses had seen Loughans between midnight and five in the morning. If this witness, who was not one of the Underground employees but only another seeker of shelter, proved to be wrong or lying, Loughans had a clear five hours in which he could have driven to Portsmouth, committed the robbery and murder, and then returned. To test whether it was possible to drive that distance and commit burglary in five hours, Casswell asked two Portsmouth detectives to try the feat. They made the return journey with quarter of an hour to spare, including a half hour 'rest' at the pub. This was the evidence that Casswell had fought to have admitted at the Old Bailey trial. He clearly felt that it could have reversed the jury's decision.

What Casswell had written implied that Loughans was lucky to get off, and that he was probably guilty. Realizing the dangerous nature of such allegations, Casswell's publishers had inserted a dryly-worded disclaimer towards the end of the account. In its wisdom, *The People* did not include such a disclaimer when they previewed Casswell's book, hence Loughans writ of libel against them.

In November 1960, the time of the article's publication, Loughans was once again in prison, in Wormwood Scrubs. Both he and his lawyer soon realized that the ill-considered *People* story was a stroke of luck, and immediately signalled their intention to sue. As a result, the serialization of Casswell's book was suspended.

Preparations dragged on until early 1963, when the case finally came to court. Acting for Mr Loughans in the case were Patrick O'Connor, QC and Stanley Waldman. Acting for the group of defendants were J. T. Molony, QC and Hugh Davidson. The proceedings took place before Mr Justice Gorman.

Defending a libel writ usually depends upon the choice of one of two lines of argument, (a) that the passage in question does not mean what the plaintiff maintains that it means, or (b) that if it does, then it is true. In an attempt to prove the former, Molony and Davidson produced the prospective publisher of Casswell's book who told them of the disclaimer that they intended to include. This effectively put the blame solely on *The People*: It had been their mistake. They could only defend their case by taking line (b): that Loughans had, in fact, murdered Rose Ada Robinson 16 years earlier.

The same witnesses were recalled. Most of them were still alive and willing to give evidence. The main exception was Sir Bernard Spilsbury, who had committed suicide in 1947. In his place, Loughans managed to convince another two doctors to testify that he could not use his right hand.

Loughans' problem in this, his third trial, was that now he had to prove his innocence. Whereas before he had only to introduce a reasonable doubt that he had committed the crime, now he would have to prove he hadn't or lose his case and be legally proclaimed a murderer.

In opposition to his counsels' evidence, Molony and Davidson introduced testimony about Loughans' other crimes. In a criminal trial this would never have been allowed; but in a civil case, Molony could legally point out that in the St Albans robbery, for which Loughans was arrested immediately after his acquittal for the Robinson case, the 'crippled' hand had sufficient strength to tie a woman to a bed with the flex of an electric fire. As Molony reeled off crime after crime it began to seem more and more like a miracle that the man's cat-burgling activities had not induced more heart attacks.

The verdict vindicated Casswell. After almost 20 years, a jury finally found Loughans guilty of Mrs Robinson's murder. Casswell, *The People*, and its editor were all acquitted of libel on the grounds that what they had said was true, and that Loughans was indeed a murderer. Nothing, of course, could be done about this since Loughans had already been tried for the crime. He was, in fact, almost beyond justice anyway, suffering as he was from terminal stomach cancer.

A few months after Casswell's acquittal, in May 1963, Loughans approached *The People* with his own story. It was a confession. Photographed by the paper writing with his right hand, Loughans admitted to Mrs Robinson's murder in a signed confession. The document appeared as an 'exclusive' the following week.

Two facts are worth noting about Loughans' damaged hand. Firstly, Professor Francis Camps, one of the doctors called upon to replace Sir Bernard Spilsbury at the libel trial, measured Loughans' grip as exerting 14 pounds, at a time when he was well into his sixties and suffering with advanced cancer. Secondly, although Loughans probably did not strangle Mrs Robinson with pressure from his crippled hand, he could easily, from his position astride her, have merely leant on her neck with both arms and hands tensed. This could have produced the bruising of the throat, and induced the heart attack. After all, Loughans' nickname in prison, derived from his skill at working with his disability, was 'Handy'.

16

The Death of the Lord of Life

King Ananda VII of Siam died from a gunshot wound to the head at around 9.20 on the morning of 9 June 1946. He was 20 years old. Lying by his left hand was a Colt ·45 revolver. He was discovered by Nai Chit Singhaseni, one of the king's bedchamber pages. These facts are undisputed; little else about the case is as uncontroversial.

'The king has shot himself!' Nai Chit screamed, and ran to find the princess mother and the guard. Princess Sangwala, when she arrived, held the bloodied body of her son and cried and threatened suicide. The ceremonial processes of washing and preserving the dead king began shortly afterwards.

Around seven o'clock that evening the country was told of Ananda's death: 'His Majesty, King Ananda Mahidol, has died in an accidental gun explosion.' Associated News Agencies carried the story around the world: 'The young King of Siam ... was found dead in a bedroom at the Barompiman Palace in Bangkok today with a bullet wound in his head ... [it was] said afterwards that death was accidental.' A silent crowd gathered outside the palace. Whether they were expecting further news or simply paying last respects was not clear.

King Ananda Mahidol VII, called Lord of Life, Brother of the Moon, Supreme Arbiter of the Ebb and Flow of the Tide, Possessor of Four and Twenty Golden Umbrellas, had been nephew to the previous monarch, King Prajhadipok. Prince Mahidol, Ananda's father, had had an affair with a commoner named Sangwala. The couple had met in America, while Mahidol was at Harvard and Sangwala had been attending Massachusetts Nursing College. Although Sangwala's low origin was deplored by the royal family and their hangers-on, she was allowed, on their return, to become a princess. Her children eventually proved to include the only blood-heir of the dynasty: young Ananda.

To follow the example of his parents Ananda was sent to be educated abroad. In his case Switzerland was selected, a preparatory school in Lausanne. The school, staffed by teachers from all over Europe, stressed the mental and physical development of its pupils. The skiing and scholarship suited the young prince and he became strongly attached to European political and intellectual principles.

The notion of returning to Siam and perhaps becoming a king must have seemed incredible and strange to this boy who was treated without ceremony by his school friends and teachers.

But in 1935, Ananda's uncle fled Siam and an uprising, and the nine-year-old prince found himself a ruling monarch. His deposed uncle decided to settle in London, from where he issued a terse, belated abdication statement.

Until the new king attained his majority, at 12, a council of regents was appointed. For the next three years Ananda skied, studied and attended plays just as he had before. Yet the necessary return to Siam and his coronation were always there on the horizon, threatening his happiness.

Finally the dreaded time came. When he stepped off the plane into his newly-acquired kingdom, the 12-year-old king was greeted by shock-waves of noise: trumpets, artillery, conch-shells, gongs, ship's sirens and fireworks. The opulent coronation was followed quickly by religious ceremonies that required Ananda's presence, fairs that needed to be opened and streams of representations from the populace.

When eventually the king returned to Switzerland to complete his education, his relief must have been enormous. Asked by a European interviewer if being king was fun, the poor 12-year-old replied that he would rather stay in Switzerland and play with his electric trains. The interviewer responded that, surely, as King of all Siam, he had bigger and better electric trains with which to play. Ananda answered: 'No, they'd never give me a chance to play with them.'

The king continued his schooling in Lausanne, taking up the saxophone and, oddly for such an apparently unaggressive child, developing an impressive knowledge of all kinds of firearms. It must have seemed something like a reprieve when, just before he was scheduled to return and finally take up the duties of kingship, Japan invaded Siam. The Japanese styled the occupation as a 'radical co-operative economic plan', and insisted that it was not in any way an issue of sovereignty. Consequently the king was informed that he was welcome to return and head a puppet administration. Ananda took the opportunity to ignore the world situation, and to remain in Switzerland, taking appropriately enough, a neutral point of view.

In his place the Siamese administration was headed

by Marshal Phibul Songgram, who gladly volunteered his own forces to aid the Japanese in their fight against the Allies. A pro-Allies resistance movement, led by a politician named Nai Pridi, took up the fight against Japan through terrorist attacks on army supply lines and general disruption. They also aided Allied soldiers in escapes from the prison camps run by Songgram's Siamese troops. The war took its course and with the collapse of the 'Greater East Asian Co-Prosperity Sphere', Nai Pridi was made head of government and Marshal Songgram was banished for war crimes. With Songgram gone, and a new order about to commence, Ananda could find no excuse to remain abroad. In December 1945 he returned to Siam.

At this time the country hovered uncomfortably between notions of democracy and feudalism. Officially the government of the country was conducted by a legislature, of which half was democratically elected. But this was combined with a system that was a hangover from centuries of dynastic rule. Ananda's grandfather King Chulalongkorn, had fathered 362 children, with the help of 84 wives. Each of these offspring was guaranteed a government post or a position high up in the army command structure. Democracy and nepotism co-existed in a continual state of tension. Ananda was the focal point of this tension: the figurehead of the dynasty who, personally, wished to abolish the monarchy.

Ananda's love of democracy and liberalism was well known to the advisers around him, forcing them to discreet but determined efforts to thwart his plans. An idea from Shaw's play *The Apple Cart* had fired Ananda's imagination: he planned to resign his royal title and stand as a candidate in a democratic election. Understandably Ananda's immediate circle of advisers counselled him against the project, insisting that now was not the right time to reverse ancient tradition.

The king's life was a depressing one. Wherever he went, people threw themselves on to the ground and abased themselves at his feet; Ananda hated this. The only royal command that they refused to obey was to stand up and behave normally. Faced with this kind of exhausting devotion, Ananda preferred to hide in his chambers in the palace. Periodically, he emerged into the courtyard to engage in target practice.

Ministers who deplored these eccentricities also had to admit that portents for Ananda's reign were inauspicious. According to tradition the greatness of a king could be measured by the number of white elephants that are captured in the country during his reign. All white elephants (they are actually only slightly pink) are the property of the king. He is expected to provide them with a home and food for the rest of their lives. In his first year Ananda only received two such beasts, and one of them was said to be a borderline-case normal elephant.

All the intellectual training that Ananda tried to bring to bear upon Siam's problems was rejected. The politics and economics that he had learnt in school were hopelessly Eurocentric. Yet Ananda naively pressed on with his schemes. Outside the palace stood a pagoda, the Wat Arun, built by one of Ananda's recent ancestors. In his wisdom this ancestor had decorated every inch of the tower's surface with European crockery and kitchen utensils. Casually suggesting that it should be knocked down and replaced with something more useful, Ananda was greeted with expressions of horror and disbelief from his associates. Patient attempts at explanation made no difference; no real communication was taking place.

Three months of this was all that Ananda could take. Although his monarchy could offer him nothing that he wanted in Siam, back in the West that he loved it would make him the friend of princes. Ananda had made Lord Mountbatten a member of the Exalted Order of the Sacred White Elephant. That should be sufficient to furnish him with an invitation to visit. He could make this trip abroad into a tour and take in America and President Truman. These plans filled him with a new optimism. But it was not to be.

As Ananda's vision of his country's future became common knowledge, his popularity with his subjects decreased. It is widely believed that the bout of stomach illness that incapacitated the king on and after 7 June 1946 was in fact a failed attempt at poisoning. Whatever the cause, Ananda was laid low with severe stomach pains for two days. On the third morning, 9 June, as we have seen, he was found dead.

The period of time between the discovery of the king's body and the announcement of his death was filled with ceremony and ablution. The police were called an hour after the body was found. After a short examination, the chief of police was sent away again and the body was thoroughly scrubbed. Finally it was placed in a huge golden urn.

Meanwhile the palace servants worked hard to remove all signs of blood and tissue from the royal bedroom. Scientific investigation of the scene of death was rendered impossible. Even the position of the body was not certain. Most accounts have it lying on the floor, some still in bed.

Towards evening, the announcement was made. The news was painful for the Siamese people, who in spite of everything felt a great affection for their monarch. The brief statement, 'killed in an accidental gun explosion,' was all that the populace was told, a situation difficult to visualize in the modern age of active electronic news-gathering. Two days after the death, a clarification of the previous statement appeared. It stated that Ananda's death must have been accidental, since he was too happy to commit suicide and the palace too secure to admit assassins. The statement also made the extraordinary claim that His Highness had been seen peering down the barrel of a gun while remarking on the lightness of its trigger mechanism earlier in the day. This only aroused suspicion. It was common knowledge that Ananda was a firearms expert. Even a hobbyist knows that the first rule of gun-care is never to stare down the barrel of a loaded weapon when the safety-catch is off.

The king lay in state, on display to the public. A silent queue shuffled sadly past his coffin. For most it was the first chance they had had to discover the nature of the fatal wound. A small red hole in the head, just above the left eye drew everyone's eyes. The bullet could still be seen, deep in the wound.

Whether the king's death had been accidental or not, it seemed more than a little suspicious. The democratic principles that Ananda had supported now began to make themselves felt in the country: the legislature started asking questions. The police even began arresting people on a new charge of 'not believing in the accidental nature of the king's death.' Yet still the legislature remained sceptical: If the shot had been fired from the king's own hand, why were there no powder burns on his face? To silence their prattle, the police sent an armed officer with a live pig to the House. There, the officer shot the pig in front of the representatives, at close range. Anyone who wished was allowed to inspect the wound, and confirm that there were no powder burns. In this way the police combined a rebuttal with an implied threat.

More scandal was on its way. Shortly after the legislature had confirmed Ananda's brother Pumipol as the next king, Prime Minister Nai Pridi resigned. It was, the government assured the nation, a routine occurrence. Naturally everyone assumed the worst. The dangerous political unrest provoked by the resignation could only be calmed by justice being seen to be done; a public enquiry was announced.

On 26 June, the evidence of 21 doctors was heard by the Commission of Inquiry. These medical men from around the world had tried to piece together some information of the nature of the king's death. They had examined the king's preserved body and removed the bullet from his head. The general consensus was that the accident theory of Ananda's death had to be discounted. Either it had been suicide or assassination, but certainly not an accident. The Colt automatic that was found near the body would not, they said, have fired accidentally in such a way; the wound was inconsistent with such a theory.

The government was now in a painful position. Whether intentionally or not they had been covering up an unlawful death. The people felt that they could no longer trust their representatives; they needed someone free of the taint of corruption to judge the evidence. Opportunely Marshal Songgram reappeared in the country. The government staggered on, the enquiry suspended, until November 1947 when Songgram, with the help of some British Army surplus tanks, headed a bloodless coup. With the new regime, Siam became Thailand.

Democracy was temporarily revoked, although Songgram's plans included a more liberal package of democratic reforms than had existed previously. These would have to wait. Songgram's purpose as ruler was, he said, to discover who had killed their beloved king. Soon Nai Chit and Butr, the king's two pages were in custody, along with Chaleo Pathumros, the king's private secretary. In their absence Nai Pridi and the king's former ADC were charged; both had fled the country.

The police began gathering information, and lawyers were assembled. Unfortunately the two original defence lawyers were shot dead while trying to escape a police patrol. Those appointed in their place were immediately arrested for plotting to overthrow the government and were forced to commute from their cells to those of their clients.

By April 1949 the police had completed their information gathering. They duly presented their case to the Director of Public Prosecutions. He resigned rather than give it his approval. A more willing successor was soon located and the hearings began. The defence, faced with a mountainous pile of documentary evidence collected by the state, asked for an adjournment in order to acquire some familiarity with it. Unfortunately this was denied and the hearings proceeded.

Nai Chit and Butr were the main suspects, in the absence of the person that Songgram would have really loved to have executed: his post-war replacement Nai Pridi. The servants were expendable and it would be easy to argue that they had opportunity, if not necessarily motive. Moreover, it was revealed that Nai Chit should not even have been at the palace on that morning. He and Butr alternated duty shifts, and that morning Butr was working. Nai Chit's explanation for his presence was

that he had been asked to measure the royal medals by
the royal jeweller, who was planning to make containers
for them.

Butr testified that he had seen the king rise on the
morning of his death to take his medicine. After this,
Butr said, he had brought the king some orange-juice.
Ananda had refused it. At 9 a.m. the king's brother
Pumipol had visited. He said that he had found Ananda
dozing lightly and had gone away. Around 9.20 the shot
was heard. Nai Chit said that he had ran back and forth
around the palace screaming: 'the king's shot himself!'

This was the wrong thing to have said, in view of the
fact that the government firmly believed that the crime
was an assassination. If one assumes that there has been
an assassination, it follows that anyone protesting that it
was in fact a suicide, must surely be covering something
up. This was the attitude of the court.

The prosecution produced its version of events. It
was, briefly, that Nai Chit and Butr had conspired
with Chaleo and Nai Pridi to remove the king and
thus precipitate a shift in the political alignment of
the country. The Colt ·45 automatic found lying next to
Ananda was, according to this argument, planted there
by Butr in order to make the death seem a suicide.

The conspiracy was not precisely described by the
prosecution; suffice it to say that all the accused were
involved. To demonstrate this the prosecution called
124 witnesses. There was certainly much evidence to
suggest that the shooting was assassination. The police
reported that examination of the bed disclosed another
bullet buried in the mattress near Ananda's pillow. They
also pointed out that Ananda's near-sightedness would
have prevented him from 'examining' the gun without
his glasses, which were lying on his bedside table. There

were even plans afoot to call Dr Keith Simpson, the British Home Office pathologist to give evidence on the scientific aspects of the police's evidence.

The hearing dragged on. Sittings only took place for three days every fortnight. The medical evidence was supplied by 15 of the doctors from the original Commission of Inquiry. One after another they told the court that the signs seemed to point to regicide. The nature of the trial was beginning to emerge clearly. Having shown that the king was probably killed by *someone*, there must be thorough investigation and eventual punishment. By the time a verdict was presented, in May 1951, the defendants had already been imprisoned in terrible conditions for two years. The findings of the committee, described in a 50,000 word judgement, were that Chaleo was innocent of complicity, and that Nai Chit and Butr could not themselves have shot the king. However, due to certain perceived oddities in Nai Chit's evidence, he was found guilty of complicity with the unknown assassins and sentenced to death.

Both sides appealed, the defence against Nai Chit's conviction, the prosecution against the other defendants' release. The appeal court was convened and considered the evidence again over a period of 15 months. In a 14-hour judgement the court found that Butr had been wrongly acquitted and he too was sentenced to death. The case then went to the Supreme Court. A further ten months passed, at the end of which Chaleo was finally also convicted and sentenced to death.

In February 1955, the three men were lashed to wooden crosses and machine-gunned at close range. They had served almost six years in prison awaiting judgement.

The manner of Ananda's death remains mysterious.

The destruction of forensic evidence by the ceremonial cleansing of the body and the bedroom made that inevitable right from the beginning. If, as is widely accepted, Ananda's illness before the shooting was caused by poisoning, it seems likely that whoever administered the poison decided to finish him off with a bullet.

In this respect Nai Chit and Butr were uniquely placed to execute the plan, and the police's suspicion of them has to be seen in the light of this. Yet there was no real evidence against them, indeed no solid indications that the king was murdered and did not simply commit suicide.

The alienation caused by Ananda's education abroad, coupled with his recorded dislike for the attitudes of his own country must have been heavy burdens for the young king. Whatever his cause of death, it seems likely that it was linked to his immense difficulty in coping with these burdens.

— 17 —

Hitchhike to Murder

On 31 October 1946, a lorry driver on the A20, near West Malling in Kent, noticed a single discarded shoe lying in the road, and stopped to investigate. In the undergrowth a little way from the road, lay the fully-clothed body of a woman. The cause of death was obvious, a series of blue, ridged bruises on her throat. The Kent police, searching the area around the body, could find no clues to her identity. Apart from the strangulation marks, she seemed to have suffered only superficial injuries; her left eyelid and cheek were grazed, while the backs of her legs were scratched. When the investigation began to stall, the local police applied for assistance from Scotland Yard.

The Yard dispatched Inspector Bob Fabian, and he was accompanied by Keith Simpson, the Home Office's chief pathologist. Simpson performed an autopsy on the dead woman that evening. She was aged between 45 and 55, and was still a virgin. At the discovery site, Superintendent Frank Smeed, Chief of Kent CID, had made the comment that the torn stockings and leg scratches on the victim could indicate that she had been dragged to her final location after death. On examining the injuries more closely, Simpson saw that this seemed likely: the gouges on her legs could be consistent with the body being pulled over barbed wire.

Time of death, which Simpson estimated by calculating how far the corpse had cooled from body temperature, seemed to be between 7 and 9 a.m. that day. In this calculation, Simpson took into account the fact that in cases of asphyxiation, the victim's temperature rises by 4 to 6 degrees.

The strangulation bruising seemed to have been caused by a length of bunched-hard cloth held tight around the victim's throat. The flesh showed no sign of a knot in the material, the markings just faded at the back of the neck, slightly to the victim's left, showing that the murderer had worked from behind, clutching the ligature closed. Simpson estimated that the strangulation had taken between 25 and 30 seconds. Despite the great pressure of the cloth upon the flesh, no impression of the pattern of its weave was left. The cloth itself was nowhere to be found.

The forensic evidence uncovered by Simpson at the autopsy provided some interesting information. After death, the blood settles in the lowest areas of a corpse and congeals there, forming a permanent record of the body's position after death. Examining the victim, Simpson found that she had remained in a sitting-position for some time after strangulation.

Furthermore, by examining the areas of the corpse that would have been in contact with a seat, Simpson established that the woman had been sitting on a hard surface. Blood had not been able to accumulate and clot on the underside of the buttocks and upper legs due to the compression of the flesh against this surface. And since the corpse was found next to a road it seemed fair to assume that she had been sitting in a vehicle. Hard, unupholstered seats immediately suggested a lorry. Thus Fabian now ordered his officers to set about the difficult and labour-intensive task of finding every lorry that had passed along that stretch of the A20 on the morning of the 31 October.

The records of haulage firms and building companies were checked, lorry drivers' journey books thoroughly inspected. Drivers that had used the road that day were questioned and investigated. Yet nothing important was discovered; the line of inquiry seemed to have petered out.

Police working in the local area had, however, succeeded in identifying the dead woman. She was a Miss Dagmar Petrzywalski, aged 47, and known more commonly to the locals as Dagmar Peters. She had lived in a cramped bungalow on Hever Avenue in Kingsdown, only 20 yards from her mother's house. Mrs Petrzywalski, devastated to hear of her daughter's death, racked her brains for anything that might provide a lead.

She explained that Dagmar got up at 5 a.m. once every week so that she would have time to hitchhike the 30 miles into London, where she would visit her sister-in-law. This had happened on the day of her death. Normally, she said, Dagmar would be carrying a purse, the key to her bungalow, a brown attaché-case that contained her lunch, and a yellow string-bag that had been crocheted for her by another sister-in-law. On that particular morning, Dagmar also had a brown and black puppy with her, a present from her mother. More importantly, Dagmar's mother revealed that on the day of her death, Dagmar had been wearing a man's vest wrapped around her neck as a scarf. She had bought the vest in Maidstone on 29 October. The vest, Dr Simpson concluded, could easily have been the ligature that the murderer used to strangle her.

As none of the items that Mrs Petrzywalski had described were found with the body, the police had good reason to hope that their discovery would yield clues to the murderer's identity and movements. Pictures of a duplicate key and purse were released to the press, in the hope of jogging someone's memory. Meanwhile, the police began once again to search the undergrowth along the A20, hoping to find a trace of the items that Dagmar Peters had carried with her that fateful morning.

The newspaper campaign produced no new information, so Fabian decided to drive to Woking to locate the sister-in-law who had made the original yellow string-bag. Since the police were unable to buy a duplicate of the bag, he asked her if she could crochet a copy of it for them to photograph. Eager to aid the investigation she stayed up all night.

The second set of newspaper photographs, featuring the newly-made bag and the headline 'Have You Seen This?', produced a more positive response. A 16-year-old boy named Peter Nash was brought to the station by his father, and told police that he had found a bag exactly like the one shown in the paper floating in the lake near his father's farm in West Malling. Unfortunately he had given it away to their next-door neighbour. Chasing the only real clue that they had the police raced to the neighbour's house, only to be told that she too had given the bag away because even after a thorough washing, she did not like the look of it. The second recipient, who had also scrubbed it well, had come to the same conclusion and passed it on again. The police caught up with it with this third owner. Having been cleaned repeatedly the bag seemed unlikely to bear any telling physical clues to the murderer's identity. Nevertheless, forensic scientist H.S. Holden, Director of the Metropolitan Police Laboratory, examined it thoroughly.

There was indeed very little left on it. Holden located three kinds of hair entwined with the yellow fibres. One was brown and black, and came from an animal, almost certainly the puppy. The other two kinds were human. One of these was matched with the hair of the sister-in-law who had crocheted the bag, the other identified as the hair of one of the women who had received the bag from Peter Nash. In disposing of the bag the murderer had left no marks upon it, at least none that had survived the thorough washing to which it had been subjected. Fabian seemed, once again, to have reached a dead end.

The next day police searching the area around the A20 uncovered the torn remains of Dagmar Peters' brown attaché case, stuffed in the hedge of Winterfield Lane. Although it offered no obvious clues, the discovery was encouraging.

Fabian and his assistant Sergeant Rawlings spent some time surveying the evidence so far. Dagmar Peters' attaché case had been found by a road, consistent with the theory that the murderer was a driver. The police had collected over 1,500 statements from lorry drivers without exposing any new information about the murder victim's fate. Yet their other clue, the yellow string-bag, had been found one field away from the road, in a lake on the other side of an 8-foot fence. Why would the murderer go to the trouble of disposing of it there? What if the lake was not where the murderer had put the bag? What if it had only ended up there? Although the link was tenuous, Fabian decided to investigate the possibility that the bag had been dumped in one of the lake's feeding streams, and that it had floated to the place where Peter Nash had fished it out.

Someone who knew the area well was needed, someone who would know the paths of the local streams. Fabian consulted the Girl Guide mistress for the area, and she told him just what he needed to hear. The lake was fed, via an underground stream, from an old water-mill at East Malling where the Guide mistress had played as a child. Messages could be sealed in bottles and dropped in at the mill, where they would disappear underground. Hours later, the bottles would bob up in the old lake by the Nashes' house. The buildings of the mill now housed a cider works, and the route to the cider works from the place where Dagmar Peters' body had been discovered lay along Winterfield Lane, the place where the police had found her attaché case. Fabian set out for the mill to investigate.

He and Rawlings began by testing their theory about the stream using a bottle. An hour after the bottle slipped away under a culvert at the mill, it surfaced down in the lake. Several bottles later, Fabian felt that a test should be carried out with the actual string-bag, to conclusively prove the possibility of the journey he was suggesting. An hour after it went into the stream at the mill, there was still no sign of the bag. Finally, after three hours of increasing agitation, Fabian and Rawlings saw the bag bob up in the lake.

To prove that the string bag *could* have been dumped at the mill did not prove that this *had* happened, as Fabian well knew. Furthermore, none of the 1,500 drivers that had used the road admitted that they had either picked up or dropped anything at the mill on 31 October.

Looking around the cider works, Fabian noticed a

neat stack of bricks that seemed to have been newly delivered. The foreman at the works was unsure of the exact origin of the bricks, but he *was* sure that they were the responsibility of the firm of building sub-contractors that he had employed recently to do some work around the mill. Thinking carefully, he said that he thought the haulage firm who had delivered the bricks was based in Cambridge.

Checking this firm, Fabian learned that they had indeed made a delivery to East Malling on the morning of 31 October. A driver named Sydney Sinclair had dropped off the bricks in a 4-ton Albion lorry. When Fabian naturally asked where Sinclair was now, he was told that the driver had left the firm a week ago, and they did not know his present whereabouts.

Fabian could not understand how this information had not been turned up by the enormous police investigations into haulage firms. And why had no officer called at this particular business?

The answer, he discovered, was that the haulage firm lay on the boundary between the jurisdictions of the Cambridge City police and the Cambridgeshire County police. Both forces had assumed that the other had investigated the firm, with the result that neither of them had actually done so. Fortunately this loophole had now been closed; the next task was to trace Sydney Sinclair.

He did not prove difficult to find, and seemed to have no objections to helping the police. Fabian was soon facing the man across his desk. He was large and thick-set, and physically powerful. Fabian was almost certain that the man's name was an alias, and so he decided to try a bluff. Announcing forthrightly that he knew that Sinclair was not the driver's real name, Fabian was rewarded with an immediate admission that he was actually called Harold Hagger.

At first Hagger denied all knowledge of the murdered woman, but after hours of patient questioning about his route, he finally cracked and admitted to concealing the case and other of her belongings. His story was that he had just found the items, but then got scared and hid them. Fabian decided to take Hagger, in a police car, along the route that he had taken that day.

As they passed just beyond the place in the hedge of Winterfield Lane where the attaché case had been found, Hagger pointed into the foliage. That, he told Fabian, was where he threw the vest. Sure enough a man's vest of coarse cloth was found hidden in the bank.

Things were looking bad for Hagger, and they looked worse when Scotland Yard's files showed that he had sixteen previous convictions, including assault on a woman. He had been discharged from the services with psychological problems, including cerebral confusion.

Meanwhile, Simpson had examined the vest and found hair belonging to Dagmar Peters attached to it. When rolled up, it formed ridges that corresponded with the bruising on her neck. It seemed that it could very easily have been the murder weapon. If it was, it must have been removed from the body after death. Was it really plausible that Hagger had hidden the murder weapon yet had had nothing to do with the murder?

Fabian did not have to wait long for Hagger's confession. In an interview on 23 November 1946, the driver admitted that he had given Dagmar Peters a lift on the morning of 31 October. He said that she had asked him to pull over, and had then interfered with his jacket, which was hanging up in the cab, making him think that she was trying to steal his wallet. In the struggle, he supposed, he must have grabbed her scarf too tightly and for too long. She had died, and he had dumped the body by the side of the road. Her possessions he jettisoned at intervals along his route.

Hagger was charged with the murder of Dagmar Petrzywalski. On the advice of his defence lawyer, Mr E.A. Morling, he pleaded 'not guilty', on the grounds that he had not been in control of himself when the killing took place. It was given plausibility by the fact that there was very little in the way of motive that anyone could point to. The defence also underlined that Hagger was prone to fits of giddiness and 'cerebral confusion'. But in spite of this medical evidence, the jury returned the verdict of 'guilty'. They were perhaps not convinced by his insistence that he was driving without his jacket on a freezing morning in midwinter.

Hagger was hanged at Wandsworth Prison on 18 March 1947.

Although the Dagmar Peters case featured some of Fabian's finest detective work, it has to be said that if the Cambridge police had not overlooked the haulage firm for which Hagger worked, the case would have been relatively easy to solve. The fact that he was in the area would have identified Sinclair/Hagger as a suspect immediately, after which his record would have placed him at the top of the list of suspects. Fabian's great skill in deduction was in fact employed to make up for a basic failure in police-work.

18

The Body in the Chalkpit

In the evening gloom of Saturday, 30 November 1946, Dr Eric Gardner was to be found carefully working by torchlight at the base of the chalkpit near Woldingham in Surrey. On the instruction of the coroner, Gardner was making a preliminary examination of a freshly-discovered corpse. The man lay in a leafy trench, 6 feet long and just deep enough to accommodate him. His face was purple and swollen; around his neck there appeared to be some sort of noose. The body was cold to the touch, but still retained a fraction of its vital heat. Gardner estimated that death had occurred about 48 hours before. With night setting in, it was clear that the full examination would have to wait until morning.

Dr Keith Simpson stood by his old companion Dr Gardner as they made more thorough notes on the body's condition at around 9.30 the next morning. The man was fully dressed, wearing a pin-striped dark suit, shirt, and vest. Under the jacket he wore a waistcoat. He lay on his right side, arms raised in front of his head, seeming, in death, to be warding off a blow.

At first the forensic evidence seemed unequivocal: the man's face and scalp were spotted and streaked with tiny red lines, fractured blood vessels, strongly suggesting asphyxiation as the cause of death. These marks also stood out prominently in the whites of the dead man's eyes. The noose around his neck was tied with a single-hitch slipknot, made from thin, frayed rope entwined with some kind of soft green cloth. The signs seemed to point to murder by strangulation.

Yet this conclusion was soon complicated. When the body was moved it became clear that the rope was not as short as it looked; it snaked about the body down to the waist. This seemed to suggest suicide by hanging rather than murder. To add to the confusion, the man's neck bore a livid inverted V-shaped strangulation bruise, with its point under the left ear. This kind of mark also seemed to signify hanging. Thus suicide had to be considered as the case.

This assumption introduced another possibility: that the man had not intended suicide at all, but sexual gratification. Partial self-suspension is a relatively common method of intensifying masturbatory orgasm. The noose, attached above head level is kept tight, but not enough to cause loss of consciousness. Not uncommonly, cases of apparent suicide by hanging are actually instances of the above practice gone wrong. In this case, the soft green cloth entwined in the noose seemed to suggest that someone had gone to pains to make the noose comfortable. Further, the man's trouser braces were detached from their front buttons. However, his trouser-flies were closed, and even if the self-suspension theory were proved correct, that still failed to explain how he had come to be in the quarry.

There was of course, the remote possibility that the man could have rolled into the quarry after trying to hang himself from one of the trees at its edge. But police officers sent to examine the trees found no tell-tale friction-stripping of bark or frayed ends of rope hanging among the branches. And if someone had transported the body to the quarry, common sense seemed to point to murder.

Further examination of the corpse supported this view. The man's jacket, waistcoat, shirt and vest had ridden up around his shoulders at the back, suggesting his having been dragged by the feet. His shoes bore none of the mud and leaf-mould that covered the chalkpit floor. More disturbingly, upon moving the body the pathologists found the trench below it filled with fresh earth. This, combined with the small amounts of earth that they had seen on top of the body suggested an attempted burial.

Identification of the body was straightforward: in one of his pockets police found his identity card. He was John McMain Mudie, aged 35, a bartender at the Reigate Hill Hotel. Police went there to question Mudie's co-workers.

The hotel was located about 12 miles from the chalkpit. The employees there remembered Mudie as a quiet and pleasant man who was in no way unusual. He had last been seen leaving the hotel around five in the evening on Thursday 28 November 1946. This, according to Gardner's estimate, must have been only a few hours before he died.

A search through Mudie's possessions in his small room at the hotel revealed nothing to suggest that he engaged in curious sexual practices. But two letters seemed to raise doubts about his honesty. These were from a solicitor, and accused him of failing to pass on three unsigned cheques. They threatened legal action if they were not returned immediately. The cheques had, according to the letters, been given to Mudie by a property firm; he had been asked to pass them on to one of this firm's directors. The first of the letters had been sent to Mudie at an address in Wimbledon. The second followed shortly after, addressed to the Reigate Hill Hotel. Were the absent cheques an issue serious enough to lead to murder? It seemed unlikely, but meanwhile, the letters were the only lead.

While the officers at the hotel quizzed staff, Mudie's body was moved to a laboratory and examined further. Photographs of the dead man's bruising revealed something that had escaped the naked eye: a second neck bruise, running laterally around, forming a fainter base to the more livid inverted V-mark. The noose seemed to have been tightened before any hanging took place. Mudie's blood showed neither alcohol or drugs. Aside from the strangulation bruising, he had only superficial wounds: a bruise on the forehead, some internal haemorrhaging, two fractured ribs on the right side and some other trivial bruising all over. Most of these marks seemed consistent with a fall to the ground after hanging. Yet although there were no obvious signs of restraint on the corpse, and no signs of having resisted an assailant, all the other evidence pointed to murder by hanging. There were no clear conclusions that the pathologists could draw. In the light of the experts' confusion, police decided to appeal to the public, publishing details of the body's discovery along with Mudie's description.

Enquiries at the firm of solicitor's who had sent the letters soon elicited the name of the property firm to which the cheques had belonged. It was called Connaught Properties and the Chairman of the Board was Thomas Ley, a returned emigrant living in Kensington. Researching Ley's background, police were soon convinced that he was hardly the type to be involved in a murder. The

66-year-old qualified solicitor was an ex-Minister of Justice for the state of New South Wales, Australia. Yet there *was* a connection. One of Connaught Properties' directors, a Mrs Byron Brook, had lived in the same house in Wimbledon as Mudie. It was to her that the dead man had been asked to pass on the unsigned cheques.

Detective Sergeant Frederick Shoobridge had been assigned by the coroner to investigate Mudie's lodgings in Wimbledon. The landlady was a Mrs Evans, who described Mudie in much the same terms as his fellow employees at the hotel – quiet and pleasant enough. He had rented his bedsit for only six weeks, and Mrs Evans had not seen much of him during that time. But one occasion she clearly remembered was when she had introduced him to Mrs Byron – known as Maggie – Brook. Mrs Brook was staying in the house for only ten days, visiting her daughter who was also a tenant. One day Mrs Evans, with Mrs Brook, had met Mudie on the stairs, and Mrs Evans had introduced the pair. Afterwards, Mrs Brook asked Mrs Evans if the young man she had met was married. When Mrs Evans said no, Maggie Brook said that would not be true for long because he had such beautiful eyes . . .

The newspaper accounts of Mudie's death soon produced new information. Two landscape gardeners told the police that they had seen something suspicious at the chalkpit on Wednesday 28 November, the day before Mudie disappeared. A man had been moving around the top of the chalkpit, but when he saw that he was observed, he ran down to a parked car, reversed it at a reckless speed, and sped away. Neither of the witnesses was certain of the man's appearance; they had only caught a glimpse. They knew the car however. It was a small model, a Ford or Austin, in a dark colour. Both remembered that the licence registration plate contained the figures '101'.

Meanwhile Shoobridge's investigations had led him to Thomas Ley's Kensington home. Ley was an imposing figure of ample girth. He explained to Shoobridge that he had instructed his solicitors to pursue Mudie through a misunderstanding. Ley had thought that Mudie was a friend of Maggie Brook's, thus he sent the cheques to her in his care. By the time Mudie had received the cheques Maggie Brook had left the house. Thus Mudie had given them to his fellow tenant, Mrs Brook's daughter, who had delayed in handing them to her mother. Hearing nothing of their fate, Ley naturally assumed that Mudie had stolen the valuable documents. Maggie Brook was also present as Ley was questioned; she told Shoobridge that she had only seen Mudie once on the stairs, with Mrs Evans. The whole thing was a mistake.

The story of the cheques seemed overly contrived to Shoobridge, and so he decided to go to the property firm's files in order to establish the facts of the bizarre transaction. Among the day-to-day records, Shoobridge discovered the carbon of the original letter to Mudie that had accompanied the cheques. There in black and white Shoobridge read: 'Mrs Brook directed us to send the cheques to her in your care.' Why would Maggie Brook receive post care of someone she met only once on the stairs? Clearly someone was lying.

Shoobridge decided to look into Ley's life a little more closely. Quietly questioning friends, he found that Ley and Mrs Brook had a relationship that reached beyond the professional level. They were lovers – to the extent that Ley's impotence would allow. Maggie Brook had been Ley's housekeeper in Australia, and had returned with him to England in 1930. Despite,

or perhaps because of his impotence, Ley was very
jealous of Mrs Brook's affections, and he kept close
track of her. A motive for murder more plausible than
a few lost cheques was beginning to emerge. Ley had,
according to friends, accused the 66-year-old Brook of
having sex with three different men living in the house
in Wimbledon.

In the face of such a distinguished murder-suspect,
Scotland Yard were called in, in the shape of Detective
Chief Inspector Arthur Philpott. Ley was now being
investigated assiduously, the jealousy motive too obvious a gift to ignore. Yet Simpson and Gardner had yet
to agree on the conclusions to their findings concerning
the corpse. Gardner was convinced, on the strength of
the forensic evidence, that Mudie had been murdered.
He told police that the superficial injuries pointed to a
'roughing up' of the dead man, prior to murder. This
was just what they wanted to hear now they had a
likely suspect. Simpson, however, pointed out the odd
inconsistencies in the findings, the lack of evidence
to disprove the idea of accidental death or suicide.
Despite the convenience of the conclusion that Mudie
was murdered and dumped, Simpson refused to agree
that the evidence either confirmed or disproved it.

Simpson's stubbornness caused some problems to
Philpott. He was, after all, investigating a murder. It
would be useful to be sure that the crime had actually
taken place. Nevertheless, the Scotland Yard man did
not let the uncertainty of the pathologist deter him.
Reasoning it out, Philpott saw that if Ley had been
involved in Mudie's death, it was more than likely
that he had help: Ley's age and weight were obstacles
to strenuous physical activity.

Philpott also thought it unlikely that this help came

in the form of professional assassins. These were, and are, uncommon in Britain. Furthermore professional killers were likely to have done a better job than in this case. Perhaps Ley's accomplice or accomplices had not been aware of the purpose of their employment, Philpott argued. Maybe they had kidnapped Mudie for Ley, but were unaware that he was now dead. If such an accomplice learned of the real situation, he would be desperate to explain the facts, and avoid a murder charge. This is why Philpott decided to publish more details – Mudie's description and the location of the chalkpit – in the national papers. He was immediately rewarded.

As soon as the story appeared, a boxer named John William Buckingham presented himself at Philpott's office. He was worried. He told Philpott that Ley had hired him to abduct and restrain Mudie, for the sum of £200. In order to do this, Buckingham had persuaded a female friend to lure Mudie back to Ley's house in Kensington. Waiting there for him was the boxer and an accomplice named Smith. They had, according to Buckingham, locked Mudie in a half-furnished office, and picked up their fee. The last time he had seen Mudie he was a worried man, but very much alive.

Ley had explained that he wanted Mudie kidnapped because Mudie was blackmailing a female friend and her daughter. The whole affair was designed to give the young man 'a scare' and to force him to sign a confession.

And now Buckingham had learned that Mudie was dead.

The boxer's accomplice proved easy to locate. Lawrence John Smith was a foreman carpenter who was carrying out repair work in Ley's house. His account of that Thursday, two weeks earlier, agreed in most details with Buckingham's, but added a new twist. When Mudie had entered the house in Kensington, Smith said, Buckingham had been waiting with a large rug. Before he knew what was happening, Mudie had been wrapped in the rug by Smith and tied at the ankles and midriff with a clothesline. Buckingham and Smith then forced him down the corridor by 'jumping' him. In the doorway of the half-furnished office, Buckingham over-balanced and Mudie fell through the open door with the boxer on top of him. Disentangling themselves, the kidnappers manoeuvred Mudie into a swivel chair and gagged him with a French-polisher's rag (very similar to the rag found wound into the noose). Smith ended his account by saying that he had left the house after Buckingham, having waited to collect the fee. Like Buckingham, Smith maintained that the last time he had seen Mudie he was alive and well.

Buckingham was shown Smith's statement and asked if he wished to amend his own. Yes, Buckingham admitted, he had used a rug to restrain Mudie, but the fall and the gag were fiction. Philpott now had found all the evidence he needed to accuse Ley. The ex-Minister of Justice, appraised of the possible charges against him, immediately drafted a statement, denying every word of the accusations.

The only problem was the lack of concurrence of the medical evidence. Philpott felt that he could not proceed with the case against the three without solid backing from both the coroner's appointed pathologist and the Home Office pathologist, meaning Gardner and Simpson. Yet despite Buckingham's statement, and a more detailed account from Gardner of how the 'roughing up' injuries could have been caused by Mudie's fall, Simpson refused to budge.

To him, Gardner seemed to be trying to tailor the facts to fit the police's case. Furthermore, Simpson felt, with justification, that his opinion outweighed that of his colleague. Gardner was only a 'GP pathologist', a part-timer. Some of the arguments that Gardner used to counter the theory that Mudie had committed suicide, such as the assertion that suicides never use single-hitch slipknots, Simpson knew from his wider experience to be untrue.

Philpott was stuck in the middle of what was becoming an argument over professional integrity. Also, in view of the charge he was hoping to bring, he was painfully short of physical evidence. For example he could not locate a place in Ley's house where Mudie could have been conveniently hanged. In desperation he asked Simpson if someone could have held the rope high enough for Mudie to asphyxiate. Simpson replied that he had never seen such a method of murder in his entire career, and furthermore that it was illogical: the lateral neck bruise proved that the rope had been tightened before hanging. There seemed to be no reason why, if murder was intended, the rope was not just tightened further until Mudie died.

Faced with the fact that despite Buckingham and Smith's statements, there was no conclusive physical evidence of murder, Philpott had to let the three suspects go.

At this point, the investigating officers turned up more evidence. Smith, it seemed, had hired a small, dark-coloured Ford a few days before Mudie's abduction. The registration number concurred with that seen by the two gardeners, FGP 101. Encouraged, the police brought

Smith back in to take part in an identity parade. Both of the gardeners viewed the parade individually. Only one of them correctly picked out Smith. The police case was still dangerously weak.

Presented with the prospect of losing all those that they thought to be responsible for Mudie's death, the police decided to ask Buckingham to turn 'King's Evidence.' In return for co-operating with the police, the ex-boxer would receive a greatly reduced sentence. Given their precarious case, it was the best that the police could hope for.

At the indictment hearing in the magistrate's court the medical disagreement was unresolved. Gardner argued that the minor injuries Mudie had sustained all pointed convincingly to attack or restraint. Simpson did not offer evidence at this stage, but his original post mortem report nestled among the evidential documents, a gift from heaven for Ley's defence lawyers.

Astonishingly, just before the trial was scheduled to start, a new witness approached Ley's lawyers. His name was Robert Cruikshank. He maintained that he had visited Ley's house on the Thursday evening of Mudie's kidnap. He had found a man tied to a chair and had, he said, pulled the rope. He wondered now if he could have been responsible for the death. Whether a genuine witness or a lunatic, Cruikshank's evidence only served to further confuse the blurred picture of events after Buckingham and Smith had left the house.

When the defence read Simpson's inconclusive post mortem report, they were so impressed by its import that they invited him to become a witness. This was a radical departure from tradition; the Home Office pathologist would rarely, if ever, have anything to say that could help a defence case. Yet in the reversed aspect of the Ley and Smith case, where one of the accused was an ex-Minister of Justice, it seemed only appropriate that a Crown consultant should help the defence. Dr Simpson drew up a list of questions with which Ley's advocates, Sir Walter Monckton, KC and Gerald Howard, KC should cross-examine Dr Gardner, who was appearing for the Crown.

In the event, even before Ley's counsels had begun to ask Simpson's questions, Gardner made an unconvincing witness. Having agreed with Simpson in the first instance, his changing opinion as the police accumulated new evidence did not inspire confidence. Monckton soon undermined him further. The evidence of hanging had not been pointed out by the Crown – understandably, since it confused the direction of their case. Gardner was soon forced to admit that there were inexplicable marks on Mudie's neck, marks that were not easily reconcilable with murder.

After providing the questions to undermine Gardner, Simpson could not expect light treatment from the Crown. During his cross-examination, both the prosecuting counsel and the judge, Lord Goddard, repeatedly expressed incredulity that Simpson was not convinced that this case involved a murder. Simpson calmly and consistently replied that although there might be a great deal of other evidence to that effect, the medical evidence remained poised and ambivalent.

In his summing-up, Lord Goddard pointed out to the jury that it did not matter in law if the prosecution could not point to a certain mode of death. The tying of rope around the victim was part of the crime, and it was reasonably certain that this had in some way led to Mudie's death. 'The man died as a result of a cruel and wicked murder.'

It took the jury only an hour to arrive at their verdict. Both Ley and Smith were found guilty and sentenced to death, but neither of the sentences was carried out. Ley was found to be insane by a medical Board of Inquiry, and was committed to Broadmoor. Smith had his sentence commuted to life imprisonment. Ley was to die only a few months later, of a brain haemorrhage.

19

The Death of Gay Gibson

On the night of 17–18 October 1947 the passenger ship, *SS Durban Castle*, was sailing off the African coast en route between Cape Town and Southampton. At just before three in the morning, Fred Steer, the assistant night-watchman, was called to Deck B by the cabin-service bell. When he arrived, he was surprised to see that the indicator for cabin 126 showed both the night-watchman and stewardess lights illuminated – indicating that both buttons had been pushed simultaneously. Fearing an emergency Steer knocked, then opened the cabin door a crack to peer inside. However, before he could discern anything of the interior, a man's right hand slammed the door in his face, and a voice said: 'All right!'

Steer remembered that the cabin belonged to an attractive young actress called Eileen Gibson – known as 'Gay' – and decided that discretion was called for . . . He went back to the night-watchman's galley and told his senior, James Murray, what had happened. They both returned to cabin 126, but found the fanlight above the door darkened and the indicator lights extinguished. Since they had no evidence that anything was actually amiss, they went back to their galley. The matter was routinely reported to the bridge officer, but he, like Steer and Murray, decided that the behaviour of the passengers in the privacy of their cabins was none of his affair.

At 7.30 a.m. Eileen Field, the cabin stewardess, knocked on the door of cabin 126, and found it open. This was slightly odd, for she knew that Miss Gibson always bolted her door before retiring. The cabin proved to be empty and the bed in a state of disarray. However, noticing that the actress's pyjamas and dressing-gown were missing, she guessed that she had gone for an early bath. It was only later, when the bathroom steward told her that he had not seen Gay Gibson, that the stewardess became alarmed and reported the passenger missing.

The *Durban Castle*'s captain, Arthur Patey, broadcast a request for Miss Gibson to make her whereabouts known, and when she did not appear, reversed the ship's engines in case she had fallen overboard. At 11.40 a.m. however, he gave orders to resume the plotted course – there was no sign of her in the sea and the ship had been thoroughly searched. If she *had* fallen overboard, he decided, she would surely be dead by now.

Gay Gibson, was an attractive, slim, brunette 21-year-old, with a quiet, friendly manner. She had joined the Women's Auxiliary Territorial Service (or ATS) during the war and had eventually found her way into acting via the services' cabaret, *Stars in Battledress*. Touring Britain, France and Germany after the war, she proved a fine actress, but had the reputation of being temperamental, even neurotic.

In 1947, she was granted a compassionate discharge from the forces to travel to South Africa with her mother. There they joined Gay's father, who was working near Durban. She soon revived her acting career, joining a repertory company and taking leading roles with considerable success. However, when the run of Clifford Odet's *Golden Boy* came to an abrupt halt due to the theatre being condemned as a firetrap, Gay decided to return to England by the first available ship. This struck her friends as odd, since she had been offered another leading role, yet had turned it down without explanation. She left on the *Durban Castle* on 10 October 1947.

The captain instigated an immediate inquiry. The evening before, she had dined with two people – an elderly gentleman called Hopwood and an RAF wing-commander called Bray. After supper she had danced with Mr Hopwood and then gone for a swim. She returned a little later, claiming to have been unable to find the ship's pool, and rejoined the dance. At 12.40 a.m., Mr Hopwood had escorted her to her cabin.

The last person to report seeing her was the boat-swain's mate. He and a deck-cleaning party had come across her smoking a cigarette and leaning on the rail of the promenade deck, at around 1 a.m. They had asked her to move to avoid wetting her feet and she had gone below. She was reported to have been in good spirits that evening; thus, if suicide was to be ruled out, accident or murder seemed the only other possibilities.

During the inquiry Fred Steer, the assistant night-watchman, came forward with a confession. He admit-ted that he had held back a detail in the first report for fear of getting a colleague into trouble. In the instant before the door of cabin 126 was slammed in his face, he had recognized the man on the other side. It had been James Camb, a promenade deck steward.

Camb was a thick-set, handsome man; 30 years old with a wife and child at home. This did not stop him, by his own admission, having occasional affairs with the female passengers. He often bragged about his victories to fellow crew members, despite the danger of instant dismissal if he was overheard by an officer. Steer had known about Camb's sexual adventures, and had automatically covered for him until the news of the disappearance had come out.

In questioning Camb, Captain Patey was careful not to reveal that he had been seen in Miss Gibson's cabin. He merely said that he had been noticed in the area at around 3 a.m. Camb denied having been there, insisting that he had gone to bed at 12.45 a.m. As the steward spoke, Patey noticed that he was wearing his full dress uniform rather than the cooler tropics kit. Wondering if Camb was trying to conceal something under the long sleeves and high collar of the dress jacket, the captain sent him down to the ship's doctor for a physical examination.

Dr Griffiths found some interesting scratches on Camb's upper body. Several parallel scrapes over the back of his right shoulder and, more suspiciously, about a dozen similar cuts on the inside of his right forearm — as if somebody with long nails had clutched him fiercely by the arm. Following the examination, Camb, now visibly rattled, sent two notes to the captain. The first reiterated his statement that he had been nowhere near the passenger cabins that night, the second explained the cuts as prickly heat scratches from his own nails and rough towels.

Captain Patey, bearing in mind the confined nature of shipboard life, allowed Camb to remain free to continue his duties until they reached Southampton. The ship arrived in the early morning of 25 October 1947, but the crew and passengers were told to stay aboard until the police had given them permission to leave.

A few hours later, Detective Sergeants Quinlan and Gibbons arrived and interviewed Camb. He continued to insist that he had gone to bed just before 1 a.m. and had been nowhere near the passenger cabins all night. However, as the interrogation progressed, he clearly began to realize that the police had evidence that he had been seen in cabin 126. 'That puts me in a tight spot,' he commented bitterly.

Eventually, Gibbons rounded on him, saying: 'You are being given the opportunity to make any explanation you may care to about this. That explanation, so far, has been a categorical denial that you know anything about the death of Miss Gibson. You may find that such a complete denial will be difficult to explain if later you are called upon to explain it.'

Camb asked desperately: 'Does that mean I murdered her and that I'll be charged with murder?'

Gibbons replied that, based on the evidence so far, he could not be certain if charges would be preferred. He then offered Camb a ray of hope: 'We have to give particular care to any explanation which you may put forward. You may be able to give a reasonable explanation of her death and her disappearance.'

Camb took the bait: 'You mean that Miss Gibson might have died from some other cause, other than being murdered,' he exclaimed, 'She might have had a heart attack, or something?'

At the later trial both sides made much of this statement. On the one hand, the prosecution said that Camb had let his guard down, momentarily showing his calculated efforts to lay a false trail for the police. On the other, the defence claimed that it was a moment of realization – that Camb had at last guessed the reason for the terrible sequence of events. Either way, he had all but admitted to the police that he knew what had happened to Gay Gibson. It took only a little while for Quinlan and Gibbons to obtain a full statement from him.

He started by pointing out that shipboard assignations between crew and passengers were far from unusual. 'Some of them liked us better than the passengers,' he boasted.

He admitted to arranging a meeting with Gay and entering her cabin at around 2 a.m. 'After a short conversation,' he went on, 'I got into bed with her consent. Intimacy took place. Whilst in the sexual act of intercourse she clutched me, foaming at the mouth. I immediately ceased the act, but she was very still. I felt for her heartbeats, but could not find any. She was at that time very still, and I cannot offer any explanation as to how the bells came to be rung, as I most definitely did not touch them myself. Thinking she had fainted, I tried artificial respiration on her. Whilst doing this, the night-watchman knocked at the door and attempted to open it. I shut the door again, saying it was all right. Then I panicked, as I thought he had gone to the bridge to report to the officer of the watch, and did not want to be found in such a compromising position. After a few minutes I could not find any sign of life. After a struggle with the limp body – by the way, she was still wearing her dressing-gown – I managed to lift her to the porthole and push her through. I am fairly certain that at the time she was dead, but I was terribly frightened. Then I went forward and turned-in. The time would be about 3.30 a.m.'

Despite the horror of his tale, Camb seemed basically unaware of his serious position. He ended his statement by saying: 'What will happen about this? My wife must not know about this. If she does I will do away with myself.' The fact that he was about to be publicly charged with murder did not appear to have occurred to him. Gibbons and Quinlan placed him under arrest, and his trial was eventually set for 18 March 1948.

It is a popular misconception that a corpse is necessary to bring a murder charge under British law. 'Corpus delicti' means 'body of *evidence*,' not a physical corpse. In fact, G.D. Roberts, KC, opening for the prosecution, pointed out that since it might reasonably be taken for granted that Miss Gibson had died, murder was an obvious possibility that demanded investigation. The jury's main task would be to determine how, not if, Gay Gibson had met her end.

In passing, it is interesting to note a rumour mentioned by Dr Dennis Hocking (who gave evidence for the defence) in his book *Bodies and Crimes*. It had been reported that a painted fingernail had been found in the belly of a shark caught off the coast where Gay Gibson disappeared. Of course, as hearsay, this was not mentioned at the trial, but if true, it was the only 'corpus delicti' in the case.

It might have been possible for the Crown to obtain a murder conviction based purely on Camb's statement – that he was only 'fairly certain' that Gay was dead when he pushed her through the porthole. This could be interpreted to mean that he was willing to risk killing her rather than lose his job. On the same basis, the prosecution could have charged him with the non-capital crime of manslaughter; a verdict they would have been certain of winning.

However, Mr Roberts decided that a more energetic attack on the defendant was called for. The prosecution's interpretation of events, laid out by Roberts in his opening address, was that Camb had forced or tricked his way into Miss Gibson's cabin, and had sexually assaulted her. He had killed her – probably by strangulation – to avoid being denounced. He had then pushed her out of the porthole to destroy the evidence of his crime.

The Crown's problem was that they had very little solid evidence to corroborate this theory. To balance matters, Roberts realized that he would have to thoroughly discredit Camb's version of events in the eyes of the jury. Camb had claimed that Gay Gibson, a healthy young woman, had died of a heart attack or some similar natural cause. Why then, demanded Roberts, did he push her body through the porthole? If he was only 'fairly certain' she was dead, why had he not called for help or gone to get Dr Griffiths? Even if he had been certain that nothing could be done for her, surely it would have been easier to quietly slip away and leave the body to be discovered the next morning? The reason Camb had behaved as he did, argued Roberts, was that the body would have proved, beyond doubt, that Gay had been raped and murdered. Camb therefore *had* to get rid of the evidence.

Roberts went on to quote from a statement said to have been made in private by Camb to a policeman called Plumley. The officer, who had recently left the police force, reported Camb to have said: 'She made a hell of a splash when she hit the water. She struggled. I had my hands round her neck. I tried to pull them away; she scratched me. I panicked and threw her through the porthole.' Roberts stressed that, as a verbal statement, the 'confession' could not be treated as strict evidence; however, if the jury believed it, they must accept that Camb had forced Gay Gibson out of the porthole while she was still alive.

In fact, Plumley's statement was open to a very obvious criticism. If the ship had been stationary, it might have been possible to hear the splash. However, since the ship was moving, any noise made by the body would have been drowned out entirely by the engines and the bow-wave. Nobody would have known this better than James Camb, so why on earth would he have said it made 'a hell of a splash'? It must be supposed that Roberts read the statement during his opening address to colour the jury's view of the defendant. When Plumley was called to give evidence for the Crown, the defending counsel made short work of him in cross-examination.

The evidence given by its own witnesses eventually led the prosecution to concede that there had indeed been some sort of relationship between the passenger and the deck steward. Camb's duties were exclusively confined to the promenade deck. However, twice during the week-long voyage, he took a tea tray down to Gay Gibson's cabin; a task he should have passed on to the cabin staff. The stewardess, Eileen Field, gave evidence that before the disappearance, Camb had told her that Gay Gibson was three-months pregnant 'by a married man' – a surprisingly intimate admission for Gay to have made to a mere steward. Finally, on the afternoon before she disappeared, the night watchman, James Murray, overheard Camb say to Gay: 'I say, I have a bone to pick with you, and quite a big one at that.' Such familiarity would have earned Camb a severe reprimand if overheard by an officer.

The prosecution, who depicted Gay Gibson as a pure and innocent young lady, interpreted this evidence in the following way. Camb had gone out of his way to

gain access to Gay's cabin, presumably in an attempt
to win her trust. He had invented the story about her
pregnancy, quite possibly to make her disappearance
seem like suicide. The 'bone to pick with you' statement,
the Crown suggested, was evidence of a grudge that
Camb meant to pay off.

The prosecution argued that Gay was a trusting and
innocent girl who had formed what she thought to be
a purely platonic friendship with a handsome steward.
Camb, on the other hand, was a cad who had intended
to take advantage of her from the start. Infuriated when
she had failed to respond to his charms, he had raped
and murdered her – quite possibly having planned the
crime several days beforehand.

The strength of the prosecution's case relied on the
Court's acceptance that Gay was both healthy and
morally upright. It was imperative to convince the jury
that she would never have invited Camb to a sexual
assignation, and that his description of her 'heart-attack'
was false. On the face of it, this might seem a very
tenuous line of argument. As in most cases which rely
heavily on circumstantial evidence, interpretation was a
double-edged weapon. We will see later how the defence
used the same evidence to a very different effect. In an
effort to reinforce their reading, the prosecution called
Gay's mother, Mrs Ellen Gibson.

Character witnesses are usually called to support a
given argument, but they rarely change the course of a
trial. Mrs Gibson, however, made a deep impression on
the court. The obviously grief-stricken mother insisted
that Gay's health had been excellent, and dismissed the
notion that she might have died of natural causes. 'She
was one of the finest types of English womanhood;
physically, mentally and morally,' she insisted. As we

will see, her words struck a chord in both the jury and the judge.

Eileen Field, the cabin stewardess, told the court that Miss Gibson's dressing-gown *and* pyjamas were missing from cabin 126 the morning after her disappearance. This undermined Camb's statement that Gay had been wearing only the dressing-gown when they made love, and therefore, this was the only item of apparel that had gone into the sea with her. Mr Roberts made much of this incongruity. If Camb was telling the truth, why were the pyjamas not found in the cabin? If he was lying, why would he have concealed what had happened to them, unless they could have shown evidence of a sexual attack?

Dr Griffiths, the ship's doctor who had examined Camb the day after the disappearance, provided the court with photographs of the scratches to the defendant's right shoulder and forearm. He confirmed that, in his opinion, these might well have been caused in a struggle with somebody with long fingernails. He added that he found no sign of any skin rash on the defendant, thus damaging Camb's claim that he had scratched himself while suffering from prickly heat.

Dr Ruth Haslam, the army doctor who had examined Gay before her discharge from the ATS, was called to report her findings. She said that Gay had been 'AW/1' – army-speak for fully fit. She admitted that the patient had seemed 'a bit wheezy,' but had put this down to a winter cold. Gay's only continuing sign of ill-health was a persistent ear infection, for which she was classified as unfit for tropical service.

The Crown also called Dr Walter Montgomery, a senior scientific officer from the police laboratory at Hendon. Montgomery had inspected the bedclothes from Gay's bed and had found two bloodspots on the top sheet. These were found to be type 'O'; Camb's blood was type 'A'. This evidence was followed up by the testimony of Dr Donald Teare, assistant pathologist and lecturer in forensic medicine at St George's Hospital, one of the foremost pathology experts in the country. Teare told the court that strangulation often caused haemorrhaging in the lungs and upper air passages due to constriction of the blood vessels. In his opinion, the blood spots found on the sheets might well have been produced under these circumstances. However, under cross-examination, he admitted that victims of major heart attacks also cough-up blood, and that this possibility could not be discounted.

This ended the case for the prosecution. The case for the defence was opened by J.D. Casswell, KC. He started with a direct attack on the prosecution's picture of Gay Gibson. She was not, as they had suggested, a blushing virgin; several witnesses who had known her in the Forces and in South Africa would be called to show this. Neither was she fully fit; witnesses would state that she had suffered from asthma and fainting fits. Camb's description of her death was not as unbelievable as the prosecution suggested. Experts would be called to confirm that Camb's story was not incompatible with several possible types of fatal attack.

Casswell called the defendant as his first witness. Camb presented a calm, self-confident composure while reiterating the details he had given in his previous statement. He said that Miss Gibson had seemed bored by her predominantly older fellow-passengers and had seemed relieved to chat with someone under middle-age. She had been very friendly with him from the start and had volunteered the information that she thought she was pregnant right out of the blue. It was she, he said, who had insisted that he personally bring her tea to her cabin, and he had done so only after pointing out that it was against the rules. He also told the court that he had prepared a special supper tray for her on the evening of 16 October, which she had not collected. This, he said, was the reason he had told her that he had a bone to pick with her.

On 17 October, she had ordered a double rum as a nightcap, and he had half-jokingly offered to take it to her cabin himself. He said that she had simply smiled in reply, which he believed to be an invitation. He had gone down at 1 a.m. but she had not been there. Returning at 2 a.m. he found the door unlocked and Miss Gibson lying on the bed . . .

Casswell's heart must have sunk as Camb gave his evidence. The entire defence case relied on the jury believing that, on finding a dead girl in his arms, Camb had panicked so severely that he had pushed her out of a porthole. The confident, unruffled composure he displayed in court was a gift to the prosecution.

Evelyn Armour, an officer in the ATS, was called to tell the court of the time she had found Gay having some sort of seizure in the barracks. When asked what the trouble was, Gay had clutched her chest and muttered 'pain'. Another army colleague, Private Peter Dalby, reported of a similar attack Gay had suffered while touring with *Stars in Battledress* in Wales. He added that it had been well known in the company that while in Germany she and a driver called Pierre had been 'infatuated with each other.'

Mike Able, a fellow actor in the South African tour of *Golden Boy*, told the court that Gay had continued to have health problems after leaving the army. She had once collapsed in a faint, he said, during which her breathing was laboured and her lips had gone blue. He also disclosed that Gay had told him she was pregnant and needed £200 to return to England for an abortion.

The wife of Gay's manager, Dr Ina Schoub, gave evidence, recalling a time when Gay had asked her advice on health matters. The young actress had told her that she had come to South Africa to help her asthma problems and that exercise made her short of breath very quickly. During the discussion they had also talked about sex, a subject on which Gay seemed fully acquainted. She mentioned that she was about to have her period, but when they spoke again, a week later, she complained that it had still not arrived.

All the defence witnesses who had known Gay reasonably well confirmed that she had an excessively flighty, even neurotic, temperament. She had enjoyed parties, drinking, and male company, and nobody seems to have been particularly surprised to hear that she was pregnant.

A new piece of physical evidence was provided by Dr Dennis Hocking, the pathologist to the Royal Cornwall Infirmary. He had examined the blood-spotted top sheet for the defence, and found two urine stains. This revelation was immediately seized upon, by both the defence and the Crown, as evidence supporting their case, since a person often releases urine during either strangulation or a fit.

The Crown pointed out that a woman lying on her back always urinates in an upward direction. Thus the sheet must have been on top of her, suggesting that she was preparing to sleep just before she died. The defence argued that if, as Camb claimed, he was lying on top of Gay, and she on the bedclothes when she died, the urine would have splashed downwards. Unfortunately for the prosecution, they had previously suggested that Gay was wearing her pyjamas when she was strangled: their two arguments were self-contradictory.

Dr Hocking had found cells from the lining of a woman's sex organs in the dried urine – thus proving it to be Gay's – but had found no blood. This, he felt, all but ruled-out the likelihood of rape or attempted rape. It was also Dr Hocking's belief that the scratches on Camb's arm were too high up to support the strangulation theory. A throttled person grabs at the attacker's wrists, not the forearm. He speculated that the scratches were more likely to have been caused by the convulsive grip of someone suffering a fit.

The last witness to be called in the trial was Professor James Webster, director of the South Midland Forensic Laboratory. He had been called in to review the evidence for the Director of Public Prosecutions, but since he had decided that Camb's statement was probably true, he had been referred to the defence. Professor Webster had been particularly impressed by Camb's description of the symptoms of Gay's death. He felt that these details were too accurate to be a fabrication, invented by a man who had no medical knowledge.

He told the court that it was possible that Gay had died from a brain aneurysm or from heart disease. The latter could have been caused by either Gay's asthma, which could have put an extra strain on her heart over the years, or her recurring septic ear, which might have caused deterioration of the heart muscle through bacterial infection. He confirmed that he had seen or knew of deaths occurring to people of Gay's age, under similar circumstances, for each of these respective possibilities. He concluded that the

chances of natural death seemed about equal to those
of strangulation.

During his four-hour summing-up it became clear that
Mr Justice Hilbery felt Camb to be guilty. When he had
finished, Mr Casswell bitterly complained that he had
not touched upon many points of evidence favourable
to the defendant. Hilbery replied: 'I have not attempted
to mention everything, and I am not bound to do so.'

The jury clearly shared the judge's opinion. After only
forty-minutes consideration, they returned a 'guilty' verdict. Justice Hilbery sentenced James Camb to death.

Casswell appealed against the verdict, citing the apparent bias of Judge Hilbery's summing-up. However, the
appeal was immediately rejected by Lord Chief Justice
Goddard, on the grounds that a judge was allowed to
assist the jury on the interpretation of the facts as well
as the interpretation of the law.

Whether Camb was guilty still remains an open
question. Mr Casswell and Dr Hocking were both of
the opinion that the verdict had come about, not because
the Crown had presented a case 'beyond all reasonable
doubt,' but because the jury were disgusted by the callousness Camb had shown in throwing Gay's body out
of the porthole. A cooler jury would, almost certainly,
have decided that the Crown's case was not sufficient to
deserve a conviction. The very fact that a contraceptive
device was found among Gay's possessions should have
destroyed the innocent virgin image presented by the
prosecution, and unless they believed that there was
a positive conspiracy among Gay's associates, the jury
should also have rejected the assertion that her health
was 'excellent'. Without these two contentions, the
prosecution's case was extremely weak.

Even the matter of the missing pyjamas, one of the

strongest pieces of circumstantial evidence against the defendant, may be less damning than it seems. It is not known where Gay was between 1 a.m. and 2 a.m. According to Camb she was not in her own cabin. In *Bodies and Crimes*, Dr Hocking mentions a rumour that a distinguished male passenger had the pyjamas in his possession, and is alleged to have promised to come forward if Camb looked likely to be executed.

As it turned out, James Camb did not hang. There was a debate over abolition of the death sentence in parliament at the time of the trial, and although the bill was defeated, the Home Secretary ruled that any capital sentences passed during the debate would not be allowed to stand. Camb's sentence was commuted to life imprisonment.

The final irony of the case was that Camb was released after 11 years, in 1959. This was roughly equivalent to the sort of sentence he would have received if he had been convicted of manslaughter – the crime of which he seems more likely to have been guilty.

20

The Undetectable Poison

For more than 2,000 years, poison was the simplest and the least detectable way to commit murder. In the 1750s, magistrate and novelist Henry Fielding was investigating a case of suspected poisoning and asked doctors if there was any reliable way of detecting poison in the human body; he was told there was not.

Just over 60 years later, all this changed when a brilliant young chemist named Mathieu Orfila launched into an extensive study of poisons, and wrote the first *Treatise on Poison, or General Toxicology*, with detailed descriptions of how various poisons could be detected. In 1836, James Marsh invented a test for arsenic that was so delicate that it could detect as little as a fiftieth of a milligram.

From then on there was an undeclared war between toxicologists and would-be murderers to find the undetectable poison. For a while, vegetable (or alkaloid) poisons like opium and nicotine defied the analysts, until new tests were devised. By the twentieth century there were hundreds of new poisons, and hundreds of new tests for detecting them.

In the mid 1950s, a male nurse named Kenneth Barlow

thought that he knew of a poison that would defy all attempts at detection . . .

On the night of 3 May 1957, a Bradford couple named Skinner were aroused by their next-door neighbour, who told them he thought his wife was dead, and asked them to go for a doctor. The general practitioner who arrived before midnight verified that Mrs Elizabeth Barlow was dead in her bath, and sent for the police.

When Detective Sergeant Naylor, of the criminal investigation division of the Bradford Police, arrived at the house in Thornbury Crescent, he was met by the doctor, and by a man with receding hair, who introduced himself as Kenneth Barlow, a male nurse who worked at St Luke's Hospital in Huddersfield. Barlow greeted the detective with apparent composure, and showed him to the bathroom, where the body of a woman lay on its right side in the empty bathtub. There were traces of vomit on the side of the bath. The doctor, who had to visit another patient, explained before he left that he suspected that the dead woman had been under the influence of some kind of drug.

Kenneth Barlow went on to describe what had happened. His wife had been feeling unwell all evening and had gone to bed at 6.30. Barlow had put his child (of a previous marriage) to bed. An hour later, his wife called and said she had been sick. At ten o'clock, she said she was too hot and decided to take a bath. Barlow had dozed off, then woke up, and when he found his wife was not in bed, had gone looking for her. She was lying in the bath, her head under the water. He had drained off the water and tried to lift her out, but found her too heavy, (although, in fact, she weighed less than 80 pounds.) After trying to administer artificial respiration in the bath he went to alert his neighbours . . .

When Naylor looked at the dead woman's eyes he saw why the doctor had suspected drugs; the pupils were dilated. Otherwise, the body bore no marks that might explain why she had become unconscious.

Glancing into the bedroom, Naylor noticed something that troubled him. Barlow's pyjamas were dry. Yet if he had tried to lift his wife out of the bath, they should have been at least damp.

Naylor telephoned Chief Constable H.S. Price and outlined the situation. Price was there almost immediately. Together, he and Naylor examined the bathroom. Price instantly commented on the fact that there was no water on the floor, and no splashes on the walls. Again, this seemed to contradict what Barlow had said. If he had tried to lift his wife, and been forced to let her fall back into the water, it would have caused a miniature tidal wave. Now thoroughly suspicious, the chief constable decided to contact the forensic laboratory in nearby Harrogate.

The telephone was answered by Chief Inspector Coffey, who promised to leave immediately with Dr David Price, the West Riding pathologist. They arrived at 3.30 in the morning. Dr Price was also suspicious of Barlow's story. He observed water droplets on the dead woman's elbows; if Barlow had attempted artificial respiration – with his wife on her back and her arms by her sides – the droplets could not have remained in that form. Price decided to take the body back to Harrogate immediately for a post mortem.

Meanwhile, Chief Inspector Coffey had found two hypodermic syringes in the kitchen, one of them wet. Barlow had a ready explanation: as a male nurse he usually had syringes around the house. In fact, he had given himself an injection of penicillin for a carbuncle.

He insisted that he had not injected anything into his wife. In view of the dilated pupils, Price found this hard to accept.

Back in Harrogate, Price began the autopsy immediately. He was looking for something that might have caused sudden collapse in the bath, such as heart failure or some glandular abnormality. The results were completely negative. The intestines were also free of any trace of bacterial infection that might explain the vomiting.

The fact that the dead woman was two-months pregnant raised another possibility: that there had been an attempted abortion. Price tested for ergometrine, one of the best known abortifacients, but again the tests were negative.

The case was baffling, and Price's frustration was increased when he learned that Barlow's first wife had died in the previous year, and that no known cause of death had been discovered. He decided to call in two other forensic scientists, A.S. Curry of the Home Office lab and P.H. Wright of Guy's Hospital. For days the three of them tested the digestive tract and the vital organs, and also the vomit, urine and blood. Results continued to be negative. If Barlow had killed his wife, he had used a poison that seemed undetectable.

The two syringes from Barlow's kitchen were tested; they showed minute traces of penicillin, confirming his story.

Four days after his first examination, Price went over the whole body with a magnifying glass. It was not an easy task because the dead woman's skin was covered with moles and freckles. But eventually he discovered something that made all his efforts worthwhile: two tiny hypodermic marks in the left buttock. Close examination showed similar marks in a fold in the right buttock.

Price carefully sliced down through the skin and fatty tissue until he found the marks that injections invariably leave under the skin. This proved that Barlow was lying; he *had* injected his wife with a hypodermic. Moreover, the injections on the left buttock were fresh; they had been made at most only an hour or two before her death. But what *was* the undetectable substance he had injected into her?

Dr Price cut out the flesh containing the injection marks, and stored it in the refrigerator. The sites of injection were the likeliest places where traces of the substance might linger.

Next, Price consulted with medical colleagues about the symptoms displayed by Elizabeth Barlow on the evening of her death: sweating, vomiting, fatigue, coma and dilation of the pupils. His colleagues remarked that it sounded like hypoglycaemia, a state due to an abnormally low blood sugar level, which leads to exhaustion and – unless glucose is administered – possibly to death. The level of glucose in our blood is controlled by a hormone called insulin, produced by the beta cells of the islets of Langerhans, which surround the pancreas. This is why insulin – first isolated in 1921 – is used on diabetics, whose blood sugar is too high.

Was it conceivable that insulin was the unknown chemical injected by Kenneth Barlow? A large insulin injection destroys blood sugar, resulting in exhaustion, sweating and trembling.

Price soon decided that this idea had to be abandoned. Examination of the dead woman's heart had showed that there was far *more* blood sugar than there should have been. Then what about the opposite of hypoglycaemia – hyperglycaemia, the condition that diabetics suffer from? This was also impossible – examination of the dead woman's urine had showed conclusively that she was not diabetic. It seemed clear that neither theory fitted the facts.

But Curry, the Home Office pathologist, came upon one interesting piece of information. Patients who died from sudden stoppage of the heart – in suffocation or drowning – often had high levels of blood sugar in the heart. This was because in a crisis, the liver – which stores sugar – floods the body with sugar to counteract the flood of hormones due to shock. They often reach the heart just as it stops. So Price's original idea of an insulin injection was still at least a possibility.

For almost three weeks the investigation marked time. Then Chief Constable Price, who had been looking into Barlow's background, brought some interesting news. When Barlow had worked at the Northfield Sanatorium, he had told a patient that a large dose of insulin was a certain passport to the next world. And he had told a fellow male nurse that insulin was the key to the perfect murder: it dissolved in the blood so that it was undetectable.

Curry was excited. None of them had been able to get the possibility that insulin was involved out of their minds. Now it sounded highly probable. The flesh of the buttocks was taken out of the refrigerator. The problem was simply how to detect insulin if, in fact, it *was* present in the tissue? There was no known chemical test.

But this was a problem that had been confronting toxicologists for almost a century, and they had found at least one solution. For example, in March 1863, a young widow named Madame de Pauw had died suddenly, apparently of cholera, in Paris. The police received an anonymous letter advising them that they ought to check whether Mme de Pauw's lover, Dr Couty de la Pommerais, would benefit financially from her death. They soon learned that Pommerais had insured her life for 500,000 francs. Was it possible that he had given her some drug that produced symptoms like cholera? The body was exhumed and sent to the famous pathologist and toxicologist Dr Ambroise Tardieu. He collected the stomach contents and made a concentrated extract. Then he tried injecting a dog with some of the extract. Its heartbeat slowed, and it soon lay gasping on the floor. Then, slowly, it recovered.

Many of Pommerais' letters had been seized by the police, and one of these mentioned that he was treating Mme de Pauw with digitalis – an extract of foxglove, used to treat heart disease.

Tardieu's problem was the same as Price's: that there was no known chemical test for the poison he suspected. What he *could* do was to inject animals with the extract from Mme de Pauw's stomach, then inject them with digitalis, and show that the same effects were produced. This is what he did, and Pommerais went to the guillotine.

Price's group tried Tardieu's method. Extracts were prepared from the samples from Elizabeth Barlow's buttocks. It was possible, of course, that if she had been injected with insulin, it had long ago been absorbed. But there was nothing but to try. First, a control group of mice was injected with various quantities of insulin, and the results carefully observed. Next, another group of mice was injected with the extract from Elizabeth Barlow's buttocks. They reacted in precisely the same way as the control group – tension, trembling, increased heartbeat and coma. The extract from the left buttock had a far stronger effect on the mice than that from the right buttock, confirming Price's suspicion that this injection had been given only a few hours before death.

Since they knew the amount of insulin that had been given to the control group, it was possible to estimate the amount present in the extract; it was 84 units. And since a large amount had been absorbed by the body, this meant that the original dose had been many times as great – more than enough to cause severe 'insulin shock.'

In court in Paris, Tardieu had found himself facing the objection that he could not be *sure* that Mme de Pauw had been poisoned by digitalis, since there was no known chemical test for it. (In fact, these objections might have led to Pommerais' acquittal if it had not been for other evidence relating to the way he had deceived the insurance company.) Price and his group had to anticipate the same problem.

Curry tried treating extracts from the dead woman's flesh with the amino acid cysteine, and with pepsin, which occurs naturally in the stomach – both have the effect of destroying insulin. When the mice were injected with this treated extract, they showed no ill effects. It was also known that guinea pigs can develop a resistance to insulin. Serum from these insulin-resistant guinea pigs was added to the buttock extract, and once again it produced no effect on the mice.

The pharmaceutical industry was asked to help. Were there any other substances that produced the same effect as insulin by metabolizing sugar? Three were mentioned: Synthalin, Carbutamid and Tolbutamed. All three were tried on the mice, in case Barlow had injected his wife with one of these. They caused a fall in the level of

blood sugar, but not the trembling, tension and coma
of insulin.

Every possible objection had to be anticipated. Someone mentioned that a tumour of the pancreas could
lead to a flood of insulin into the blood. But the
examination of Elizabeth Barlow's pancreas showed no
such tumour.

This conclusion was finally reached on 28 July 1957;
on the following day, Kenneth Barlow, age 38, was
arrested by Detective Superintendent Cheshire of Scotland Yard, and accused of murdering his wife by an
insulin injection.

Barlow's first reaction was shock; it was obvious that
he had believed that insulin was undetectable. A few days
later, he decided to change his story. Now he admitted
that he had injected his wife – but with ergometrine, to
procure an abortion. Price was in the position of being
able to counter that immediately: ergometrine was one
of the substances he had tested Elizabeth Barlow for in
the first few days, and it was undoubtedly not present
in her body.

In December 1957, the trial of Kenneth Barlow opened
in Leeds Assizes before Mr Justice Diplock. Opening the
case for the prosecution, Sir Harry Hylton-Foster, the
Solicitor General, suggested that Barlow's motive in
murdering his wife may have been that he objected to
her pregnancy. This was the only motive that anyone
was able to suggest.

He went on to describe the finding of the body,
Barlow's denial that he had injected his wife, then his
admission — when injection punctures were found —
that he had injected her with ergometrine to terminate
her pregnancy.

The weight of the evidence was, of course, based on

the findings of the Harrogate laboratory. The jury sat through many hours of complex scientific evidence. A century ago – perhaps even half-a-century ago – these complications would almost certainly have led to the acquittal of the accused; juries have always taken a pride in being sceptical and hard-headed. In fact, the famous Marsh test for arsenic was developed because in 1832 a Kent jury had acquitted a man named John Bodle, who was accused of poisoning his grandfather with arsenic. The jury flatly declined to believe Marsh's explanations about how he had proved that the elder Bodle had died of arsenic poisoning. (In fact, John Bodle later confessed to the murder.) Marsh was so furious at the jury's stupidity that he vowed to invent a test for arsenic that would convince the most hidebound jurors.

But modern juries have become accustomed to scientific evidence, and in this case, they could see that the chances of a whole team of forensic investigators being mistaken about insulin were minimal. Mr Bernard Gillis, for the defence, tried hard to persuade Price to agree that carbolic soap might have produced Mrs Barlow's convulsions, but Price pointed out that the vomit and the damp and sweaty pyjamas proved that she was already ill before she entered the bath. Gillis at least gained ground when he led Price to admit that he should have taken samples of flesh from other parts of the body besides the buttocks. This point was pursued with another expert witness, Dr Maurice Gurd, who agreed that if Mrs Barlow's pancreas had been abnormal, it could have produced large amounts of insulin which would have flooded her system. Yet it could also be argued that, in agreeing that the cause of Mrs Barlow's collapse was insulin, Gillis was neglecting his one real line of defence: that since no *chemical* test for insulin existed,

Price and his team might simply be mistaken about the cause of her collapse.

Gillis called only one expert: Dr Hobson of St Luke's Hospital in London. Hobson was frank enough to admit that he had been a stranger to the subject until the previous day, when he had studied as much of the literature as he could find. What Hobson went on to suggest was that fear may produce a flood of adrenalin, which leads to an automatic increase in the sugar content of the blood. Mrs Barlow may have experienced panic as she felt herself slipping under the water, and unable to prevent it. In that case, her pancreas would attempt to correct the balance by discharging large quantities of insulin.

Dr Price was called back to the witness stand, and had no difficulty in refuting this theory. If the insulin in Mrs Barlow's body was due to shock, then why had it concentrated itself in the area of the needle marks in the buttocks? Surely it would flood throughout the whole body? And in order to flood the whole body to the same concentration found in the buttocks, Mrs Barlow's pancreas would have had to produce about 15,000 units of insulin. And that was simply beyond the capacity of the human pancreas.

It could be argued that, in calling Hobson, Gillis had damaged his own case. Before Dr Hobson appeared, he seemed to have succeeded in implanting in the minds of the jury a certain suspicion of the findings of the scientists, which might have led them to decide to give Barlow the benefit of the doubt. But Price's refutation of Hobson's theory was so decisive that it had the effect of removing all doubts about the tests.

In his summing-up, Diplock underlined the fact that *if* Barlow had injected his wife with insulin, then his purpose must have been to kill her; there could be no other reason. 'This is murder or nothing.' So everything depended on whether the jury accepted that the immense care taken by the Harrogate scientists had proved beyond reasonable doubt that Barlow had injected insulin.

The jury took only a very short time to make up their minds. The foreman delivered a 'guilty' verdict, and Barlow was sentenced to life imprisonment. Asked if he had anything to say, Barlow replied: 'I am not guilty . . . I had no reason to murder my wife.'

Barlow was in prison for 26 years, and was finally released in 1984 at the age of 65 – Britain's second longest-serving prisoner. (Straffen, the child murderer, is the longest-serving.) He continued to maintain his innocence.

Obviously, the central mystery of the case is: Why did he do it? The answer is: we do not know. Yet another question: How did he do it? may provide some clue. Unless Barlow knocked his wife unconscious to inject the drug (and that would have involved the obvious risk of leaving a bruise), we must assume that he convinced her that he was injecting some fairly harmless drug. This could have been some tranquillizer – or it could have been, as he himself claimed, ergometrine, with the purpose of procuring an abortion. If so, we must assume that Elizabeth Barlow wanted to terminate her pregnancy – perhaps because she wanted to continue her work as a nurse.

But if Barlow's motive in killing her was – as the prosecutor suggested – desire not to become a father for the second time, then he would have solved this problem by injecting her with ergometrine instead of insulin. It follows that the motive of terminating her pregnancy is not the answer to why he committed murder.

Then what is the answer? As far as we know, he was
not in love with another woman – although, of course,
it remains a possibility. All we *can* be certain of is that
after six months or so of marriage, he had decided he
preferred to be single again. If the pregnancy was an
accident, and Elizabeth Barlow agreed that it should be
terminated, he may have felt that this was the perfect
opportunity. Insulin, he believed, was undetectable, so
all he had to do was inject her with a massive dose and
watch her lose consciousness. He injected her first in the
right buttock, but this failed to induce a coma. So a few
hours later he told her she would need a second injection.
This itself is the most powerful argument for the theory
that Elizabeth Barlow believed she was being injected
with ergometrine – if she thought it was a tranquillizer
or some other harmless drug, Barlow would have had
no obvious reason to administer a second injection.

It seems unlikely that she climbed into the bath of her
own accord. Someone who feels sick prefers to lie still in
bed. So it seems likely that Barlow watched her fall into
a coma, then carried her to the bath and drowned her.
After that he left her in the bath for an hour, to support
his own story of falling asleep. (It is hard to determine
time of death with complete accuracy, but it would
hardly be worth taking the risk.) Then, presumably, he
drained off the water and went to alert the neighbours.

He forgot two things: first, that since his wife was a
very light woman, his statement that he had been unable
to lift her out of the bath might arouse suspicion. (In fact,
no one seems to have questioned it.) Second: to support
his story by splashing water on his pyjamas. It was this
second mistake that aroused the suspicion that led to
his downfall.

There is another interesting question: why did the

insulin injected by Barlow fail to disappear, as he expected it to? It was Dr A.S. Curry, the Home Office investigator, who found the explanation. After death, enzymes cause some tissues to become alkaline, particularly the viscera, and alkalis dissolve proteins like insulin. But at the same time, lactic acid develops in the muscles, and insulin does not dissolve away when acid is present. So an obscure internal process had preserved the insulin in the muscles of Mrs Barlow's buttocks even when it had vanished from the rest of her system . . .

Barlow obviously hoped that the fact that he had no obvious motive for murdering his wife would weigh heavily with the jury, and there is some evidence that it did. But in this case, the painstaking scientific evidence accumulated by Price's team weighed even more heavily. Like Tardieu's solution of the death of Mme de Pauw, the Barlow case remains one of the classics of medical detection.

21

The Sleeping Strangler

At nine o'clock on the chilly morning of 2 January 1961, a van driver named Sidney Ambrose pulled up in a lay-by near the village of Ridgewell, Essex, and walked a few yards into a field to answer a 'call of nature.' There, in the ditch under a blackberry bush, he saw the body of a girl. He rushed to the nearest telephone, and in less than an hour, Detective Chief Inspector H. Burden had arrived on the scene. A brief examination revealed that the girl was dead, and scratches on the neck suggested murder.

One thing was clear: she had not walked into the field. The ground was muddy, and the soles of her bare feet had no mud on them. Moreover, no girl would be so scantily clad on a cold January day; she was wearing only a cotton blouse, a black gaberdine skirt, pink knickers and a black bra. This also argued that she had not been hitch hiking when she died, unless her killer had kept the rest of her clothes. Another curious feature was that most of her hair had been clumsily hacked off, presumably with scissors.

In the mortuary, the pathologist Dr Francis Camps confirmed that the girl had died of manual strangulation; traces of semen in her vagina indicated that she had

engaged in sexual intercourse not long before her death.
She was little more than a teenager, and had been pretty.
The temperature of the body, and the fact that rigor
mortis had started to disappear, suggested that she had
been dead more than 24 hours. (Rigor mortis sets in after
five or six hours and disappears between a day and two
days later.)

A missing persons check soon revealed the identity of
the dead girl: she was 20-year-old Jean Sylvia Constable, who lived in the village of Halstead. Her parents
reported that she had left home on New Year's Eve,
intending to go to a party in London, but had not
contacted them since. A little more investigation revealed
that Jean Constable was well known at the American jet-
fighter base at Wethersfield, half-a-dozen miles from her
home. And her friend, Veronica Benfield was able to tell
the police that on New Year's Eve, Jean had travelled no
further than a hotel called the Bell, in Braintree, another
popular resort for American servicemen. Veronica and
an American named John Smith had been in the Bell
with Jean Constable, and a young Englishman named
David Sault, whom she had picked up that evening. Also
present had been an American sergeant named Boshears,
and at closing time, he had invited the four young people
– Jean and David, Veronica and John – back to his flat in
nearby Dunmow. Veronica and John had declined, but
– as far as they knew – Jean and David had accepted.

Two days after the finding of the body, Detective
Inspector Leonard Jeavons, of the Braintree CID, went to
the air-force base at Wethersfield. The provost marshal
there had already spoken to serviceman John Smith, and
confirmed that he had seen Jean Constable and David
Sault leave the Bell soon after 10 p.m. with Staff
Sergeant Boshears. And when Jeavons showed Boshears

— a crew-cut 29-year-old — a photograph of the dead girl, he immediately identified her as Jean Constable.

'Where did you last see Miss Constable?' asked the detective inspector.

'On New Year's Eve, at the Bell.'

'And then?'

'That was it,' said the young man. But a few moments later he was admitting that Jean Constable and David Sault had accompanied him back to his flat in Dunmow, where they had drunk vodka. Boshears claimed that he had passed out — from drinking too much — and that when he woke up in the morning, the couple had gone.

Jeavons knew better. He had talked to David Sault, and learned that Sault had left in the early hours of the morning, asking Boshears where he could find a taxi, and leaving Jean Constable undressed and asleep on a mattress in front of the fire. Unless Boshears was too drunk to remember what had happened, then he knew that Jean Constable and David Sault had not left together.

When the detective intimated as much — and also enquired about some scratches on Boshears' face — the sergeant began to hedge, then suddenly said: 'I guess I'd better tell you the truth.'

The truth, he now admitted, was that after Sault had left, he had lain down beside Jean Constable on the mattress, and gone to sleep. He had awakened to feel something 'pulling at my mouth', and realized that he was on top of the girl, with his hands round her throat. Moments later, he realized the girl was dead.

'That sort of sobered me up,' he admitted. He dressed her, and carried the body into the spare room, then went back to the mattress and went to sleep. In the morning, he thought that it must have been a bad dream – until he saw Jean Constable's body in the next room.

Too frightened to go to the police, he decided to wash the body to get rid of evidence. He also washed the sheets and blankets. The body lay in his flat for another day-and-a-half before he decided to get rid of it. First, he cut off the girl's long and attractive hair, hoping to make her less recognizable. Then, at 11.30 on the Monday night, he carried her down to his car, drove north to the lay-by near Ridgewell, and carried her into the field, where he dumped her in the ditch.

Boshears was taken to the Braintree police station, where he was charged with the murder of Jean Constable. The news media gave the case wide publicity. Boshears was a Korean war veteran with distinguished service (he had been awarded two medals), and a married man with two children – his wife June was at her parents' home in Ayr, Scotland, giving birth to a third child, at the time of the murder. She broke down when two policemen arrived with the news of her husband's arrest.

The fact that Boshears was an American serviceman presented certain difficulties. Both the police and the US Air Force were anxious to preserve good relations. In the magistrate's court, Major Carl B. Prestin, of the US Judge Advocate's Department, requested that Boshears should be held by the US Air Force until his trial. The police objected on the grounds that it might cause bad feeling among the locals if the killer seemed to be receiving special privileges. So the magistrate denied the request and ordered that Boshears be held in civil custody.

The trial of Eugene Boshears opened at the Chelmsford Assizes on 14 February 1961. It was there that the full story of that evening finally emerged.

Jean Constable left the Bell Hotel at closing time. She had been drinking vodka-and-soda all evening. Her friend Veronica Benfield stated that she was not drunk, but 'tiddly.' This was also the impression of the taxi driver, Donald Mills, who had driven Boshears, Sault and Jean Constable to Dunmow. He described how Jean had said: 'I know what you're thinking. You're thinking I'm going to sleep with this American. Well you're wrong. Eugene's a respectable married man . . . I'm going to sleep with the civilian.'

According to David Sault, Jean was 'merry', while Boshears was sober.

Mrs Clara Miller, Boshears' neighbour from the flat above, described how she had been forced to bang on the ceiling to get him to turn down the radiogram. Clearly, a party was in progress.

At some point, said E.G. MacDermott for the prosecution, Jean had proceeded to remove her clothes in front of the two men. Boshears then retired to the bedroom, while Jean and David Sault had sex on the rug in front of the fire. Then, after more drinking, Sault and Jean retired to the bedroom, and made love again. Boshears went into the bedroom and invited them to return to the lounge.

Boshears had asked them to stay the night; he accordingly moved a mattress into the lounge, in front of the fire. Jean curled up in the blankets and went to sleep; Sault joined her on the mattress. Boshears lay on the floor beside them, wrapped in blankets. But Sault did not go to sleep; a few minutes later, he got up, dressed, and asked Boshears where he could find a taxi. He left some time between 12.30 and 1 a.m. Boshears then joined the naked girl on the mattress.

Clara Miller, the neighbour, testified that she heard

someone sobbing at about 1 or 1.30, and a girl saying: 'You love me' or 'You don't love me.'

Then, according to Boshears, he had awakened to find himself on top of Jean Constable, with his hands around her throat, and realized that she was dead. He carried her to the spare bedroom and dressed her, then took the sheets and blankets off the bed and put them in the bath. After that he went to sleep.

Boshears told the court: 'There was no quarrel or argument. At no time did I make any overtures of sexual relations to her. Nor did I have any desire to kill her or harm her in any way. I cannot throw any light on how I came to have marks on my face. I have no more knowledge of how Jean met her death than I have told the police and jury.' But he did admit that he had lied when he told the police he had no idea of why he carried the body to the ditch. He knew exactly why he did it: to hide the crime.

Dr Francis Camps told the court that death was due to manual strangulation, maintained for perhaps 30 seconds. Asked by Mr Gerald Rees, for the prosecution, if he thought that Boshears might have killed the girl in his sleep, Camps replied: 'I should think it is certainly within the bounds of improbability.' Strangling someone, he said, would take a certain amount of time, and he felt that Boshears description of finding her dead failed 'to fit in with that type of death.'

In his summing-up, the judge, Mr Justice Glyn-Jones, asked the jury whether they could believe that a man could strangle a girl in his sleep.

The jury had a difficult task, and it took them nearly two hours to make up their minds. On the surface, the case seemed straightforward enough. David Sault had left a naked girl alone in the flat some time before 1 a.m. Boshears admitted that he then climbed in bed beside her. Some time after 1 a.m. Clara Miller had heard the girl sobbing and saying 'You love me' or 'You don't love me.'

When Boshears found that he had killed Jean Constable, he dressed the body, then put the sheets and blankets in the bath. That seemed to argue a desire to conceal evidence – possibly semen on the sheets. Boshears had then decided to conceal the body – again evidence of guilt, as he himself admitted. He had kept it in his flat for almost two days, cut off and burnt the hair, and also burnt the girl's other clothes – her fur coat, stockings, suspender belt and jacket, as well as her handbag. He had even thrown away her ring as he drove away to dispose of the body.

The prosecution case was that Boshears had attempted to have sex with Jean Constable and strangled her when she resisted. And under the circumstances – having watched her get undressed, having been aware that she had twice had sexual intercourse with David Sault – it would surely not be unusual for a man, left alone with a naked girl, to also want to have sex with her?

Nevertheless, there were certain points in Boshears' favour. He had invited the couple to stay the night, and had placed a mattress on the rug for them: that seemed to argue that he had no sexual designs on Jean Constable. His neighbour had heard the girl sobbing, but if what she really said was 'You don't love me', that remark would be more appropriately addressed to David Sault than to Boshears. As to the time – between 1 and 1.30 according to Mrs Miller – it could easily have been slightly earlier, while David Sault was still in the flat. Or David Sault himself may have been mistaken about the time he left . . .

But assuming they believed Boshears' story of having made no sexual advances to Jean Constable, could the jury accept that he could have strangled her in his sleep? If he felt 'something scratching and pulling at my mouth', then presumably the girl was alive when he became conscious. Yet he claimed that when he removed his hands from her throat, she was dead. Dr Camps certainly thought it unlikely that he could have killed her in his sleep. But was it, nevertheless, a possibility?

Faced with the possibility of finding an innocent man guilty, the jury decided to give him the benefit of that doubt. When the verdict of 'not guilty' was announced, a voice from the gallery shouted: 'Why?' But a US Air Force representative spoke for a relieved officialdom when he stated: 'he has been acquitted of the charge of murder, and that is the end of the matter.'

June Boshears certainly found it in her heart to forgive her husband. Whether the US Air Force took the same view is not clear: the following July, Boshears was dismissed under what were described as 'less than honourable conditions.'

One thing *is* clear: the notion that a man can commit murder in his sleep has made British legal history.

22

The Uses of Maggots

Maggots make ideal fishing bait, especially if they can be found just before they pupate to become insects. At this stage they are at their fattest, making a very appealing meal for the fish. Any fisherman who came across a large mass of such maggots could count himself very lucky.

This is why Tony King and Paul Fay, two boys out to spend their Sunday by the river, were keeping an eye out for a dead hedgehog or other possible nurseries for free bait. They were not disappointed; as they walked through Bracknell Woods in Berkshire, they came upon an enormous pile of gently wriggling maggots. These completely obscured the body of the carrion upon which they were feeding. It had to be something big. The two children were not really concerned about their bait's meal, so great was their elation at finding such a large selection.

The heaving mass of larvae were wriggling on what looked like a mound of earth, only a few feet from the path. It was concealed by a pile of tree branches that seemed to have been deliberately cut. Casting these aside, the boys suddenly became aware of a rotting human forearm sticking out of the mound. They lost no time in heading for the nearest police station.

By five o'clock that Sunday, 28 June 1964, Detective Superintendent Arthur Lawson of the Berkshire CID stood by the mound, together with the pathologist Keith Simpson. A police photographer hovered around, taking pictures of the disinterment as it progressed. Another spectator was Superintendent Faber, of Gloucestershire police. During the obligatory check of Scotland Yard's missing persons list, police had turned up a report on a Mr Peter Thomas who had disappeared around 16 June. Faber, the investigating officer on Thomas's case, had heard of the body's discovery and, on an intuition, raced to Berkshire.

The local police soon noticed that the branches covering the grave were oddly out of place in Bracknell Woods – they were sprays of beech, a tree that did not grow in the vicinity. This suggested that the victim had died elsewhere, perhaps, as Faber suspected, in Gloucestershire, and had then been brought to Bracknell Woods. Yet the surrounding area showed no signs of either footprints or tyre marks.

When the maggots and earth had been cleared away it became obvious that the body was male. A towel was wrapped around the head. The flesh was badly decomposed and the police had originally estimated that the body had been buried six to eight weeks. Simpson was able to correct their error. He judged that the period was more like 12 days. Any more and the larvae would have pupated and become flies. The maggots that Simpson was examining and storing away were in that final sluggish stage, about to metamorphose. Taking an average maggot lifecycle to be more like 10 days than 12, and adding a day or two for the laying process, Simpson arrived at a likely time of death around 16 or 17 June.

The police had decided to learn as much as possible

before moving the body from the discovery site. In its present state, no one could be sure that it would survive the process. The larynx of the corpse was exposed through the action of maggots, and peering into the cavity, Simpson saw a pool of blood. Probing further he found the tiny bones of the larynx crushed and loose in the throat. Simpson knew that this does not happen easily, since the throat is protected and supported by tough rings of cartilage. So it seemed very likely that this wound had been the fatal one. But the crushing ruled out strangulation – this damage had been caused by a single heavy blow, from a bottle or a fist. Superintendent Faber, who had been trained in unarmed combat in the Forces, pointed out to Simpson that most soldiers were taught to kill with a sharp karate chop to the throat. The country was full of ex-servicemen who would have known how to commit the murder.

Disinterred and still relatively intact, the corpse was taken to a mortuary for further examination. The towel on the body's head concealed nothing, the skull was unfractured. Since death the man's brain had dissolved into a kind of sludge. There was, therefore, no way of discovering if any other blow had been responsible for his inability to defend himself. In the absence of any other wounds Simpson found that death was caused by the blow to the throat. Was the corpse that of Peter Thomas? Further investigations showed that it might very well be. The heights matched: both the missing man and the unidentified corpse were 5 feet 2 inches tall. The ages also tallied; Thomas was 42, the corpse was between 40 and 50. Dental records agreed in as much as Thomas had had none; the corpse's teeth were rotted and uncared for. Faber's man had broken his left arm early in life; examination of the dead man showed that he had done the same. Finally Simpson suceeded in removing fingerprints from the dead man's hands. These matched Thomas's, which the police had on file.

Having identified the victim, Berkshire police learned that Faber had spared them the trouble of investigating his background. Peter Thomas had lived in Lydney, a small town on the Welsh border, in an ill-repaired wooden bungalow. He and his dog lived alone. He had no job, living on the dole. The only clue that Faber had uncovered so far was related to a sum of £5,000 that Thomas had recently inherited from his father. Searching around for good investment opportunities, Thomas had found an advert in the newspaper that promised high immediate returns on investments in an agricultural project. Having been warned about the risk he was taking by both his family and his bank manager, Thomas nevertheless invested £2,000. The man who had placed the advertisement was a Mr William Brittle, a heating engineer and salesman of Hook in Hampshire, with an army background.

Faber had travelled to Hampshire and questioned Brittle on his business dealings with Peter Thomas. Yes, Brittle admitted, he had been lent £2,000 by the missing man. He had paid it back, however: he had driven down to Lydney on 16 June, the day Thomas had disappeared. Brittle's story was unconvincing, but Faber had no proof that Brittle was responsible for Thomas's disappearance. Now that Thomas's body had been found, Faber decided it was time for a further interrogation.

This time he was more direct: where had Brittle got the money to repay Peter Thomas? After all, police investigations had shown that he had substantial debts. The money, Brittle said, had come from an accumulator bet on the horses. He could not, however, name any of the animals or jockeys that had provided this almost miraculous win, or where he had placed the bet. No local bookmaker recognized a photo of Brittle shown to them. Police who had looked into Brittle's background found much circumstantial evidence that the heating salesman was supplementing his income with fraud. He repeatedly set up business schemes and encouraged investment by claiming to know influential people. Despite Brittle's insistence that he had paid Thomas his money, the sum was nowhere to be found on Thomas's body or in his bungalow. Brittle maintained that he had taken a receipt from Thomas for the repayment of the money, and had posted it to Thomas's solicitors. They said that they had never received it. This behaviour seemed odd in itself: why not just keep it? The evidence seemed to point to a failed fraud that had been covered up with murder . . .

Police took Brittle's car to pieces, testing all stains and examining all hairs and threads that they found inside. They also tested his clothes for blood. The results were inconclusive. The car had no bloodstains, though police found a single beech leaf under the driver's mat. The sleeve of one of Brittle's jackets tested positive for blood of the same type as that of the murdered man, but this was rendered equivocal by the discovery that Brittle shared the blood group, common type 'O'. To add to the uncertainty, Brittle told police that he had picked up a hitchhiker on his way back from Lydney. After some effort, police traced the man, who fully confirmed Brittle's story. Would he really have picked up a hitchhiker if he was concealing Thomas's dead body in the boot? The sane answer had to be no, yet stacked against this, police had a welter of suggestive evidence. The facts that the police were gathering were confusing and ambiguous.

As the balance of evidence stood poised, Faber's investigations turned up a statement that weighed heavily in the suspect's favour: Thomas had been seen alive after the pathologist's theorized time of death. A nylon-spinner named Dennis Roberts told police that he was certain he had seen Peter Thomas alive at the bus station on 20 June, four days after Brittle's visit to his house. Roberts was certain that the man was Thomas, whom he knew from work, as they had exchanged greetings. He was also completely certain of the day; it was the only day of his life on which he had been on strike. This was the kind of testimony that defence lawyers pray for, and it cast very serious doubt on whether the police could even convince the DPP to begin prosecution, let alone eventually win their case.

Roberts's statement contradicted Keith Simpson's estimate of the time of death. In order to prop up their sagging police case, Faber asked Simpson to draft a statement himself. Simpson did so, stating conclusively that Thomas must have died before 20 June.

The case was presented to the DPP in London, who took some time in considering it. Did the unbiased testimony of a member of the public outweigh the scientific evidence of the Home Office pathologist? In this case it seemed it did. The DPP, having taken the issue on advisement, found the police's case to be too weak to try. As there was to be no criminal case brought, a coroner's inquest was begun at Bracknell where the body had been found.

The coroner, Mr Wellbelove, heard much evidence over the seven days of the inquest. New witnesses had come forward to say that they had seen Thomas alive after 20 June, confirming the statement of Dennis Roberts. On balance it seemed inevitable that the jury should decide that Thomas was murdered by a person or persons unknown. Mr Wellbelove, however, had other ideas. His summing-up stated the facts in such a way as to leave no one in doubt that he believed that Brittle was involved in the murder. Following the coroner's hints, the jury's verdict astonishingly named William Brittle as Peter Thomas's killer, on or around 17 June 1964.

Brittle was now returned to police custody, to await trial for murder. Mr Gibbons, Brittle's solicitor, applied to the High Court to quash the jury's decision on the grounds that the verdict was against the weight of evidence. After all, the only new testimony introduced since the DPP's considerations had in fact supported Brittle's version of events. The plea was rejected; the case was to proceed.

The murder trial was to take place at Gloucester Assizes. Brittle's defence was to be conducted by Quintin Hogg, QC, later to become Lord Hailsham. Hogg had enjoyed a successful political career, and the Brittle case represented his trial return to the bar. There was much media attention to his preparations for the case; the expectations of the public were high.

Ralph Cusack, QC presented the Crown's case. Brittle's suspiciously odd alibi and the circumstantial evidence against him, were all paraded before the jury. To end on a note of positive certainty, Dr Simpson was the last prosecution witness.

Simpson went into the detail of the life cycle of the maggots that he had found feeding on Thomas's corpse. The fat larvae, *Calliphora Erythocephalus*, that had covered it were of the 'third instar', meaning that they had shed their skins twice and were preparing to become bluebottles. In the absence of outside circumstance leading to acceleration of the process, the bluebottle larvae needed at least ten days to mature to the third instar. Therefore Thomas *must* have died at the very latest on 18 June.

Instead of attacking Simpson's scientific evidence directly in cross-examination, Hogg decided to call a distinguished entomologist, Professor McKenny-Hughes, as a defence witness. McKenny-Hughes certainly outranked Simpson in terms of his knowledge of insects, yet he seemed to be totally unaware of his position in the defence's case. As Hogg questioned the professor, his evidence seemed barely relevant. It emerged that McKenny-Hughes agreed completely with Simpson in all important aspects. His replies to Hogg's carefully framed questions were rambling, and what was far worse, damaging to the defence in their total acceptance of Simpson's suppositions. Nothing useful to his case had been established; Hogg was eventually forced to dismiss him.

Despite the embarrassment of having a defence witness support the Crown's case, Hogg proceeded undeterred. He was on far safer ground with the three witnesses who had seen Thomas after the time that the Crown maintained he must have died. Dennis Roberts was called, and confirmed the details of his statement. A shopkeeper remembered Thomas coming in to buy some matches on 21 June, the day after Roberts identified him. A third witness saw Thomas on the road walking towards Blakeney on the same day. All were certain of Thomas's identity, and of the date. How could each of these witnesses be mistaken? Was a Peter Thomas lookalike in the area around the twentieth? For the prosecution, Cusack tried to cast doubt upon the three witnesses' testimony. He stressed the intervening time, nine months, and asked if they could not possibly be mistaken. Each stuck to his story. The prosecution could offer no explanation for the sightings, their only recourse was to point to the scientific evidence and the shady nature of Brittle's past.

In summing-up for the defence, Quintin Hogg, QC stressed the flimsy nature of the Crown's case. He cast doubt on the notion that Brittle could 'fell an ox at a single blow', although any karate expert could have proved him wrong. More tellingly he drew attention to the complete absence of blood or tissue in Brittle's car. Finally, he pointed out, Dr Simpson could not prove that Thomas had died on 16 June. Indeed, the three subsequent sightings of him strongly suggested the contrary.

Mr Justice Phillimore summarized for the jury and in doing so, followed the example of the coroner at the Bracknell inquest and dropped some hints that implied that he thought Brittle to be an unscrupulous man.

The jury followed his lead and found Brittle guilty of murder and he was sentenced to life imprisonment.

Twice then, William Brittle had been found guilty on evidence that was circumstantial and inconclusive. It was perhaps the ease with which the police established that Brittle was a fraudster that destroyed his case. Despite the fact that there was no evidence that Brittle had been involved in violence, let alone that he had been violent towards Thomas, he was seen to be a liar with an obvious motive for murder. For both juries, this was enough.

23

The Bloodstained Handkerchief

Returning home from an office party at eight o'clock on the evening of Wednesday, 7 February 1968, Bernard Josephs was surprised to find that all the lights in his flat were off. His wife of five months, Claire, should have returned to the flat at least two hours before. Moving from room to room turning on lights, Bernard Josephs first found evidence that his wife *had* returned: unfinished cooking on the stove, unwashed coffee cups and biscuit crumbs on the kitchen table. In the bedroom he found his wife. She lay motionless, and the floor around her was soaked with blood. Her head was almost separated from the body by several huge gashes to the throat.

Detective Superintendent John Cumming was assigned as chief investigating officer. Soon after the discovery the flat, in Deepdene Court, Shortlands, Kent, was crammed with policemen. The pathologist, Dr James Cameron, crouched over the body and made preliminary investigations. Claire Josephs' throat had been both stabbed and slashed repeatedly. The slash-wounds had an irregular edge, suggesting that the blade that had caused them had been serrated. Her body was still warm — the death must have occurred within the last few hours. It could be reasonably surmised that Claire had returned home from work as normal at around six, switching the lights on. The murderer, to conceal his exit, must have extinguished them.

Officers searching in the kitchen noticed that the breadknife was missing from its slot in the knife block. A breadknife could well have been the murder weapon. While making sure that it was not in the flat, a police officer discovered a bloodstained handkerchief, swept haphazardly under the doormat. From the size and design it seemed to belong to a man. Police did not suspect Bernard Josephs of the murder – his shattered state on the discovery of his wife and his solid alibi discounted it. It seemed far more likely that the killer had been a friend of the Josephs', and that he had shared coffee and biscuits with Claire Josephs. The police officer in charge of forensics took the coffee cups for testing, and Dr Cameron had the body removed for an autopsy.

In the absence of significant leads, the police announced the discovery of the body to the press, and appealed for witnesses. They were particularly anxious to find out if unfamiliar cars had been parked in the area in the period between 5.30 p.m. and 7.30 p.m. on the previous day. Many local witnesses came forward, and most of them told the same story: a white Triumph sports car had been parked at Deepdene Court in the early evening. No one seemed to have seen its owner.

Detective Superintendent Cumming made a televised appeal on the following evening. He described the sports car that neighbours had reported seeing and ended by saying: 'The killer may strike again. It was a senseless killing in every respect. There appears to be no motive at all at this stage.' Without explicitly saying as much,

DS Cumming had conveyed the impression that the killer was a maniac, who might strike at any time.

The autopsy results revealed that, before cutting her throat, the killer had stabbed Claire Josephs four times and attempted to strangle her. The cause of death was established as haemorrhage, combined with an air embolism.

Other investigators were examining the items that had been removed from the flat: the handkerchief, the coffee cups and specimens of the bloodstains that covered the walls. Dr Margaret Pereira, who had been involved in the development of a new method of blood grouping two years previously, was responsible for the classification of the stains. In 1968, a test that could link one bloodstain to a single individual, such as genetic fingerprinting, had yet to be developed. But refinements of blood grouping had already made it possible to narrow the focus of the search far beyond the four basic blood groups: A, B, AB and O.

Cutting the bloody handkerchief into tiny squares, Dr Pereira tested each section for its grouping. The blood proved to be mainly that of Claire Josephs, as was to be expected. But Dr Pereira was interested to discover that her blood type was an extremely rare one, known as AB-MN/PGM21. Statistically, only about 100 people in Britain would have this type of blood. Its extreme rarity meant that it was a perfect marker. A single drop on a suspect's clothing would be strong evidence of involvement.

But there was also another blood type present on the handkerchief in small amounts – a rare 'O' subgroup. This could be the killer's own blood. Further tests showed that saliva on one of the coffee cups matched the rare AB subgroup blood type, and that saliva on the other was consistent with the 'O' bloodstains.

In addition to the scientific data that the police were accumulating, enquiries in the Shortlands area had produced a number of possible leads. One woman told police of an untidy-looking man who toured the area every Wednesday offering to cut wood. *The Times* of the next day carried a story featuring the description of this wood-cutter, asking again for any witnesses. In case the white sports car turned out to be unconnected with the crime, detectives looked into other possible methods of escape that the murderer might have employed. All local bus drivers were asked if they had carried anyone whose clothes were stained with fresh blood on the night of 7 February.

A third area of investigation focused on friends of the Josephs family. The police examined all documents and letters that they could find in the flat, and checked everyone mentioned. It was in this way that police came across the name of Roger John Payne, a local bank clerk.

Bernard and Claire Josephs had been invited to Payne's wedding about two years earlier, and had kept the invitation as a souvenir. Payne's name was placed among the others on a long list of individuals to be questioned. Later in the process, a check of the criminal files revealed that Payne had two convictions involving attacks on women. In one of the attacks, dating from 1959, he had broken into a girl's room and attempted to rape her at knife-point. Another attack was even more recent, dating from 1965. Payne was clearly someone to whom the police needed to talk.

The Times of 13 February mentioned the wedding invitation, but did not name Roger Payne. The same piece reported that the police were now almost sure that the murder was not a random attack. Meanwhile the investigating officers, frustrated by the absence of a murder weapon, had invited ten Royal Engineers to search the woodland surrounding Shortlands with metal detectors.

Roger Payne was still at work when the police called at his house in Ivens Way, Harrietsham, but they were able to speak to his wife Mary. Since it was important that, at this stage, Payne should not realize that he was a suspect, the detectives confined themselves to routine questions about the friendship between the two couples, and when they had last met. It was in the course of this conversation that Mary Payne mentioned in passing that her husband had known that Claire Josephs would be alone on the night of the murder – Mary herself had told her husband that Bernard Josephs would be away at an office party.

While they were still talking, Roger Payne arrived home, and the police were interested to see that he was driving a white Triumph. They also noted that his cheeks and forehead were covered with scratches.

Payne's attitude did not seem to be that of a wholly innocent man – in fact, it bordered on hostility, and he declined to answer questions, except in the presence of his solicitor. It was Mary Payne who told the police that the scratches had been caused when he was looking at the Triumph's engine, and the bonnet had fallen on his head. After Payne's solicitor had been summoned, Payne accompanied the detectives to the police station, where the solicitor joined them. There Payne agreed to answer questions about his whereabouts on the day of the murder.

He had, he explained, tried to visit some friends at

about four o'clock, but had found them out. He had then
decided to drive to his mother's home in Carshalton. On
the way there, his car had broken down, and it was then
that he received the cuts and scratches, when the bonnet
fell on his head. It was raining, and his clothes were wet
and grease-stained by the time he got to his mother's
house at about seven. After staying there for about 40
minutes, Payne set off home. But on the way, his car
broke down again, and it was nearly ten o'clock by the
time he eventually got back to Harrietsham.

It was during this account that Payne made a comment
that threw doubt on his protestations of innocence; he
remarked that it would be no use questioning his wife,
because she would have no idea of where he was at
seven o'clock that evening. The policemen glanced at
one another and Payne's solicitor grimaced. No one had
told Payne that the murder had taken place around seven
o'clock, and the newspaper reports had not mentioned
the time . . .

The next step was to test Payne's car and clothing for
bloodstains. But the suit he had worn that day had been
cleaned – Payne explained that it had been covered in
mud and oil after his struggles to repair his car. When
the police pointed out signs of bloodstains on his hat,
Payne insisted that it was his own.

This was obviously going to be a point of crucial
importance; if Payne was telling the truth, then it was
still conceivable that he might be innocent. The hat was
sent to Margaret Pereira's laboratory. Her tests quickly
revealed that Payne had been lying: the blood belonged
to Claire Josephs' rare blood group. Moreover, blood
found on the seat of the white Triumph also proved
to be Claire Josephs'. So did a 9-inch stain in the
shape of a knife in the pocket of the driver's door –

it was even possible to make out the serrated edge of the blade.

The case against Payne was virtually complete – although, of course, circumstantial. In fact, the only evidence in Payne's favour was his mother's claim that he had been with her at seven o'clock, and the police decided that this was outweighed by the highly convincing evidence of the bloodstains. An old lady could easily be mistaken about the time on a dark and rainy February evening.

Roger Payne's trial began on 15 May 1968, at the central criminal court of the Old Bailey. The Crown's case was presented by Mr John Buzzard, while the defence was represented by Mr Wilfred Fordham, QC. Fordham decided to put his client on the witness stand to present his alibi in person, which Payne did at some length. But in his cross-examination, Mr Buzzard pounced on the weak point of the story: Payne's claim that it had taken him no less than two hours to repair his car on each occasion. Payne's answer was that he had also been to a café for a cup of tea – a fact he had forgotten to mention earlier.

When Payne's mother was in the witness box, Buzzard gently probed her reasons for being so certain that her son was in her house at seven o'clock. Without actually pressuring her into an admission, Buzzard succeeded in making it clear to the jury that she could easily have been mistaken about the time Payne had called, and that the actual time had probably been an hour earlier.

The crucial evidence was, of course, that of the forensic expert Dr Margaret Pereira. She explained about blood types, then went on to speak about the rarity of Claire Josephs' blood group, and how it was virtually impossible that the stains in Roger Payne's car and on his hat could have come from anyone but the victim. She also described how the saliva found on one of the coffee cups had been found to be of Payne's relatively rare blood group, and how hairs from his coat had also been found on Claire's body. When asked how blood could have found its way on to Payne's hatband, she replied that it was one of the most likely places for it, since a cut-throat stroke of a knife causes blood to spurt upward and over a long distance.

According to the Crown's reconstruction of that night, Payne left his mother at some time after six o'clock and called on Claire Josephs, knowing that he would almost certainly find her alone. She welcomed him in and gave him coffee, but when he tried to make sexual advances, pushed him away. Payne tried to throttle her into submission, but she escaped and ran into the bedroom. Payne followed her with the breadknife, and during the struggle that followed, his own face was cut and scratched. He stabbed her in the neck at least four times, then cut her throat. After that, shocked by the amount of blood and sobered by the struggle and her screams, he left in haste.

Payne's only comment in reply to all this was that it was impossible, 'because there is only one woman in my life, and that is my wife.'

In the light of the forensic evidence the jury found this unbelievable, and he was sentenced to life imprisonment.

One revealing piece of evidence was not presented at the trial, since it related to Payne's previous offences which, according to British law, may not be revealed to the jury. When Payne was asked by a police officer about the violence of his two previous attacks, he explained that in spite of his powerful sexual urges, he was impotent and unable to complete an act of rape. The violence of the attacks was aggravated by sheer frustration.

24

Murder by Paraquat

Peter Lindsay fell ill after supper on 4 July 1974, and his wife Anne summoned the doctor the following day. The problem was a severe stomach ache, accompanied by a sore throat and diarrhoea. As she stood by the bed, watching Dr Torquill Sinclair examine her husband, Anne Lindsay mentioned that she had also suffered the same symptoms, but was now feeling better. Both of them thought the illness might be associated with a can of Paraquat weedkiller that had been in the kitchen the day before. The doctor said that was unlikely; Paraquat would have to be ingested into the system to produce ill-effects.

The Lindsays ran Foulden Hill Farm in Berwickshire, together with Peter's brother Quintin. Peter, several years his wife's senior, had met her while he was working in Australia – she had become his mistress when she was 12 and was pregnant at 16 – and invited her to return to Britain with him. Reluctant at first, she had eventually accepted, and now the two seemed to lead a contented existence with their two children Douglas and Rhona.

The doctor's opinion was that Peter Lindsay was sickening for flu. The notion of Paraquat poisoning struck him as so unlikely that he joked: 'That is the sort of thing you can get a divorce for.' After prescribing an anti-flu drug, he told Anne Lindsay to contact him if her husband's condition failed to improve.

The doctor was back the next day. According to his statement: '[Peter's] condition had entirely altered. I examined him and the first thing that he complained of was his mouth. I was horrified to see that his tongue was red-raw and bleeding in some places.' Dr Sinclair consulted with Anne Lindsay and told her that her husband might have to be admitted to hospital. Anne replied that she thought that this would be a good idea, as she really did think that she had accidentally spilt some Paraquat into Peter's meat stew.

Dr Sinclair was dumbstruck; his impression had been that the Paraquat had just been placed accidentally in the house, not splashed about near food: 'It is difficult to describe my reaction. It altered the whole situation.'

Peter Lindsay was admitted to Berwick Royal Infirmary that day. He was now in terrible pain at all times; opiates were used to make his waking hours bearable. The doctors at the hospital could not know if Peter Lindsay had ingested Paraquat, or if so how much. Certainly his wretched pain and red-raw mouth and throat seemed to indicate that he had some Paraquat in his system. Time would reveal if he had swallowed a fatal dose.

Lindsay was moved to the Edinburgh Royal Infirmary for observation. There he could be attended by Dr H.J.S. Matthew, a recognized expert in the field of poisoning.

Members of Peter's family came to visit him in hospital every day. His mother and father were divorced, his mother, Betty, had remarried and was living in Middlesex under the name Kingzett. Peter's father lived locally, having turned the management of his farm over to his two sons. Peter's brother Quintin and their father rarely left the bedside.

It soon became clear that Peter Lindsay had little chance of surviving. His condition deteriorated rapidly. It now seemed clear that his intake of Paraquat must have been far greater than the fatal dosage. Mrs Kingzett was summoned to Edinburgh by a phone call that told her her son had only two more days to live. Anne was told of the situation by Dr Matthew himself. He said afterwards that she seemed unaffected by the news.

Dr Matthew, as he was required to do in a case of poisoning in suspicious circumstances, contacted the procurator fiscal. The case was deemed to require investigation, and Detective Inspector Andrew Suddon was sent to interview the dying man.

Lindsay told DI Suddon that he believed that his wife had poisoned him deliberately. There were two insurance policies on his life, one for £3,000, the other for £13,000. There were also shares worth £17,000 that passed to Anne on his death. Speaking painfully, Lindsay explained that his marriage had been difficult for some time. Anne hated Scotland and was homesick for Australia. She missed a friend that she had made while committed to a mental hospital in Adelaide. Peter told Suddon that he believed that Anne had taken the notion to poison him after reading about a similar murder case in the *Daily Telegraph* of 3 July. The idea of Anne murdering her husband for his money had been a running joke between them for years. Now Peter was wondering at which point the joke had turned serious.

Police officers sent to search the farmhouse at Foulden Hill discovered two letters from Anne Lindsay, one to 'Joe' and the other to 'Steve'. The envelopes had not been addressed. Meanwhile Anne was being asked for a full account of the events of 4 July by Dr Matthew.

The Lindsays' young daughter Rhona had, Anne said, somehow found a tin of Paraquat and was playing with it in the house. Anne had grabbed it and poured it down the sink, beside which was sitting a bowl of stew waiting to be reheated for dinner. Peter had complained that the stew contained too much rosemary. He ate most of it however. Anne had sat down to eat slightly later and had rejected her portion because it tasted disgusting. What little she had eaten, she told Suddon, had made her very sick.

Finally, on 15 July Peter Lindsay died in agony. Dr Matthew told police that before his death Peter had told him some interesting facts. Firstly Peter believed that Anne was in love with someone else, the 'Steve' of her letter. Steve had been a fellow patient at the Hillcrest Mental Hospital in Adelaide, where Anne had spent some time after an overdose. He also told Dr Matthew that Rhona could not have dragged the Paraquat into the house herself: she was only two years old and the can was stored in a high-sided tea-chest in the garden shed.

Although the news that her husband was going to die had, apparently, not upset Anne greatly, his actual death came close to unhinging her. She threatened suicide and was sent to a hospital in Morpeth to be under psychiatric observation.

The police were now, unsurprisingly, interested in interviewing Anne. The story she told to DI Suddon differed significantly from her previous versions. Now, she maintained that *she* had brought the Paraquat container into the house, unaware of its contents, in order to adapt it into a watering can. While she was pouring out its unwanted contents, with the stew poised on the edge of the sink, Anne's attention had been distracted. Rhona had been behaving badly, and Anne had turned to her right in order to look at her daughter. This, she said, could have been when the Paraquat entered the stew.

The fact that Anne's story had changed fundamentally aroused the suspicions of the police. When they asked around Peter's family about the Lindsays' marriage, Quintin, Peter's brother, told police of a 'letter' that Anne had written that was now in his possession. Peter had found this 'letter', entitled, 'Essay on my Life' and had shown it to Jan, his sister. Jan had passed it unread to Quintin.

The piece was sharply self-critical; in it Anne describes herself variously as 'mercenary', 'selfish', 'hard-hearted' and 'cruel'. The main thrust of the essay, however, was contained in the quote: 'I am moderately attractive and moderately intelligent so why should I bury myself in a strange house in a strange country without any hope of fulfilling my hopes?'

Although this letter contained an insight into the distaste with which Anne regarded her husband and family, it did not, of course, give the police enough evidence to prosecute. There would have to be more solid evidence. To this end, the police asked the University of Strathclyde to simulate the situation in which, as Anne Lindsay maintained, the poison had entered the stew. Hundreds of times an unfortunate graduate student was forced to pour liquid carelessly down a sink, measuring after each time the amount that had slopped into a bowl placed nearby. One teaspoon full of Paraquat is the minimum fatal dose, thus police needed to show that this amount could not enter the bowl accidentally. One set of results showed that the splash-volume was always less than a teaspoonful. Another 'splash test', replicating Anne Lindsay turning to see her child, *did* achieve fatal levels easily, but also flooded the draining board with deadly poison, something that Anne Lindsay had not reported happening.

This evidence, combined with the testimony of Peter Lindsay's family, convinced the authorities to prosecute. Anne Lindsay was charged with murder. Her defence was to be conducted by Mr W.I. Stewart. R.I. Sutherland, QC presented the prosecution case.

Among testimony from Peter's parents and brother, all reporting that Peter had been convinced that his wife was responsible for his poisoning, one interesting fact emerged. Peter's father told the court that he had received a letter from Anne about four months before the poisoning. In it Anne said that if anything were to happen to Peter, she would renounce all claim to his insurance and estate, allowing it all to pass on to the children. The prosecution read out sections from Anne's essay and from her letters. In these letters, Anne talked of escape from Scotland. In one, she even spoke of a plan that she had to get away, without elaborating on the plan's nature.

After the witnesses' testimony, which in itself could not be decisive, the prosecution brought in Dr Fletcher, of the University of Strathclyde. Dr Fletcher told the court of his group's findings, even demonstrating the methods employed on a replica sink-unit erected in the courtroom. The findings seemed unequivocal. Combined with the post mortem report which showed that Peter Lindsay had ingested at least five teaspoonfuls of Paraquat, it became damning.

Anne herself took the stand in her own defence. She explained the conflicting nature of her two alibis by saying that at first, when she was not aware of the seriousness of Peter's illness, she had just made up a story that would give no cause for Peter's family to criticize her, as they were wont to do. The second story was, she said, the truth. The 'plan' referred to in her letter was not a plot to murder Peter but a far more innocuous escape: a short trip to Ireland. Yet it was clear that she had no hope of winning. The *Edinburgh Evening News* after four days of coverage that made it quite clear that they considered Anne Lindsay guilty, did not even bother reporting on the final verdict until the day after it was announced.

On 9 January 1975, Anne Lindsay was sentenced to life imprisonment for the poisoning of her husband.